Getting to know Office 2010

IF YOU'VE EVER attempted to pick up one of those 1,000-page tomes explaining the ins and outs of Microsoft's Office, you're probably still suffering nightmares from the intense, worthy and dull advice contained within. Detailed guides to everything you could possibly imagine, and much more you'd prefer not to. Or perhaps you've suffered a simplified guide full of cartoon faces and bullet lists.

Well, this guide is nothing like either of those.

It's printed in colour, for a start, so the screenshots actually make sense. It contains many step-by-step tutorials, but they're not there to patronise you; we assume that if you're looking for advice on using Office 2010 (and you've been wise enough to pick up this guide) you're probably from intelligent stock. And it's 100% independent of Microsoft, so we've included criticism where it's due.

But, to be fair to Microsoft, there's far more to like about Office 2010 than there is to dislike. Even users of Office 2007, which was a massive leap forward from 2003, will find plenty to tempt them.

Our first chapter is dedicated to helping you choose the right version of Office 2010 for your needs, and if you haven't already taken the plunge we should be able to help you save some money in the process.

Then comes the meat of this guide: a chapter dedicated to each of the applications in the suite, from Word to Excel, Publisher to PowerPoint. You'll soon see that whatever your current level of knowledge, there'll be something to build upon and challenge you. Our aim is to really tap into the power these applications have to offer, whether you're using them at home or in the office.

So read on, enjoy, and good luck in getting to grips with one of the finest pieces of software Microsoft has ever produced.

Tim Danton
Editor, PC Pro
editor@pcpro.co.uk

Q&A

Q: How do I find my way around this guide?
A: The following two pages give you a full overview, with previews of the introductions to each chapter: turn to these pages for detailed listings of contents. You'll find a full index to the whole book on p160.

Contents

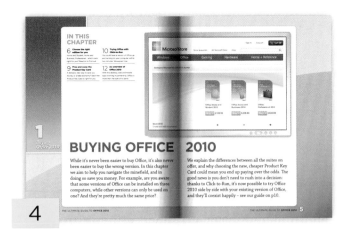

BUYING OFFICE 2010

While it's never been easier to buy Office, it's also never been easier to buy the wrong version. In this chapter we aim to help you navigate the minefield, and in doing so save you money. For example, are you aware that some versions of Office can be installed on three computers, while other versions can only be used on one? And they're pretty much the same price?

We explain the differences between all the suites on offer, and why choosing the new, cheaper Product Key Card could mean you end up paying over the odds. The good news is you don't need to rush into a decision: thanks to Click-to-Run, it's now possible to try Office 2010 side by side with your existing version of Office, and they'll coexist happily – see our guide on p10.

4

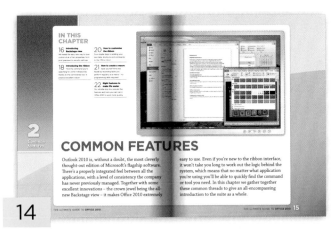

COMMON FEATURES

Outlook 2010 is, without a doubt, the most cleverly thought-out edition of Microsoft's flagship software. There's a properly integrated feel between all the applications, with a level of consistency the company has never previously managed. Together with some excellent innovations – the crown jewel being the all-new Backstage view – it makes Office 2010 extremely

easy to use. Even if you're new to the ribbon interface, it won't take you long to work out the logic behind the system, which means that no matter what application you're using you'll be able to quickly find the command or tool you need. In this chapter we gather together these common threads to give an all-encompassing introduction to the suite as a whole.

14

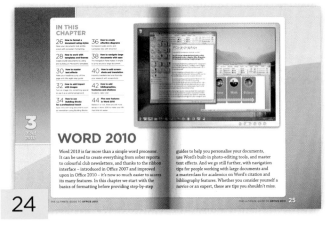

WORD 2010

Word 2010 is far more than a simple word processor. It can be used to create everything from sober reports to colourful club newsletters, and thanks to the ribbon interface – introduced in Office 2007 and improved upon in Office 2010 – it's now so much easier to access its many features. In this chapter we start with the basics of formatting before providing step-by-step

guides to help you personalise your documents, use Word's built-in photo-editing tools, and master text effects. And we go still further, with navigation tips for people working with large documents and a masterclass on Word's citation and bibliography features. Whether you consider yourself a novice or an expert, these are tips you shouldn't miss.

24

EXCEL 2010

Excel is an immensely powerful program, and this chapter helps you tap into that power. We start by introducing the fundamental terms, the simplest functions and how to string them successfully; all the basics you need to know to get started with a spreadsheet. You don't need to be a genius to use Excel to take control of your household finances, with templates ready and

waiting to be adjusted to your needs. And our guide to using formulae will tell you everything you need to know – all within half an hour. Then, if you're looking for more of a challenge, we show you how to dive deep into your data; how to present complicated results in a simple manner; how to link to external sources, and how to use Microsoft's famous PivotTables.

46

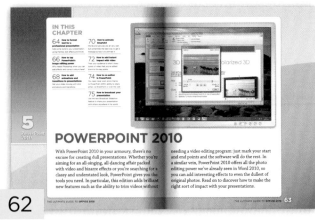

POWERPOINT 2010

With PowerPoint 2010 in your armoury, there's no excuse for creating dull presentations. Whether you're aiming for an all-singing, all-dancing affair packed with video and bizarre effects or you're searching for a classy and understated look, PowerPoint gives you the tools you need. In particular, this edition adds brilliant new features such as the ability to trim videos without

needing a video editing program: just mark your start and end points and the software will do the rest. In a similar vein, PowerPoint 2010 offers all the photo editing power we've already seen in Word 2010, so you can add interesting effects to even the dullest of original photos. Read on to discover how to make the right sort of impact with your presentations.

62

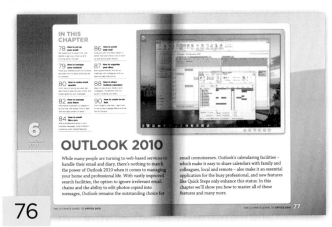

OUTLOOK 2010

While many people are turning to web-based services to handle their email and diary, there's nothing to match the power of Outlook 2010 when it comes to managing your home and professional life. With vastly improved search facilities, the option to ignore irrelevant email chains and the ability to edit photos copied into messages, Outlook remains the outstanding choice for

email connoisseurs. Outlook's calendaring facilities – which make it easy to share calendars with family and colleagues, local and remote – also make it an essential application for the busy professional, and new features like Quick Steps only enhance this status. In this chapter we'll show you how to master all of these features and many more.

76

92

ONENOTE 2010

It's far too easy to dismiss OneNote as a makeweight application, thrown into the various Office suites to make up the numbers. Certainly Microsoft doesn't see it like that: it's one of the first apps to have been converted into a Web App (see chapter 12) and has been cleverly designed for use in conjunction with Word, Internet Explorer and PowerPoint. And, as

we'll see in this chapter, if you choose to embrace its abilities OneNote could make your life a lot easier and more organised. You can use it to take notes in meetings, to draw up action points, to analyse Word documents sent to you by colleagues, to research and create in-depth projects... if you use your imagination, there's very little it can't do.

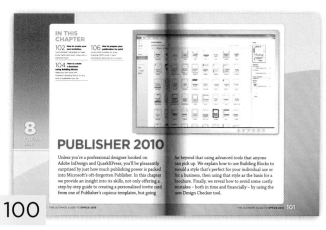

100

PUBLISHER 2010

Unless you're a professional designer hooked on Adobe InDesign and QuarkXPress, you'll be pleasantly surprised by just how much publishing power is packed into Microsoft's oft-forgotten Publisher. In this chapter we provide an insight into its skills, not only offering a step-by-step guide to creating a personalised invite card from one of Publisher's copious templates, but going

far beyond that using advanced tools that anyone can pick up. We explain how to use Building Blocks to mould a style that's perfect for your individual use or for a business, then using that style as the basis for a brochure. Finally, we reveal how to avoid some costly mistakes – both in time and financially – by using the new Design Checker tool.

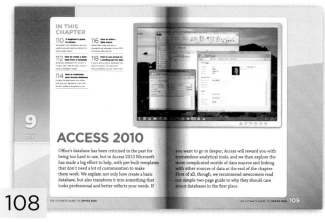

108

ACCESS 2010

Office's database has been criticised in the past for being too hard to use, but in Access 2010 Microsoft has made a big effort to help, with pre-built templates that don't need a lot of customisation to make them work. We explain not only how create a basic database, but also transform it into something that looks professional and better reflects your needs. If

you want to go in deeper, Access will reward you with tremendous analytical tools, and we then explore the more complicated worlds of data macros and linking with other sources of data at the end of the chapter. First of all, though, we recommend newcomers read our simple two-page guide to why they should care about databases in the first place.

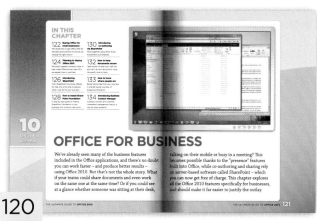

120

OFFICE FOR BUSINESS

We've already seen many of the business features included in the Office applications, and there's no doubt you can work faster – and produce better results – using Office 2010. But that's not the whole story. What if your teams could share documents and even work on the same one at the same time? Or if you could see at a glance whether someone was sitting at their desk,

talking on their mobile or busy in a meeting? This becomes possible thanks to the "presence" features built into Office, while co-authoring and sharing rely on server-based software called SharePoint – which you can now get free of charge. This chapter explores all the Office 2010 features specifically for businesses, and should make it far easier to justify the outlay.

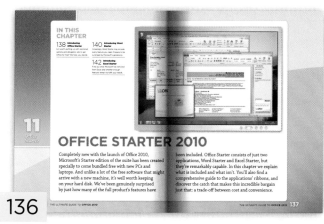

136

OFFICE STARTER 2010

Completely new with the launch of Office 2010, Microsoft's Starter edition of the suite has been created specially to come bundled free with new PCs and laptops. And unlike a lot of the free software that might arrive with a new machine, it's well worth keeping on your hard disk. We've been genuinely surprised by just how many of the full product's features have

been included. Office Starter consists of just two applications, Word Starter and Excel Starter, but they're remarkably capable. In this chapter we explain what is included and what isn't. You'll also find a comprehensive guide to the applications' ribbons, and discover the catch that makes this incredible bargain just that: a trade-off between cost and convenience.

144

OFFICE WEB APPS

For the first time, Word, Excel, PowerPoint and OneNote will now be available not only as desktop or mobile software, but also through a web browser. No longer will you need Word installed on your PC to make changes to a document, or PowerPoint on your laptop to run through your slides. All you'll need is a web browser and a broadband connection.

But don't be lulled into thinking the Office Web Apps could replace Office: they're more of a complement than a replacement. Most of the suite's features are unavailable if you try to create a document from scratch, although many more come into play if you're editing a file already created in Office 2010. Here we reveal what each of the Web Apps can and can't do.

IN THIS CHAPTER

Microsoft

Windows

Compare Microsoft® Off

Word 2010
Create and edit documents

1

Buying Office 2010

BUYING OFFICE

While it's never been easier to buy Office, it's also never been easier to buy the wrong version. In this chapter, we aim to help you navigate the minefield, and in doing so save you money. For example, are you aware that some versions of Office can be installed on three computers, while other versions can only be used on one? And they're pretty much the same price?

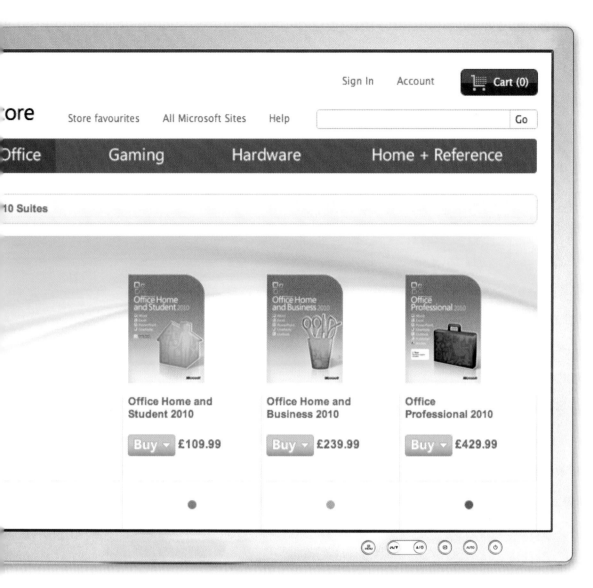

2010

We explain the differences between all the suites on offer, and why choosing the new, cheaper Product Key Card could mean you end up paying over the odds. The good news is you don't need to rush into a decision: thanks to Click-to-Run, it's now possible to try Office 2010 side by side with your existing version of Office, and they'll co-exist happily – see our guide on p10.

THERE ARE A BEWILDERING NUMBER OF OFFICE EDITIONS TO PICK FROM, SO HOW DO YOU MAKE SURE YOU BUY THE BEST VERSION FOR YOUR NEEDS?

Choose the right edition for you

It's tempting to rush into a decision about which version of Office 2010 to buy. Home and Student appears to do all you want and more, and the Product Key Card is clearly the cheapest way to get it. So open the wallet, whip out the credit card, job done. Or perhaps the sales person at your local computing emporium has explained that Professional is the only edition for business users, and despite the high price you bite the bullet and write out the cheque.

Hold on, because either way you could make a costly mistake. With Office available in so many different configurations, there are a number of traps you could fall into that would result in you spending too much money, or not getting what you need, or both.

Over the next three pages, we cover the five key choices you have to make. Read carefully, as the right decision could save you time, money and aggravation. And if you're going to university, or you're a lecturer, do make sure you read about the Professional Academic version (far right).

CHOICE 1 IS STARTER ENOUGH? The good news is that time is certainly on your side. If you've bought a new PC then there's every chance it includes Office Starter, which includes cut-down versions of Word and Excel. The table on p8 shows at a glance what's included in Word Starter and what isn't, and for more detail on the restrictions we've dedicated Chapter 11 of this guide to Office Starter.

While those omissions will be enough to put off a lot of people, the real annoyance stems from the sidebar that sits constantly to the right of your Word or Excel window. The fact that you can't remove or resize this would be grating enough, but an arguably even greater irritation is that a distracting advert rotates within it as you work.

Nevertheless, for casual use Word and Excel Starter are both perfectly adequate, and if you're at all uncertain about your needs we'd recommend you live with them a while rather than succumbing to an in-store sales pitch and upgrading immediately.

CHOICE 2 PRODUCT KEY VS RETAIL BOX That sales pitch is likely to include a few sentences dedicated to the all-new Product Key Card. We explain more about this on p9, but the important facts to remember are these: buying a Product Key Card allows you to install Office on only one computer, and that doesn't mean one computer at a time, it means *one computer*. When that computer comes to the end of its natural life, you won't be able to move your copy of Office to a new machine; you'll have to buy it all over again.

Both of these restrictions are in stark contrast to the boxed editions (note that Microsoft calls these "Fully Packaged Products", which is why you might see the abbreviated FPP if you search for products online). If you buy the boxed version of Home and Student, you're actually

TECHNICAL SUPPORT

When you buy the Product Key Card or the boxed version of Office 2010, you're entitled to full free technical support by phone and email. Importantly, this isn't just for solving technical problems; they can also help with the "how do I...?" types of questions.

If you buy Home and Student or Home and Business, this free support lasts for 90 days. With Office Professional, that extends to a year. Note that those days start ticking away the moment you activate the product on a PC; this is a change in policy from previous versions of Office, when the 90 days (or year) of support started from your first support call.

Once that time has run out, you can either rely on Office discussion forums (and goodwill from your better-informed fellow users), or pay Microsoft for additional support as and when you need it.

Office Starter comes with no support at all, although you still have the option of trawling Microsoft's website. Head to www.pcpro.co.uk/links/officehelp.

---

entitled to load that single product onto three computers simultaneously. Then, if you decide you don't want Office on the netbook but on the laptop instead, for instance, you can uninstall and reinstall it with impunity. Your three copies can exist on any three PCs indefinitely.

In this light, the Product Key Card doesn't seem such good value. After all, the "cost per licence" for Home and Student works out at £30 if you buy the boxed version, compared to £80 for the Product Key Card. (Prices may be lower if you shop around.) What's more, with the boxed version you receive an installation disc; if something goes wrong with an Office installation based on a Product Key Card, you'll have to download it all again (go to www.office.com/backup) or pay Microsoft to send you a disc.

We also asked Microsoft what would happen if you activated a copy of Office on a computer that then failed completely, so you had to get a replacement. It advises that

if you call the helpline with a credible story, the company will be sympathetic and allow you to reuse your licence key.

One final important note: part of the licence agreement for both the Home and Student and Home and Business editions is that each PC must belong to your household. It might seem obvious, but you're not supposed to buy a copy of Home and Student and then let a neighbour have the third licence key for their own PC. If one of your own children is heading off to university, though, this is covered by the licence – they're still part of your household.

CHOICE 3 HOME AND STUDENT VS HOME AND BUSINESS

On paper, the decision whether to buy Home and Student or Home and Business looks straightforward. If you want Outlook you choose Home and Business; if you don't, stick with Home and Student. Considering Home and Business is twice the price, that surely becomes a simple decision?

Office Professional and Academic

If you're a student or lecturer in higher education, you can buy Office Professional Academic 2010 for just £50. It's identical to Office Professional, and an absolute bargain: you get Word, Excel, Outlook, OneNote, PowerPoint, Access and Publisher. Just use your .ac.uk email address to order direct from www.office.com.

Office editions

	OFFICE STARTER	OFFICE HOME AND STUDENT 2010	OFFICE HOME AND BUSINESS 2010	OFFICE STANDARD 2010	OFFICE PROFESSIONAL 2010	OFFICE PROFESSIONAL ACADEMIC 2010	OFFICE PROFESSIONAL PLUS 2010
Retail box: official price inc VAT	—	£110	£240	—	£430	£50¹	—
Retail box: street price² inc VAT	—	£90	£200	—	£360	—	—
Product Key Card: official price inc VAT	—	£90	£190	—	£300	—	—
Product Key Card: street price inc VAT	—	£80	£170	—	£260	—	—
Microsoft Word 2010	Starter	●	●	●	●	●	●
Microsoft Excel 2010	Starter	●	●	●	●	●	●
Microsoft Outlook 2010	•	•	●	●	●	●	●
Microsoft OneNote 2010	•	●	●	●	●	●	●
Microsoft PowerPoint 2010	•	●	●	●	●	●	●
Microsoft Access 2010	•	•	•	●	●	●	●
Microsoft Publisher 2010	•	•	•	●	●	●	●
Technical support	•	90 days	90 days	1 year	1 year	1 year	1 year
Licence details	With retail PCs only	Up to three PCs	Up to two PCs	Volume licensing	Up to two PCs	One PC only	Volume licensing

¹ Academic edition available direct from Microsoft only (see above right)
² Street prices subject to constant fluctuation

If it wasn't for the fact that Outlook 2010 has so many neat features that could genuinely save you time, we'd say yes. In particular, this version makes it much simpler to manage a busy inbox (see p82) and to create classy-looking emails (see p80). Before you make this decision, we suggest you read Chapter 6, starting on p76.

The other key advantage of Home and Business is that it's licensed for commercial use; Home and Student isn't. The downside is that you receive a licence for only two installations, as opposed to three for Home and Student. Finally, it's worth noting that Home and Business doesn't include Publisher 2010. This unheralded application offers a lot to sole traders and home users, including the ability to create decent brochures. While Word can step into the breach on occasion, it's no substitute for a dedicated DTP package.

CHOICE 4 THE PROFESSIONALS If you need Office for professional use, you face the toughest choices of all. First, you must decide if you need Publisher and Access (both included with Office Professional, but not Home and Business). While we like Publisher a lot, it's unlikely to be a vital part of your business armoury. Access, on the other hand, may well be. If you're currently using Access 2003, then the step up to Access 2010 is a significant one; heavyweight improvements include the way it works with external data and the new Macro Designer (see p116). The other benefit of Office Professional over Home and Business is that you receive a year of technical support instead of just 90 days.

The biggest decision you'll have to make, however, is how you buy Office. The Professional edition, either via Product Key Card or retail box, is expensive, so it makes sense to investigate the Volume Licence schemes. This also gives you the option to buy Office Standard, which includes Publisher but not Access. We go into more depth on the choices in Chapter 10.

CHOICE 5 WHERE TO BUY The most tempting place to get Office is a bricks-and-mortar shop, especially if that's where you've just bought your new PC. But make sure the price is competitive with your second option: online retailers. The likes of Amazon offer very good deals for software. Note that many sell both Product Key Cards and retail, boxed versions of Office, and it isn't always clear which is which: look for phrases such as "PC (DVD)" or "FPP" if it isn't clear, as those indicate a boxed version. If, when the package arrives, you find it isn't what you expected, don't open the retail box: you have the right to return it with seven days, no questions asked, but software that's been opened is specifically exempted from this.

A simpler way is to buy from Microsoft. As we see on p10, you can download a trial of Office 2010 that lives side by side with your existing Office installation. If you then decide to buy Office 2010, all you need to do is enter a new product key. The downside is price: Microsoft will never offer the most competitive prices.

Another (and rather drastic) choice is to buy Office abroad. For example, Home and Student costs $120 in the US (excluding sales tax where it's applied) and Professional $500. Depending on the exchange rate, that could lead to a substantial saving.

Q&A

Q: What if I already own Office 2003 or Office 2007? Presumably I can get a cheaper upgrade edition of Office 2010?
A: Unfortunately not. With this release, Microsoft has decided to scrap upgrade schemes completely: you have the same options regardless of whether you've bought Office before. Sorry.

Word Starter: what's missing?

Formatting	Word 2010	Word Starter
Fonts: styling (eg bold)	●	●
Fonts: type (eg Calibri)	●	●
Text Effects	●	●
Styles (eg Heading 1)	●	●
Themes	●	●
Drop caps	●	●
Illustrations		
Pictures	●	●
Clip-art	●	●
Shapes (eg flowcharts)	●	●
Charts	●	●
WordArt	●	●
Textboxes	●	●
Insert screenshot	●	·
The little things		
Customisable ribbon	●	·
Full-screen reading	●	·
Macros	●	·
Side-by-side windows	●	·

The professional touch	Word 2010	Word Starter
Cover page	●	●
Headers & footers	●	●
Page numbering	●	●
Symbols	●	●
Watermarks	●	●
Mail merge	●	●
Table of contents	●	·
Citations	●	·
Bibliography	●	·
Insert object (eg Excel worksheet)	●	·
Review		
Spelling & Grammar	●	●
Thesaurus	●	●
Translate	●	●
Word Count	●	●
Commenting	●	·
Track Changes	●	·
Compare Documents	●	·
Protection	●	·

PROS AND CONS
BUYING A PRODUCT KEY CARD

You don't have to buy a boxed version of Office. Microsoft is introducing an alternative route that promises to be easier, cheaper and greener.

With this latest release of Office, Microsoft has introduced a new way of buying the software: the Product Key Card. This has been designed for use with new PCs that come with Office Starter (see Chapter 11), because those computers actually have the full version of Office 2010 installed – but hidden away. To unlock them you need a serial number, which can be found on a Product Key Card.

Product Key Cards can be bought from Microsoft or from other online retailers and computer shops. They may look good value, but do note that they allow you to use Office on just one computer. Not one computer at a time – one specific computer, forever. That means you'll only ever be able to use Office on the PC you bought Office Starter with; there's no way (or at least no legal way) to transfer it to your next PC in two or three years' time.

In contrast, when you buy a retail boxed version of Office 2010, it includes a licence that can be used multiple times. Home and Student allows you to install on three computers at the same time, Home and Business on two. What's more, your licence isn't tied to any particular PC: so long as you uninstall it from one PC first, you can re-install it on another – for example, when you upgrade your computer.

BENEFITS OF THE PRODUCT KEY CARD Given this major limitation, why would anyone buy a Product Key Card? First, because it might still work out cheaper than the boxed versions. If you have only one PC, and you plan to keep it for long enough that when you buy a new one you'll also be ready to buy a new version of Office (bearing in mind Microsoft no longer offers upgrade pricing to existing users), then you stand to lose nothing. Plus, buying a Product Key Card is a straightforward saving: see our price comparison chart on p7.

It's also convenient. If Office Starter is preinstalled on your computer, all you need to unlock the full version is to enter the key. The computer will go online, activate your copy and hey presto – within a few minutes you'll have a fully working installation.

Finally, there's a slight "green" advantage, because you don't have to buy a DVD. This is somewhat offset by the fact that the Product Card comes in a plastic box. (Apparently, Microsoft initially planned it to be just a card, but people felt that if they were paying almost £100 for a product they wanted to feel like they owned something physical. It's no wonder the

environment is in trouble, really.) But it's still smaller than the normal retail box, and doesn't contain a DVD.

WHERE TO BUY A PRODUCT KEY CARD So you've decided you want a Product Key Card; where are they available? Certainly from high-street retailers, who we expect to heavily promote the cards, especially to people who've just bought a new PC with Office Starter installed.

You can also buy Product Key Cards from online retailers; they'll simply post them to you as they would a normal piece of software. Finally, you can buy direct from Microsoft itself. The advantage here is that you can access the code there and then, so you don't need to wait for the physical card to arrive before you can start using Office.

Finally, can you take advantage of the Product Key Card if your PC doesn't already have Office Starter installed? Yes, for the moment. Microsoft says that during the "transition period", while many PCs are shipping without Office 2010 preinstalled, customers can download the software that matches their Product Key Card by heading to www.office.com.

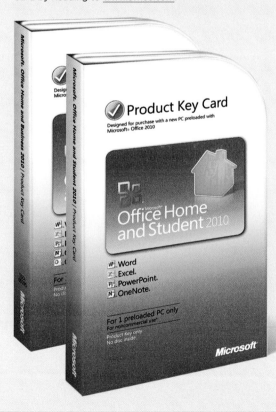

Q&A

Q: What happens if my PC gets a virus and I have to reinstall Windows? Will I still be able to use my Product Key Card?
A: Yes. You can restore your PC to its factory settings, or download the software again from Microsoft, or ask for a backup of the Office software to be sent to you (at a cost). Whichever option you choose, all you then need is the product key – although you may need to phone up Microsoft to activate Office, to confirm that you're not installing it on a different PC.

Trying Office with Click-to-Run

Traditionally, if you wanted to try a new version of Office you had to install a trial version, and in the process uninstall your existing copy of Office. This was all well and good if you went on to buy the new edition, but if you didn't you had to suffer the pain of uninstalling the trial version and reinstalling your old version.

Microsoft has wisely moved away from this scenario with Office 2010. Although trial DVDs will still be available, the best way to decide if the new edition is worth the upgrade is to use a new service called Click-to-Run. One key difference between this and simply downloading a piece of software is that it's instantly available – Microsoft reckons home users on a broadband connection can be up and running in less than 90 seconds.

HOW IT WORKS If you've ever watched a video over the internet, you've experienced something similar to Click-to-Run. The idea is to "stream" the software direct to your computer; Office will then install itself inside a virtual bubble on your PC. All the most important parts of the program are delivered first, which is why you could be using Office in under two minutes. If you try to use a feature that hasn't yet been installed, it will deliver that feature next. There'll be a brief delay, but nothing dreadful.

When Office has been fully installed, you're free to disconnect from the internet and use it just as you would normally. While it's online, the software will occasionally check for updates, then simply download the new code and upgrade itself as necessary.

NOT JUST FOR SHOW While we expect most people to use Click-to-Run to trial Office, what if you actually want to buy Office this way? It is possible, and in many ways more convenient than the hassle of inserting a DVD and pressing Next. Click-to-Run is really just a new delivery method, just as we've moved from buying software on discs to downloading files over the internet.

There are some very good reasons to opt for Click-to-Run over those traditional methods. For a start, you're always going to get the latest (and thus most secure) version of Office, with no annoying message saying "Updates available". Disadvantages are few. Because of the way Click-to-Run installs, some add-ins won't work. And... that's about it.

SO HOW DO I GET IT? The only outward sign of this new technology is likely to be hidden away in the small print: just head to www.office.com and follow the "Try Office 2010" signs. Press the relevant button and follow the instructions (you'll need a Windows Live account) .

If and when you do want to remove whatever version you've installed, note that you'll need to uninstall Microsoft Click-to-Run, which installs itself as a separate program, as well as Office 2010 itself.

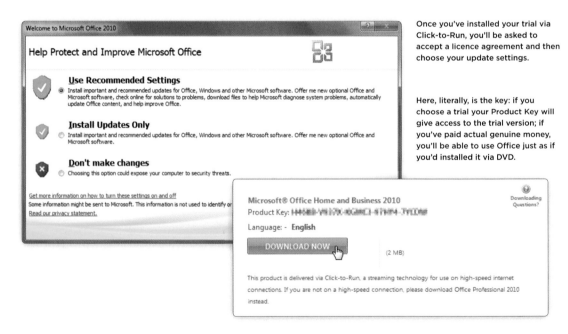

Once you've installed your trial via Click-to-Run, you'll be asked to accept a licence agreement and then choose your update settings.

Here, literally, is the key: if you choose a trial your Product Key will give access to the trial version; if you've paid actual genuine money, you'll be able to use Office just as if you'd installed it via DVD.

WE SPEND MUCH OF THIS GUIDE DETAILING THE SPECIFICS, BUT IT'S WORTH STEPPING BACK FOR A MOMENT TO SEE HOW EVERYTHING FITS TOGETHER.

An overview of Office 2010

Most of us are used to thinking about Microsoft Office as a collection of desktop applications: Word, Excel, PowerPoint, Outlook, Publisher and Access, plus OneNote and other bits and bobs. With this release in particular, though, Microsoft has bigger ambitions. It's well aware that rivals such as Google have introduced strong competitors that work online, and we assess their relative strengths and weaknesses elsewhere (see p156).

With the Office Web Apps, however, Microsoft isn't just releasing a rival to Google Docs. It sees its new online offering as a cog in the larger Office 2010 wheel. In this overview, we'll explain how those various cogs mesh, how you can take advantage, and what role Office Mobile has to play. It's all about having the same basic functionality available wherever you are and whatever device you're using – not by cobbling together a number of just-about-compatible solutions, but in a seamless way.

GREATER THAN ITS PARTS To take a very simplistic view, you could say the desktop version of Office is there to create documents; the online version, Office Web Apps, is there to share them with colleagues; and the mobile version, Office Mobile, is for viewing them on the move.

While that's largely accurate, what's clever about Microsoft's trio of offerings is that they're mutually non-destructive. That is, if you edit a Word document on your mobile phone and then open the edited file in Word on your desktop PC, the only changes will be to the words you edited. All the formatting, the tables, the fancy charts you may have created, will still be intact, even though they weren't fully available to view or edit in the mobile app.

Exactly the same holds for the Web Apps – which is one of the key advantages Microsoft's online suite holds over Google Docs. If you upload a Word file to Google, it will convert it to a format Google Docs understands, and that means you'll probably lose the fundamental feel of your document. When you save your edits and later open the result in Word, that missing formatting won't come back.

SAME DIFFERENCE Microsoft has deliberately kept the interface very similar across the Web Apps and the desktop applications. The idea is that you may lose some of Office's features when you switch to the online version (which you might be using on a second machine, such as a netbook, or on someone else's computer), but you should always know where to look for the commands that do exist.

If you create your document in the desktop application (right), the web application (overlaid here) will make an excellent fist of reproducing it online. You can see the 3D-effect chart isn't supported by the Excel Web App, but the meaning of the figures is still perfectly well conveyed.

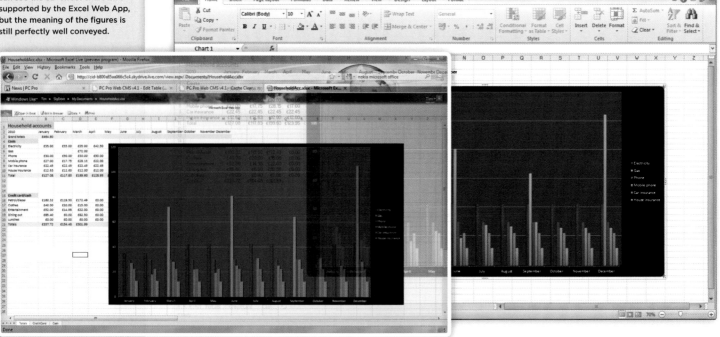

OFFICE MOBILE

Office Mobile 2010 is a new suite of Microsoft apps for Windows Mobile 6.5 smartphones. As you might expect, the features as well as the screen display are severely cut down compared to the familiar Office desktop applications, but if you do use a Windows Mobile device it's well worth having a look at what Office Mobile could do for you.

This consistent interface is true whether people are viewing documents they've saved to their Windows Live SkyDrive (see p146) or on SharePoint (see p126). Once they open a spreadsheet in the Excel Web App, the ribbons and the whole environment will look exactly the same. Microsoft hopes this will make it easier for people to get to grips with the ribbon interface and reduce the need for training.

LIMITED MOVEMENT The final piece in the Office puzzle is Office Mobile. This is a very cut-down version of the software, and that restriction extends to the number of applications included: Word, Excel, PowerPoint, OneNote and Outlook are all covered, but Access and Publisher aren't.

As can be seen from the gallery of screenshots (right), there's no way Office Mobile apps can come close to matching the features offered by their desktop equivalents, and nor will you be able to see Word documents on your handset as they're meant to be printed.

There are more caveats too. While Microsoft won't be charging any money for Office Mobile, it's currently only available for phones running Windows Mobile 6.5 or later. Nokia has announced that it will also be releasing a version of Office Mobile, but hasn't yet committed to a delivery date.

As such, Office Mobile should be seen as a handy extra if you happen to use a Windows Mobile phone; it isn't a vital part of the operation.

BEHIND THE SCENES The final ingredient in the Office "system" applies only to businesses. We cover this in far greater detail in Chapter 10, but if you want to use Microsoft Office to its full capability, your business should investigate SharePoint (and Microsoft's other supporting software).

The mere word "SharePoint" can strike terror into grown men, but as we show on p128 it's surprisingly easy to install if you have any experience of server software, and with SharePoint Foundation now free there's all the more reason to experiment and introduce it to your network. In return, you could make collaborations between team members far easier and more productive.

There are caveats: you'll need to be running suitable Microsoft system software on your servers, and that doesn't come cheap. Rolling out a more sophisticated SharePoint setup also requires specialist expertise. However, the rewards can be quite stunning, and if companies you work with also invest in this area, that collaboration can extend to partnerships as well.

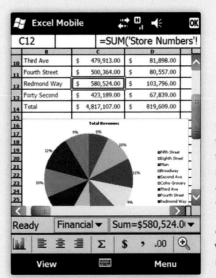

Excel Mobile packs a lot into a small space, and could be handy to show figures. You wouldn't want to present in **PowerPoint Mobile**, but it's possible to flick through and check your slides.

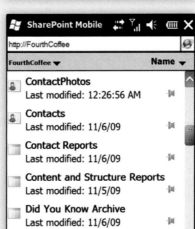

In **Word Mobile**, you'll find all the main formatting tools at the bottom of the screen – but we recommend you mainly use the app for making small amendments to text rather than sweeping changes to the document.

Outlook Mobile supports Conversation View. Here the "(8)" means there are eight messages you can drill down and see.

OneNote Mobile supports pictures and audio clips, but is best for viewing simple pages. You can also view **SharePoint** to access and manage shared files.

IN THIS CHAPTER

2
Common features

COMMON FEATU

Office 2010 is, without a doubt, the most cleverly thought-out edition of Microsoft's flagship software. There's a properly integrated feel between all the applications, with a level of consistency the company has never previously managed. Together with some excellent innovations – the crown jewel being the all-new Backstage view – it makes Office 2010

RES

extremely easy to use. Even if you're new to the ribbon interface, it won't take you long to work out the logic behind the system, which means that no matter what application you're using, you'll be able to quickly find the command or tool you need. In this chapter, we gather together these common threads to give an all-encompassing introduction to the suite as a whole.

MICROSOFT PROVIDES A WHOLE NEW WAY TO CONTROL A FILE'S PROPERTIES IN OFFICE 2010, AND IT COULD SAVE YOU TIME AND HEARTACHE.

Introducing Backstage view

"Backstage what?" is the natural response we hear when we try to explain the purpose of the Backstage view. It isn't so much a feature you'll come to love in Office 2010 as something you'll come to use as if Microsoft Office has always worked this way.

You access the Backstage view by clicking File, which always sits on its own solid-coloured tab at the top left of the screen. In Word, it's blue; in Excel, green, and so on. It's equivalent to the old File menu in Office 2003 and earlier, and you can even see this heritage in the list of commands down the left-hand side: Save, Save As, Open...

Things get more interesting when you click on the other entries. These vary by application, but there's a large amount of overlap, so we'll go through all the main options.

Before we do, though, we should address the concept behind the Backstage view. In essence, it brings together all the *properties* associated with the file and application, as opposed to the *contents* of the file. If you think of a "file" in the conventional meaning – as a bundle of papers, say – this is the front of the file that tells you everything you need to know about who wrote it and why.

INFO In the likes of Word, Excel and Publisher, the Info tab will provide a summary of your document's key statistics:

for example, the name of the author, when it was created and how long it's been edited for. All very worthy, but there are also a number of tools on offer. Perhaps the most useful is Manage Versions. This can jump back to older versions of files, which can be a life-saver if you unthinkingly save a document only to regret the changes you've made.

If you open an older document – for example, one created in Office 2003 – then pressing Convert will re-save it in the Office 2010 format. This not only compresses the file, but also enables advanced features, such as Text Effects in Word or Sparklines and Slicers in Excel.

The Info area also allows you to encrypt Word, Excel, Access and PowerPoint files, or check for potential problems before you share the file. The exact tools on offer depend on the application, with Publisher using the Info tab to manage commercial print settings, for instance, but the common thread is obvious to see.

RECENT Gone are the days when you could only jump to the four files you opened last. Now you can click Recent and see the past 20 at a glance. Just as useful for power users, the likes of Word and Excel also point to the most recent folders you accessed, greatly reducing the need to browse manually through nested folders.

Tip

If you don't like the default colour of Office 2010, change it. Whichever app you're in, click on File | Options, head to General, and click on the dropdown bar next to "Color scheme:". You have three options – Blue, Silver or Black – and we think Blue is the least offensive. You may also be wondering how to get rid of the transparency effect that allows you to see through the title bars. This is a setting in Windows 7 (or Vista) that can be turned off: type "window color" into the search field, choose "Change window glass colors" and untick the "Enable transparency" checkbox.

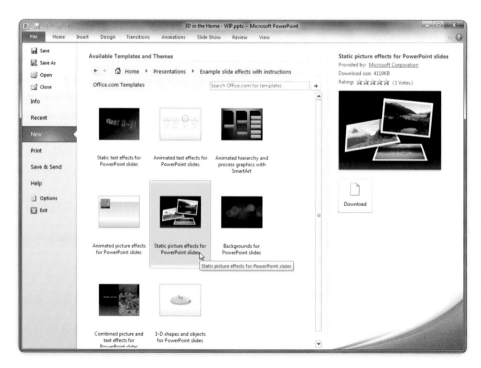

Templates can make a big difference to your documents, whether they're figures-based such as in Access or Excel, or – as here – image-based, such as in PowerPoint. You're not stuck with the installed templates either, because Microsoft has made it easy to access new ones saved to its Office.com website.

NEW As everyone has come to expect, most of the Office applications offer a number of templates on which to build a new document. While the sample templates preinstalled with the application are often useful, we generally find the best templates can be found on Office.com. However, no-one wants to launch Internet Explorer each time they're looking for a new template, so Microsoft has made them much easier to access direct from the applications.

For instance, if you were in Excel and looking for a budgeting template, you'd head to File | New and then double-click on Budgets underneath the Office.com Templates bar. You can then see a selection of pre-selected templates, complete with star ratings and a preview. Simply click Download and the document will automatically open as soon as the download is complete.

PRINT This is one of the best features in Office 2010. Microsoft has deviously made it simple to see exactly how your chosen document will print on your chosen printer by integrating the print preview into the Print tab.

In a stroke, this means hundreds of wasted print jobs will never make it to the output tray. Say you're about to print a colour document to a mono laser: you'll see the output is in greyscale, and will cancel the job (although note, sometimes printers aren't correctly identified as mono). Or perhaps you didn't realise the document was going to print on two pages, or you notice that it's going to print in landscape mode rather than portrait...

It sounds mundane, but trust us: this feature alone will save you time, money and annoyance. Our only gripe is that the feature isn't so well implemented in Outlook (where you get a page preview, but have to press Print Options to change the page range being printed) or OneNote (which doesn't even show the print preview).

SAVE & SEND You might be wondering why Microsoft has bothered to create a Save & Send tab. After all, Save and Save As are both included at the top of the Backstage view, so why bother? The reason soon becomes clear, with a plethora of choices on offer.

The default option is normally Send Using E-mail, which leads to a choice of formats in applications such as Word and Excel. For example, you could send a document as a PDF, as an internet fax, or just as a standard attachment.

Reflecting Office 2010's sharing abilities, two further options are typically on offer if you're using Word, Excel, PowerPoint or OneNote. Clicking Save to Web allows you to save the file direct to your Windows Live folder (see Chapter 12), while companies that have implemented SharePoint (see p126) can publish to a shared workspace.

PowerPoint even allows you to create a video, package a presentation for CD (or a USB flash drive) that will automatically run on other computers, or broadcast your slideshow over the internet (see p75).

HELP As its name implies, this is one way to access each application's help files – but it's easier to simply press

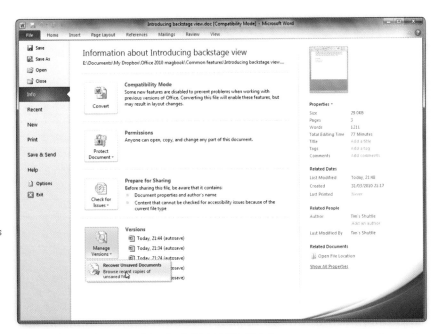

Above: Here's the Backstage view of a Word file. The tabs down the left – such as Info, shown here – allow you to jump to the task you're interested in. Info isn't just for information: you can encrypt the file using the Protect Document command, or recover autosaved versions if you make changes you later regret.

Above left: While the most likely use for the Save & Send tab is to quickly send a file by email, more advanced options are on offer – particularly in PowerPoint, which allow you to do all sorts of crazy things with your presentation.

Left: We're huge fans of the Print feature built into most of the Office 2010 apps, as it makes it far less likely that you'll output a document to the wrong format of paper. Its implementation in OneNote, unfortunately, leaves much to be desired.

the question mark button that sits at the top right of the program's window. Possibly more useful is the link to a Getting Started guide (note that this is online, not stored with the app). You can also see your product key and double-check which version of Office you're actually running.

OPTIONS The final button worthy of note is Options. Whichever app you're using, this provides a quick way to access its advanced options. For example, you might want to adjust how many recent documents you can see, change the document's language settings, or switch to a different colour scheme. There's really very little you can't do from Options, so it's well worth taking a look to see what you can and can't tinker with.

DON'T FEAR THE RIBBON! WHILE IT MAY SEEM STRANGE AND UNFAMILIAR AT FIRST, THIS INNOVATION MAKES IT QUICKER TO FIND THE FEATURES YOU NEED.

Introducing the Office ribbon

Q&A

Q: Help! The ribbon has disappeared! How do I get it back?

A: You can make the ribbon disappear by double-clicking on any of the tab names – for example, Home. To make all the tabs reappear, simply double-click on any of the names again.

Microsoft introduced the ribbon concept with Office 2007, and it would be fair to say it received a mixed reaction. Some people hailed it a huge step forward for usability; others called it a wretched curse upon the world, and begged Microsoft to bring back the old menu system. Indeed, many people refused to upgrade from a previous version simply because they despised the ribbon so much.

No-one disputed the fundamental problem Microsoft was attempting to solve. With every release of Word, Excel, PowerPoint and friends came a new swathe of features. The toolbars were being overrun with options, and you had to be an Office guru with 20 years' experience behind you, and an intricate knowledge of Microsoft's way of thinking, to find the precise command you wanted.

There was another problem too. The only option Microsoft had in its arsenal if it wanted to "promote" a command so everyone could see it was to position it as a small icon on the toolbar. There wasn't enough space, and because the icons were so small it was tough to see what task they were meant to perform.

The ribbon doesn't provide a magic wand for all these problems, but it does perform magic of sorts: it makes it far easier to find the tools you're looking for, while presenting the new ones in a way that invites you to experiment. The result is that everyone can create better documents faster, and with Office 2010 Microsoft has improved things to such an extent that even people who swore they'd never use the ribbon may just be persuaded otherwise.

ANATOMY OF THE RIBBON Each ribbon consists of a number of tabs. For example, the Insert tab in PowerPoint collects all the most popular commands associated with inserting elements into your presentation – you can add a new chart, embed video, place a textbox, and much more besides.

Rather than randomly throwing all these tools and commands onto the tab, Microsoft groups them. So the Insert tab in PowerPoint is split into seven groups: Tables, Images, Illustrations (such as charts), Links, Text, Symbols and Media. This makes it far easier to jump straight to the command you're interested in. Sometimes, there just isn't enough room for Microsoft to squeeze in all the commands it wants to. On these occasions, you'll see a tiny arrow to the right-hand side of the group's title. Pressing this launches a dialog box to give you the control you need.

Taking PowerPoint as our example again, the Font group on the Home tab includes just such an arrow, and pressing it launches the Font dialog box (see below left). From here you can add effects such as a double strikethrough, which isn't available from the tab itself.

Here, we provide a brief guide to what you can expect to see in each application's tabs.

THE HOME TAB As its name suggests, the Home tab is the default tab you see when you first launch an Office application. Microsoft has attempted to include the most common tasks here, so you don't need to jump around the tabs simply to find the Bold command in Word, for example.

Although the Home tab contains different commands depending on the application you're using, there are some easily identified patterns. Almost all the apps offer the Clipboard at the far left, providing tools such as Copy, Paste and Format Painter (which applies the formatting of text currently selected to another block of text).

To the right you'll generally find more advanced text-formatting tools (such as the text highlighter), followed by paragraph formatting (bullet lists, increase line spacing, indent) and then styling options. As we explain in depth in Chapter 3, which covers Microsoft Word, styles allow you to give different documents a consistent look and to change the appearance of a document dramatically within seconds.

Additional controls

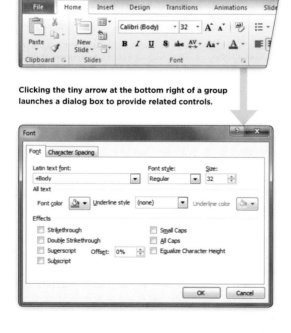

Clicking the tiny arrow at the bottom right of a group launches a dialog box to provide related controls.

The Home and Insert tabs

THE INSERT TAB The Insert tab needs little explanation. In short, if you ever want to add anything into a document – be that a web link, an obscure symbol or even a screenshot – the Insert tab is the place to go. The exact commands vary depending on which application you're using, but there's a surprising amount of common ground – clip-art, tables, time and date being just a handful of examples.

Not every application includes the Insert tab, with Access and Outlook being obvious exceptions, but the rule of thumb is that if an application involves graphical elements then the Insert tab will be ready and waiting.

THE PAGE LAYOUT TAB Common to Word and Excel, the Page Layout tab offers a huge amount of control over both the page design and how the final document will be printed. From here, you can adjust the margins, switch between landscape and portrait orientation, add a picture as a page background and, in Excel, choose whether to see the gridlines. The Page Design tab in Publisher offers similar tools, but presents extra controls over the design – hence the change in name.

THE VIEW TAB Sitting at the far right of the ribbon in Excel, Word, Publisher, OneNote and PowerPoint is another tab worthy of note. Again, the precise commands vary depending on the app – for instance, PowerPoint offers control over how the speaker's notes look – but they have much in common as well. You can control the zoom from here (or use the command at the bottom right of the application window) and, a little incongruously, create and record macros.

TABS WITHIN TABS When you're working with charts in Excel, tables in Word or images in PowerPoint, you'll notice that a new tab appears. This is specific to that element. For example, tables need to be formatted – but you wouldn't want all those formatting tools to be available when you're just typing away at a report.

The new tabs appear towards the right of the ribbon, typically after the View tab, and once you click away from the table, chart or image – or whichever type of object you happen to be working with – the tab will disappear. Until you click on the object again.

Different designs

PowerPoint has the Design tab to control the appearance of your slides, while in Publisher, another visually led application, it's the Page Design tab that offers formatting, alignment and colour options.

Reference work

Unique to Word, the References tab provides commands to help students, academics and report writers manage footnotes and endnotes, citations and bibliography, tables of contents and cross-referencing.

Similarly, Excel devotes a whole tab to one of its specialist subjects, Formulas. Note the More Functions dropdown.

AND THE REST... Most of the Office applications provide six or seven tabs; typically, the ones we've described above, plus three or four more tied in with the core needs of that app. In Word, for example, the References tab is an aid for students and report writers, with options for adding a table of contents and inserting citations. In Excel, Microsoft dedicates an entire tab to formulae.

As we discuss on the following page, however, there's also room for adding your own custom-made tabs for the commands you regularly use.

HOW LONG?

Don't spend too long on your first ribbon; trial and error will sort it later.

HOW HARD?

It's easy to add your own ribbon; slightly harder to fine-tune it.

Q&A

Q: When I rename a group, I'm asked to choose a picture. It doesn't seem to appear anywhere, though, so why does it matter?

A: It still makes sense to find a picture that has some link with your group name, because if the ribbon gets too crowded it will show the icon rather than your commands. Click the small down arrow to access the commands.

HOW TO...
CUSTOMISE THE RIBBON

You don't need to live with the ribbon exactly how Microsoft imagined it. Add your own shortcuts and commands with this simple step-by-step guide.

One of the biggest criticisms of the ribbon in Microsoft Office 2007 was its rigidity. While someone with programming knowledge could customise it and add tabs to the default ones, such skills were beyond the typical Office user. All this has changed in Office 2010, and now you need absolutely no coding skills to adjust and customise the ribbon as you see fit.

① START CUSTOMISING We'll use Word as our example, but the method holds true for all the Office applications. The first step is to launch the Customize Ribbon dialog, which you can do in two ways: by going to File | Options and clicking on the Customize Ribbon tab, or by right-clicking any empty space on the ribbon and choosing "Customize the Ribbon…". The dialog box that appears shows two long lists, each with a dropdown menu at the top.

On the right are the ribbons already in your template, while the left-hand list displays the commands that exist in Microsoft Word and are thus available to be included on your ribbon. They're grouped in nine ways, such as "Popular Commands" and "Commands not in the

Ribbon". If you choose All Commands, you'll notice the number of options is huge – there are around 1,000 tools.

② CREATE A TAB Click New Tab. You'll see a new entry pop up, usually just under Home in the list. By default it's empty – your blank canvas. The first thing you should do is give it a meaningful name: click Rename and type something suitable. Now comes the step-by-step process of creating your tab.

③ ADD GROUPS Your new tab includes a New Group by default, which again you should rename. After this, pick the commands you'd like to include in this group. It makes sense to follow Microsoft's cues here: stick similar commands in groups and name them sensibly. You can click OK at any time and you'll see your ribbon in action.

④ SPIT AND POLISH Add more groups using the New Group button until you're happy with the results. And that's it. From now on, your new ribbon will appear whenever you create a new document.

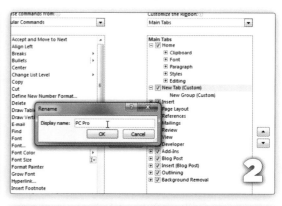

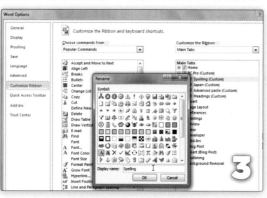

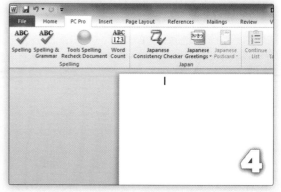

HOW TO...
PROGRAM A MACRO

If you perform a particular set of tasks routinely, you can save time by recording a macro. Macros sound daunting, but that's partly just their name; if they'd been called Time Savers, they'd probably be used much more. In reality, they're simply a way of pre-recording a set of actions. Let's say you often create a table with the same headings, and all you ever change is the values. Macros are a fine way to add that table instantly into your documents.

Here, we'll create such a macro using Microsoft Word; the same method works in the other Office apps.

(1) NAME YOUR MACRO The Macro command sits, confusingly, in the View ribbon. Click the down arrow and choose Record Macro. You're asked to give it a name, the default being Macro1; try to choose something more descriptive. In our example, we'll opt for PasteTable. Note that no spaces are allowed in names.

You can also add a description and choose whether you want your macro to be available in all documents or just this one. In most cases, you'll want it in all documents. You then click the Button or Keyboard icon, depending on whether you want your macro to be launched by clicking on an icon or pressing a key shortcut.

(2) QUICK ACCESS Once you select Button or Keyboard, you'll see a menu rather similar to Customize Ribbon. This is asking if you'd like to add the macro to the Quick Access bar, which by default sits above the ribbon on the left. Click on your macro (which will be named Normal.NewMacros.PasteTable, if you chose PasteTable as the name in step 1) and press Add. A flow-chart-style icon will now appear in the Quick Access Bar.

(3) PRESS RECORD Time to put your plan into action – and we should emphasise that planning is important. Every action you perform will be recorded, so each mistake you make will be made over and over again when you play it back. With a clear idea of what you want to do, perform your task step by step, then press the tiny Stop button at the left of the status bar that runs along the bottom of the Word window. Alternatively, head to View | Macros and click Stop Recording.

(4) EDITING Your macro is now ready and waiting: just click the Quick Access shortcut you created in step 2. If you want to edit it at a later stage, you can: go to View | Macros and select Edit to see the macro broken down into code. While advanced editing may be a step too far for most users, it's quite easy to change a name, for instance, and even if you have only basic programming knowledge you'll be able to strip out any unnecessary code.

HOW LONG?
Creating a macro can take seconds, once you get the hang of it.

HOW HARD?
Much simpler than it appears, honest!

Q&A

Q: While I'm recording my macro, I can't select or double-click text to copy it. Why?
A: Selecting text with a mouse is very difficult to translate into simple code, and beyond the limits of macros. You'll have to stick with key commands such as <Ctrl-A> to select all, <Ctrl-C> to copy and <Ctrl-V> to paste, rather than dragging and dropping.

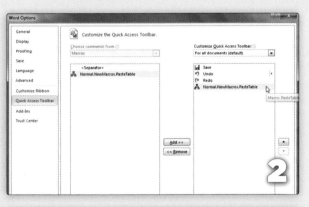

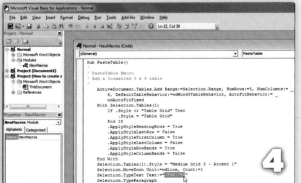

Eight features to make life easier

Office 2010 is littered with little touches that make it easier to work with your documents. Some are new, others were introduced in Office 2007, and some have been around for years but hidden away deep beneath the surface where few people found them. Here, in no particular order, are eight of our favourite features that could make a big difference to your everyday computing life.

1 ADVANCED PICTURE EDITING The cliché still rings true: a picture can be worth a thousand words. What the cliché never explained was how a drab picture could take away from your document's impact, which is why PowerPoint presentations and Word documents the world over have bored their readers to tears. Office 2010 may rectify this, as it brings some pretty powerful photo-editing tools within Word, Excel, PowerPoint, Outlook and Publisher. Insert your photo and you'll be able to perform procedures that used to be exclusive to more advanced tools such as Adobe Photoshop: removing backgrounds, add Polaroid-style borders, and even (with care, please!) apply artistic effects.

2 PASTE WITH LIVE PREVIEW This new feature allows you to see what any copied data will look like – before you paste it. For example, say you're pasting a chunk of text from an email into Word. Right-click in Word and you'll see four Paste Options: Use Destination Theme, Keep Source Formatting, Merge Formatting and Keep Text Only. If you hover your mouse over each option, the document will update live in front of your eyes and show the result. No more paste, undo, repeat ad infinitum.

3 BEAM PRESENTATIONS ACROSS THE INTERNET PowerPoint is one of the most improved apps in Office, and frankly it needed to be. While its headline improvements are support for embedded video and much-improved transitions, we particularly like the fact you can instantly broadcast slides live to an audience all around the world – they don't even need PowerPoint. For more details on exactly how to perform this trick, turn to p75.

4 QUICK ACCESS TOOLBAR This handy little collection of commands sits almost unnoticed at the top of each Office app. In both Word and Excel, it's home to the Save,

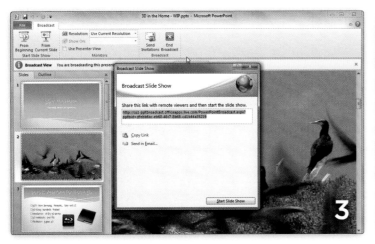

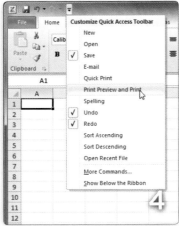

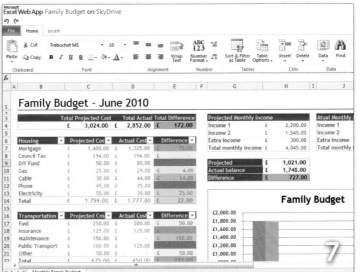

64-bit processing is just one of the less visible innovations in the Office 2010 apps, and if you buy a boxed version of Office then you'll have the option to choose 32-bit or 64-bit. There are some good reasons to stick with 32-bit for now, though, as we discuss on p124.

Undo and Redo commands – but it can do so much more. If you constantly find yourself adjusting page margins, why not add this command? Or in OneNote, add a Print Preview. Then each of those commands are just a click away. You can quickly add commands Microsoft has chosen by clicking the down arrow to the right, but as with the ribbon you can also add your own commands or even macros.

5 **OPENTYPE TYPOGRAPHY** Available in Word and Publisher, OpenType fonts allow you to add amazing flourishes to your text. While they should be used wisely – think of those early newsletters where every font under the sun was squeezed in to make it look "lively" – the impact can be stunning. We explain more about the wonders of OpenType in our chapter on Publisher (starting on p100).

6 **LINKING WITH ONENOTE** We all get information from many sources, and trying to keep track of it inevitably results in a mess. That's exactly the type of thing OneNote was born to deal with, but it's only in Office 2010 that Microsoft allows you to "link" notes. You dock OneNote to your desktop, then take notes while working in Internet

Explorer, Word or PowerPoint; when you review your notes, you'll see exactly what you were doing at the time, so you can dive straight back to the source.

7 **ACCESS DOCUMENTS ON THE WEB** Office Web Apps still feels like a product in embryo, but the fact that you can now view Word, Excel and PowerPoint documents wherever you are – and you don't need the corporate-strength SharePoint to do so, only a web connection and a Windows Live account – is a massive shift. Yes, we've had services such as Google Docs for years, but these rip out your formatting; with Web Apps, you know your document will look just as good as it did when you created it.

8 **64-BIT SUPPORT** The processors inside new PCs and laptops have supported 64-bit computing for some time, and finally Microsoft is offering a 64-bit version of Office. All you have to do is select 64-bit during the installation process. As we discuss on p124, there are caveats to consider. But if you need to work with huge spreadsheets, for example, this is a long-awaited option – and if nothing else, a step in the right direction.

IN THIS CHAPTER

Word 2010

WORD 2010

Word 2010 is far more than a simple word processor. It can be used to create everything from sober reports to colourful club newsletters, and thanks to the ribbon interface – introduced in Office 2007 and improved upon in Office 2010 – it's now so much easier to access its many features. In this chapter, we start with the basics of formatting before providing step-by-step

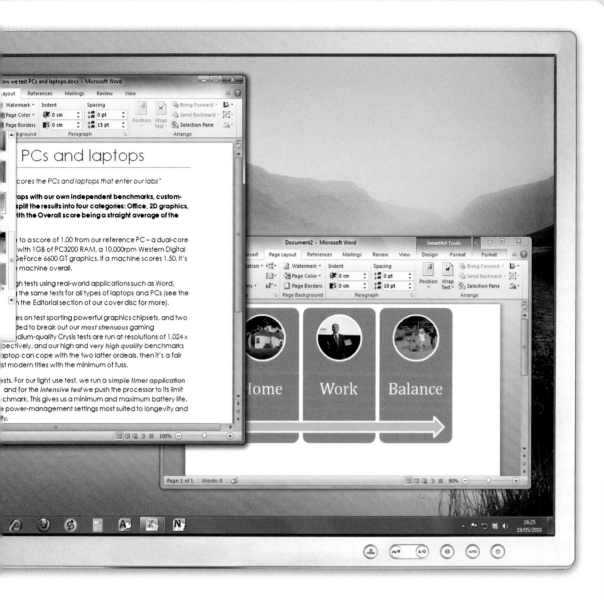

guides to help you personalise your documents, use Word's built-in photo-editing tools, and master text effects. And we go further still, with navigation tips for people working with large documents and a masterclass for academics on Word's citation and bibliography features. Whether you consider yourself a novice or an expert, it's advice you shouldn't miss.

3
Word 2010

HOW LONG?
20 minutes now will save you lots of time in the long run.

HOW HARD?
Once you see how it works, very easy.

HOW TO... FORMAT A DOCUMENT USING STYLES

Format your text as you go along and you'll end up with a document that looks like a greengrocer's stall. Use styles to save effort and ensure consistency.

For years, Word has had the most advanced and usable formatting controls of any word processor, allowing a sophisticated and efficient approach to type and colour, and enabling anyone to create professional-looking documents. The tragedy is that many of us don't make full use of these controls. We either leave everything at default and just start typing, or we format every element by hand, using the Font and Paragraph sections of the ribbon to do all the work. This isn't the way things are meant to be. To make the most effective use of Word, you need to get to grips with styles and themes.

You can get some sense of the importance of styles within Word from their appearance on the default Home tab of the ribbon, with the Font and Paragraph options. Think of them as a set of preset formats for the main elements you might use in any document; the main text (or "body"), headings and subheadings, titles, quotes and so on. There are two good reasons to employ them. First, using styles will save you time. By selecting the right style before you type or selecting a block of text and applying a style, you can be sure that the text in question will have the appropriate font, size, colour, alignment,

spacing and indent. What's more, this will be consistent throughout – the key to professional-looking documents.

Second, using styles makes it much easier to apply widespread changes later. If you decide, say, to change the font used for subheadings across a 30-page business report, there's no need to change each instance separately: just modify the style and watch your change roll out across the whole document. This becomes even more useful when you remember that styles also work in conjunction with themes. Found across Office, these ready-made collections of fonts, styles and colours are designed to help you create neat, attractive documents where all the elements on a page sit well together. If you use styles correctly, altering the theme will change all the text on every page to match. With a single click, you can transform the whole look and feel.

Styles are customisable, and you can alter the existing ones or add your own. Be aware that styles "cascade". The Normal style, for example, is the foundation for several others, so picking a different font, say, will apply this change across the other styles in your document. Useful, as long as you know what to expect.

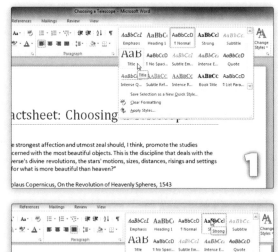

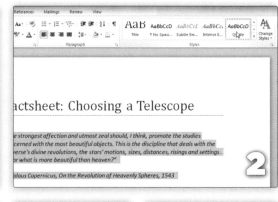

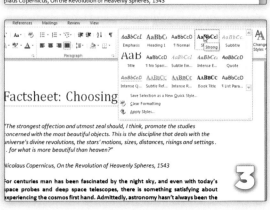

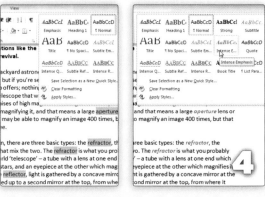

① STYLE THE TITLE We start with a page of basic, unformatted text, cut and pasted into a blank Word document with the default Office theme and Calibri font. First, let's apply a style to the title. Click and drag over the title to highlight it, then go to the Styles section of the ribbon (click the Home tab if you can't see this) and click on the lower down arrow to expand the Styles panel. Note how the styles are previewed as you mouse over them. Click on the Title style to select it.

② FIX THE QUOTE Now select the quote below the title and select the Quote style from the Styles section. Click on the upper down arrow to scroll through to it, or the lower to expand Styles as before.

③ ADD EMPHASIS For this first section of body text we want a font with a little more impact. Highlight the paragraph (the quickest way is to triple-click) and click the Strong style in the Styles panel.

④ INTENSIFY Certain words need to stand out. We could colour them, but the Emphasis styles may work better and will give us more options later. Highlight words by clicking and dragging while holding the Ctrl key, then select the Intense Emphasis style.

⑤ CHANGING COLOURS If we do want to change the colour, we can customise the style. Right-click Intense Emphasis in the Styles panel, then select Modify from the menu that appears. This lets you alter any aspect of the style. For now, we'll just change the colour to the "Red, Accent 2" colour from the Office theme (to see the colour names, just mouse over them). The change rolls out across every block of text with that style applied.

⑥ MAKE AN INDENT The quote style needs some tweaking too: an indent from both the left and right margins will give it more impact. Select the text, then click on the Page Layout tab. Use the Indent options in the Paragraph group to nudge the indents, say, 0.4cm inwards on either side.

⑦ SAVE A NEW STYLE We can save this change to our existing style or use it as the basis for a new style. Right-click on the selected text and go to Styles | Update Quote to Match Selection (where "Quote" is the name of the style) or Styles | Save Selection as a New Quick Style. Give the new style a name and click OK. The new style will also reflect any changes you make to alignment, spacing or colour.

⑧ TOTAL TRANSFORMATION Here's the other advantage of styles. Click the Page Layout tab of the ribbon, then click the Themes button. Mouse over the themes to see how your various elements change all at once in font, size and/or colour.

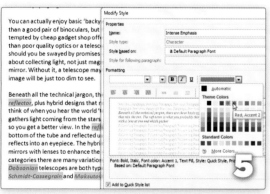

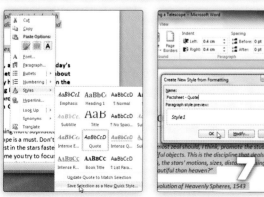

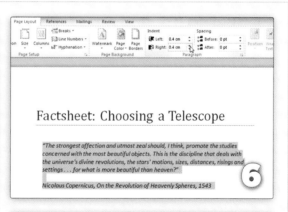

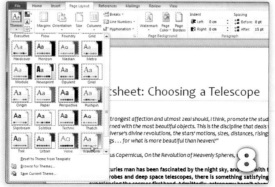

Q&A

Q: If I try to update the Normal style using "Update <style> to match selection" from the Style menu, it just overwrites my existing style. How do I get around this?

A: Word prevents you making major changes to the Normal style because it's the basis for other styles in the document. Instead of updating Normal, use "Save Selection as a New Quick Style" to make a variant and call it something descriptive, such as "Normal–Justified", then use this to style your body copy.

HOW LONG?

A lot less time than it would take to build a template from nothing.

HOW HARD?

We explore some more complicated changes here, but stay with us and you'll make a big impact for little effort.

HOW TO... WORK WITH TEMPLATES AND THEMES

Word's supplied templates may not always look brilliant, but by using them as a foundation you can get a head start on making stylish documents.

While the most basic text pages can always be built from scratch, it makes sense to use templates for documents like newsletters, reports and CVs, which demand more complex layouts. The problem can be finding a ready-made format that fits your needs. True, there's a growing selection available to download from within Word 2010 at the www.office.com website, but they're generally skewed towards an American market. And some of the older Office templates are now looking very tired indeed.

The trick is to see the template not as a finished product, but a springboard for your own designs. Amending one needn't be difficult or time-consuming. By mixing and matching themes, modifying elements and amending styles, you can make the template your own without having to tweak every chunk of text.

As templates are tied in to themes, the easiest way to effect a quick, global transformation is to change the theme. You'll find the Themes panel in the Page Layout tab. Click the button to expand the Themes gallery, and you'll see the results previewed in real-time as you mouse over the various options. Themes, however, are more flexible than you might think: using the three

buttons to the right you can select the colours, fonts or effects of an entirely different theme, allowing you to combine what you like from one with elements of another. Take the fonts and text styles from Austin, the bold colours from Perspective and the effects from Origin, say, and you have your own hybrid theme ready to go.

Beyond that, you can drill down and alter every style, every colour and every effect in the template (although it makes sense to stick within the parameters of the current theme if you want to avoid the more hideous colour clashes). Experiment with the various styles and themes, using Word's Live Preview to get some idea of how your changes will affect the final result. Then, when everything suits your tastes, save it. You have a custom template you can reuse for years to come.

(1) **CHANGE THE THEME** Click the File tab to go to the Backstage view, then select New and take a look at the templates supplied. Here, we're going to use a rather dowdy old template, Executive Newsletter, from the sample collection. It's pretty drab as supplied, so click the Page Layout tab and then the

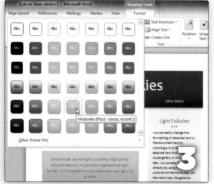

Themes button, then mouse through the selection to see how the template might look with another theme applied.

2 **CHANGE THE SCHEME** The Waveform theme looks good, but the colours aren't ideal. Time to mix and match. Click the Theme Colors button (topmost of the three next to the main Themes button) and look down the list. Here, we've gone for Slipstream.

3 **FIX THE BACKGROUND** The pull-out quote panel lacks impact, and has a slightly cheesy gradient effect to boot. Click on it, then on the Drawing Tools Format tab. Go to the Shape Styles section and click on the lower down arrow to expand the Shape Styles panel. Again, mouse over the various options. This time we've chosen "Moderate Effect – Green, Accent 3".

4 **MODIFY STYLES** The text comes next. Click the Home tab, right-click on the Heading 1 style in the Styles panel and select Modify. Change the font to Calibri and size to 18. Using the B and I buttons, switch on bold and switch off italic, then click the paragraph spacing up button twice to give the heading more room. Click OK. Highlight the subheading text and apply the Strong style from the Styles panel (use the down arrows to scroll or expand the Styles panel if you can't see it). Finally, amend the Quote style. Set Bold and change the colour to "Green, Accent 4, Darker 50%".

5 **DROP CAPITALS** Let's add a drop cap. Highlight the first letter of the main story, click on the Insert tab. In the Text section, click the Drop Cap button (you'll have to write some text; the template uses dummy text). Select the simple Dropped style.

6 **MAKE ROOM** Just because the template doesn't have an image, it doesn't mean we can't add one. First, we need to make room. Click and drag the quote box down to the bottom of the page. Switch on gridlines to help you align the edges (click the View tab, then the Gridlines checkbox in the Show panel), and resize the box if necessary by dragging the corner handles.

7 **INSERT AN IMAGE** Click the Insert tab, then the Picture button in the Illustrations panel. Navigate to an image and click Insert. Click on the image's bounding box and drag the image around to fit. If you need to, resize it to fit within the column.

8 **WRAP UP** Finally, you might need to adjust how the text wraps around the image. Click on the picture and the Picture Tools/Format tab will appear. Click Wrap Text and select Square from the menu. The revised template is now ready to go. Save it as a template before you exit: go to File | Save As, then choose Word Template from the "Save as type" dropdown menu.

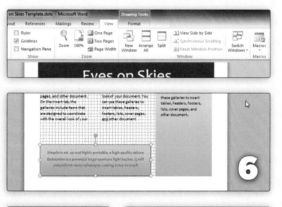

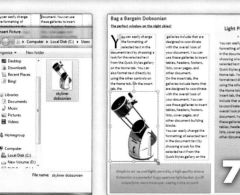

Q&A

Q: Some of Word's dialogs and options don't give me a live preview. What's up?
A: Some of the Text Effect and Font options dialogs don't offer live previews – for example, when you're modifying a style. This is annoying when you're working with Stylistic Sets or Ligatures, but there's just no way to see some of the effects in action without clicking OK. You can always undo or tweak the results afterwards.

HOW TO...
MASTER TEXT EFFECTS

Need titles and headlines that jump off the page? Word 2010 has the text effects tools to make it all happen. Here's how to use them for maximum impact.

Sometimes a new version of Office brings features that, rather than being totally new, give us a more effective way of handling an old task. For over a decade Word has had options to create heavily stylised text for titles, headings and spot effects in the form of WordArt, a built-in set of simple, scalable graphic text effects. Now, Word 2010 has new, more flexible ways of giving text special treatment.

In the past, you inserted WordArt onto the page, typed in your text and positioned it. WordArt wasn't treated in the same way as regular text; it didn't benefit from the full range of formatting options, and wasn't spellchecked and grammar-checked in the usual way.

That all changes with the new Text Effects. These are preset and customisable treatments that you can apply to any block of text, anywhere on the page – just like a change of font, font colour, underline or bold. Text Effects can even be applied to styles, and the results saved as a new Quick Style (see p27). Galleries of presets make it easy to try different options, particularly as you get a real-time preview before they're applied. Any changes you make can be reversed instantly. What's more, text with Text Effects is dealt with by Word's proofing tools in exactly the same way as normal text. You need never worry about an embarrassing typo in a headline.

The Text Effects button can be found in the Font panel of the ribbon's Home tab: it's the glowing blue capital "A" next to the highlighter icon. Text Effects also work in conjunction with themes. Altering your colour theme, for example, changes the colours in Text Effects.

Text Effects aren't the only new way to spice up text. While the options are more deeply buried than in Publisher, Word can also exploit some of the advanced features of OpenType fonts, enabling you to play with ligatures (where specific letter combinations are joined into a single shape) and alternative style sets (stylistic variations on the typeface). By combining these new controls with Text Effects, you can come up with results that are sure to grab attention. Just don't overdo it; as always, restraint works better than excess.

(1) **SET FONT AND THEME** There's nothing special to look at here, just a block of text in Candara 24pt, with a background tint on the page and the theme (Page Layout | Themes) set to Perspective.

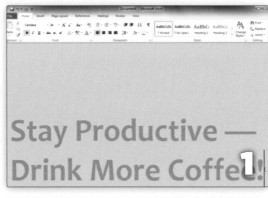

2 ADD TEXT EFFECTS Click and drag over the text to highlight it, then go to the Home tab and click the Text Effects button in the Font panel. You'll see the default gallery of preset effects. Mouse over them to see how each will affect your selection; note the description summarising the colours and effects applied.

3 MIX YOUR OWN EFFECTS There's no need to stick with the presets, however. Click on the Outline, Shadow, Reflection and Glow menu options below and you can expand the gallery of preset effects. Here, we've opted for an Orange fill with an "Indigo, Accent 5, Darker 50%" outline and an Offset Diagonal Bottom Left shadow.

4 FINE TUNING To get more control over Shadows, Reflections or Glows, click the relevant Options button; for example, to adjust Shadows go to Text Effects | Shadow | Shadow Options. These give you the ability to alter every parameter by dragging sliders. We've created a new shadow effect with Transparency 24%, Size 100%, Blur 5pt, Angle 174° and Distance 6pt.

5 3D EFFECTS Click on the small arrow at the bottom right of the Font panel to open the Font dialog box. Click on Text Effects to see the Format Text Effects dialog, which gives you access to a range of 3D treatments through the 3-D Formats tab.

This allows you to add bezels, surfaces and translucency or transparency effects to your text. This time we'll opt for a preset top bevel with the Material set to Plastic.

6 A NEW STYLE Now let's wipe the slate clean. With the text still highlighted, click the Clear Formatting button (in the Font group of the name tab). Change the Font to Gabriola, click Bold, set the font size to 24, then click Text Effects and select "Gradient Fill – Black, Outline – White, Outer Shadow".

7 PLAY WITH LIGATURES Now right-click on the text block and select Font from the menu. This brings up the Font dialog box. Click the Advanced tab of the Font dialog, then go to the OpenType features and click the Ligatures dropdown. Select "Standard and Contextual", and note how the two "f" characters now crowd in and join together. You'll see similar effects on other common ligatures, depending on the words and OpenType typeface used.

8 STYLISTIC SETS Finally, we can have some fun with the Stylistic sets. In the Advanced tab of the Font dialog, click on the Stylistic sets dropdown, and change the set being used from the Default option to set 5. As you can see, in this font certain letters' strokes now get exuberant "swash" flourishes – perfect for an elegant headline that will get itself noticed.

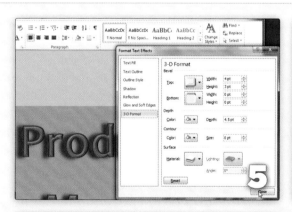

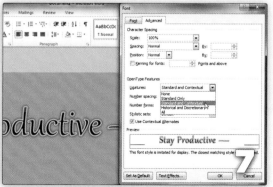

Tip

The beauty of using Text Effects is that they can be applied to any block of text, including body text, headline text or titles. In fact, if there's a text effect that works well in, say, a heading, you can update a Heading style to use it or save your own new style with the text effect applied. Just right-click on your text, then go to Styles | Save Selection as a New Quick Style. See p26 for our detailed guide to using styles.

HOW TO...
ADD IMPACT WITH IMAGES

Word's graphic-handling capabilities just keep getting better. With this much editing power, you may not even need to use a separate photo application.

As time has gone on, the Word document has moved from being a primarily text-based creation to one that may include a range of graphic elements, from a simple letterhead to diagrams, photos and backgrounds. While more elaborate projects are still better suited to Publisher, Word 2010 packs in a lot of image-manipulation power.

Insert a picture into your Word document and you'll now find a range of tools and options waiting for you under the Format | Picture Tools tab that appears on the ribbon. Divided into four panels, it gives you the ability to perform the most common image adjustments without needing to launch a dedicated image-editing app.

These tools are surprisingly sophisticated. Remove Background, for example, makes it reasonably easy to isolate an object in a photo – say, a product or person – from the background by identifying the area to focus on, then clicking on those areas you want to keep and those you wish to remove. Other tools enable you to make simple colour, brightness and contrast adjustments just by clicking on one of a selection of thumbnails.

Monochrome and sepia treatments are also a click away, while borders and effects can be applied from galleries in seconds. You can also crop images within Word, moving markers to isolate which portion of the shot will appear on the page. Word helpfully greys out the unselected chunk to show the effect of your changes.

Finally, Word's options now extend to a gallery of filters known as Artistic Effects. These cover a range of natural media such as watercolours, chalks and pastels; a selection of textures including film grain, glass and cement; and some – let's be polite – wackier options for glowing edges or a weird plastic-wrapped look.

Click on Artistic Effects Options beneath the main gallery and you can even configure many of these filters. True, their flexibility and power is limited compared to the range of effects found in a dedicated photo editor, but if you just need a quick and dirty fix for a photo you're dropping into a report, guide or newsletter, then Word 2010 has you covered.

1 **SET THE THEME** Here's our initial text document, waiting for images. We've already applied the Title text style to the first paragraph and set the theme to Composite (Page Layout | Themes | Composite).

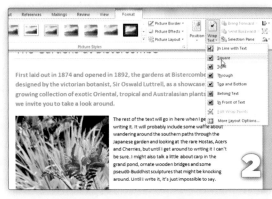

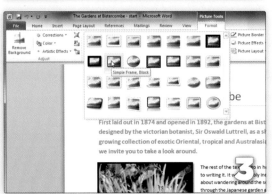

HOW LONG?

Word's only similarity to chess is that its image-editing tools take moments to learn but longer to master.

HOW HARD?

It may take some tinkering to get the exact result you want, but it's surprisingly simple once you know where the tools are.

2 INSERT AN IMAGE Time for the first picture. Click before the first word of the body text and then click the Insert tab on the ribbon. Select Picture, navigate to an image file and click the Insert button. Click on the handle at the right-hand corner of the image and drag it inwards or outwards to scale the picture. You'll notice that the photo has scared away all the text. No problem: with the Picture Tools Format tab active, select Wrap Text | Square.

3 APPLY PICTURE STYLES We'll apply a basic effect to help the picture stand out. Click on the down arrow next to the gallery of Picture Styles to expand it, and select the effect of your choice. Here, we've gone for "Simple Frame, Black".

4 INSERT ANOTHER IMAGE This next move might seem odd at first, but bear with us. Click before the first letter of the title and insert another image. If it messes up the layout so far, don't worry. Select Wrap Text | Behind Text to put the shot at the back, then move and rescale the picture so that it covers the whole top section of the page.

5 CROP Let's cut that image down to size. Still in the Picture Tools Format tab, click the Crop button. Now use the crop markers to select only the portion of the image that sits behind the title.

If you need to, you can always click inside the crop area and drag it around to select which part of the image will appear within the crop. When you're done, press Enter on your keyboard.

6 ADJUST BRIGHTNESS AND CONTRAST You can't read the title here, so we'll fix that. With the Picture Tools Format tab active, go to the Adjust group on the left and select Corrections. Hover over the thumbnail shown below, which should say "Brightness: -40% Contrast: -40%", then select it to knock both contrast and brightness back by this amount. The picture gets greyer and lighter, returning the text to prominence.

7 COLOURISE THE IMAGE The colours behind the text are still distracting, though. Click the Color button next to Corrections. You'll see a whole range of tone and saturation controls; this time, we want to recolour the image. Select the "Lime, Accent color 1 Light" thumbnail (if you can't see Lime as an option, make sure you're using the Composite theme – or pick an alternative of your own).

8 APPLY ARTISTIC EFFECTS Finally, we'll add an artistic effect to make the background even more abstract. Click on the Artistic Effects button, then select the Cutout thumbnail at the bottom left of the gallery.

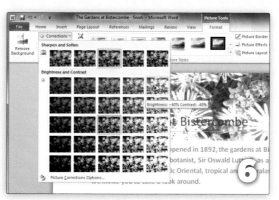

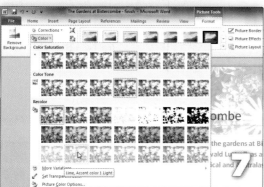

Tip

It's easy to set an image to use as a Page Background: go to the Page Layout tab, select Page Color from the Page Background panel, click Fill Effects and hit the Picture tab. However, if the image is too strong to make the text readable over it, a better plan is to follow steps 4 to 8 in this tutorial, but with the image scaled to cover the whole page.

Word 2010

HOW TO... USE BUILDING BLOCKS FOR A PROFESSIONAL TOUCH

Creating templates for longer documents can be time-consuming, but Word's built-in Building Blocks make the process much simpler and more effective.

Complex documents such as club newsletters and company reports can take a lot of time to set up, and while there are always templates to rely on, these might not match the content and image you want. But creating a document from scratch means setting up each textbox or graphic element step by step, which requires a certain level of expertise, and then you have the problem of keeping to a consistent style. Before you know it, your document looks amateurish.

Fortunately, there is a halfway house. Word 2007 introduced Building Blocks: ready-made cover pages, headers, footers, quote boxes, tables and sidebars that you slot into your document as and when they're needed. And Word 2010 continues with the concept. Many building blocks are intended to be used within existing templates, but don't let this put you off. All can be customised, and as they've all been set up using Word's preset text styles and colour themes, it's easy to make global changes to integrate them into your new template.

You'll find all these components under the Insert tab of the ribbon. Go to the Pages section and you'll see a Cover Page button that leads to a gallery of fully formatted cover pages: all you need to do is amend the existing text, or select dates using the pop-out fields. Or click the Table button in the Tables section next door and select Quick Tables to find a range of ready-made calendars, tables and lists ready for you to use.

It's in the Text panel, however, that things become really interesting. The Text Box gallery gives you an extensive selection of quote boxes and sidebars in a variety of styles; if you can't find what you're looking for, click the Quick Parts button and select the Building Blocks Organizer to browse through Word's entire selection of cover pages, equations, headers, footers, watermarks and textboxes. Many building blocks – including headers, footers and sidebars – automatically cling to a specific area of the page, but others, such as quote boxes, can be moved, with any text on the page wrapping around them.

You're not solely reliant on Microsoft's own building blocks, or the others you can download from www.office.com. If you create your own textboxes or graphic elements, these can be saved back as new blocks. Create them once and you can use them again and again throughout your document, and in other documents too.

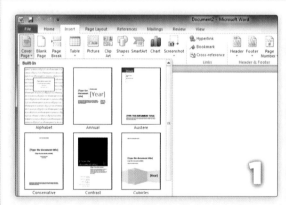

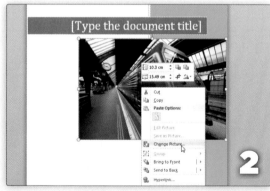

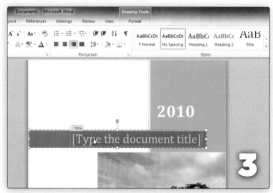

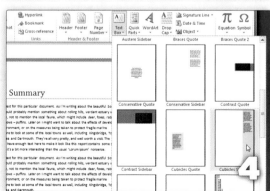

1 **ADD A COVER PAGE** In this report for a (fictional) countryside trust, we'll take a cover page from Office's ready-made line-up. Click the Insert tab, then the Cover Page button. We'll use the Motion option.

2 **INSERT YOUR OWN IMAGE** Obviously we need to change the image, so right-click on the train photo, select Change Picture from the context-sensitive menu, and navigate to an image file. Click Insert.

3 **AMEND THE FIELDS** For the rest of the changes, just type into the fields laid out on the page to change their contents. For the dates, click on the arrow and select a date – you don't even need to type.

4 **ADD A SIDEBAR** We've pasted in our summary. Here, it's vital we style our title and body text using styles (Home | Styles) instead of formatting by hand using the Font panel. Next, we'll add a sidebar. Click the Insert tab, then the Text Box button, and choose a sidebar from the gallery. Here, we're using the Cubicles Sidebar. Now just alter and re-style the text in the sidebar. Sidebars are designed to be brief, eye-catching snippets of info, so keep it short and pithy or use a bulleted list to highlight key points.

5 **DIY QUOTE BOX** For the next page (click Ctrl-Enter to insert a page break) we've reused the Cubicles Sidebar, but this page needs a quote as well. We could use a pre-built quote box from the Text Box gallery, but this time we'll create our own. Click the Insert tab, then go to the Illustrations panel, click Shapes and choose a simple Rounded Rectangle.

6 **ALTER THE COLOURS** Once you've drawn the rectangle shape, the Drawing Tools | Format tab will activate. Use the fill and outline options in the Shape Styles panel to make the colours more subdued (sticking to theme colours if you want consistency). Now click the Wrap Text button and choose Square.

7 **SAVE YOUR TEXTBOX** With the box selected, start typing and the text will appear in the box. Style your text, again using Home | Styles. You can then save your quote box for later use. Click the box to select it, then go to the Insert tab, click the Text Box button and select "Save Selection to Text Box Gallery" from the menu. Give the box a name and description, make sure the Options entry is set to "Insert content only", then click OK.

8 **REUSE YOUR BOX** When you want to reuse your textbox, simply click on the page where you want it, then on the Insert tab. Click the Text Box button, scroll to the bottom of the gallery, and your new quotes box will be there, ready for action.

Tip

The problem with mixing and matching building blocks is that you can end up with a mess. The best way to fix this is to apply a new global theme over the top (find this option in Page Layout | Themes). This will tie all the fonts and colours together, although you may need to go back through and alter text sizes and spacing to make the new theme work. As ever, themes provide a quick means of making dramatic changes to a document's overall look and feel.

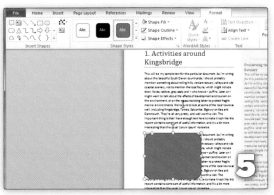

HOW TO... CREATE EFFECTIVE DIAGRAMS WITH SMARTART

Numbered lists and bullet points are so 1990s. Turn your text into clear, explanatory diagrams with Word 2010's SmartArt feature.

HOW LONG?
You can create a diagram in 20 minutes – or longer if you're an inveterate tweaker.

HOW HARD?
A little fiddly, but fairly intuitive considering the capabilities on offer.

We'd seen clip-art. We'd done WordArt. Then, with Word 2007, we had SmartArt. Enhanced and improved for Word 2010, SmartArt is essentially a collection of pre-built, modular sets of shapes and textboxes that you can use to build your own diagrams in minutes. Whether you're after a simple Venn diagram, a flow chart, a family tree or an organisational diagram, you can create it within Word with no design expertise and very little hassle. Even if you just want to make a list with more visual impact than the old-school bullet points option, SmartArt can help.

You'll find SmartArt on the Insert tab of the ribbon, where it sits between the Shapes and Chart buttons in the Illustrations panel. The SmartArt gallery organises the available diagrams in categories, such as Process diagrams to show a flow of information from start to finish or the self-explanatory Hierarchy diagrams. Each choice comes with a preview image and a description that explains the features of that piece of SmartArt and its likely applications. Your choice couldn't be much easier.

But the really cool things happen when you insert SmartArt on page. You can drag and drop the bounding box to reposition or resize it, or type into the boxes just as you would any other textbox. The item will also be accompanied by a specific text-entry box (click the arrow on the left or right edge if it doesn't appear), and you can type into this as if typing a normal bullet list: Word places the entries automatically. If the SmartArt doesn't quite fit your needs – say, it's designed for three items, but you need five – don't worry. Press Enter after typing the third item, and a fourth will appear. Repeat, and so will the fifth, with the SmartArt resizing and scaling the existing elements to fit the new shapes and textboxes.

SmartArt is also fully customisable through a series of preset styles and colour schemes. These are tied into your current global theme, so as long as you stick to this, whatever you choose will always work with your document as a whole. What's more, word wrap options can be applied in exactly the same way as any other graphic object, giving you real control over how the piece of SmartArt fits into the page.

While specialist graphics products such as CorelDRAW or Microsoft Visio will always have their place, SmartArt puts a lot of diagram-building power into the hands of the average user. Let's give it a whirl.

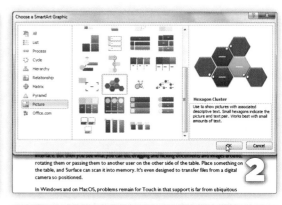

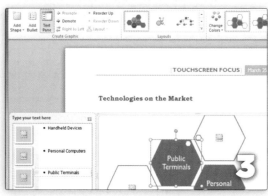

1 THE BARE TEXT Here's a rather staid page of text just waiting for some extra bling. We could add some clip-art or a bullet list to add some extra weight, but this time we're going to let SmartArt do the heavy lifting and give us a stronger result.

2 ADD SMARTART Click before the first character of the first line of body text, then click the Insert tab and hit the SmartArt button. Unless you know what you're looking for, it's good to scroll through the gallery and take a look at the options. Here, we're just trying to differentiate between basic types of product in a visual way. The Hexagon Cluster, in the Picture section, will be ideal. Pick it, then click OK.

3 TYPE YOUR TEXT There's no need to type on the drawing itself: type items into the "Type your text here" panel, pressing Return after each. Word will size and position the text automatically to fit.

4 CHANGE THE IMAGES Changing the images is just as easy. Either click on the picture icon next to each text item in the "Type your text here" panel, or click on the picture in the diagram itself. In each case, browse to your desired image and click Insert.

5 RESIZE AND REPOSITION Grab one of the corner handles on the bounding box and resize the image to take up one-sixth of the page. To position a diagram easily, ensure it's selected, then click the Format tab that appears under SmartArt Tools in the ribbon. Click Position (found in the Arrange group to the right), go down to the With Text Wrapping section and choose "Position in Top Right with Square Text Wrapping".

6 MORE STYLE It's still a bit drab, so let's add some impact. Click the Design tab under SmartArt Tools, then the Change Colors button near the middle of the ribbon. Pick whichever option you like; we've gone for "Colorful Range – Accent Colors 2 to 3". Now click the down arrow next to the SmartArt Styles gallery to expand it, and pick a new style. Ours is 3D.

7 BUILD A LIST We'll now use SmartArt to create a more detailed bullet list. Go to Insert | SmartArt once again, but this time visit the List category and choose Vertical Box List. Typing in the box will again replace the main item text; to add subcategories, simply click in the space under the blue bar and start typing.

8 MAKE THE LIST LOOK GOOD You can adjust the colours, style and positioning as in steps 5 and 6. In this case, we want to keep the colour scheme consistent between the two diagrams, but we've opted for a more basic flat style and chosen "Position in Bottom Left with Square Text Wrapping".

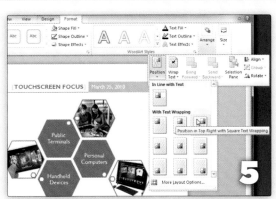

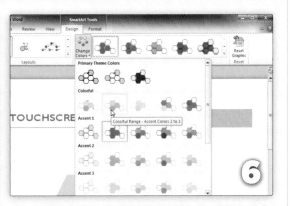

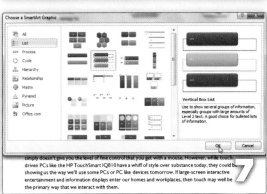

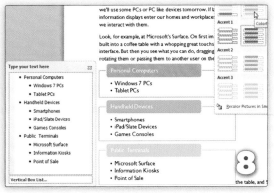

Tip

Word sometimes struggles to wrap text around more complex, non-square items, including many SmartArt diagrams – and particularly so if you use the Tight or Through options (SmartArt Tools | Format | Arrange | Wrap Text). However, you can give it a helping hand. Go back to the Wrap Text menu and pick Edit Wrap Points. Click and drag the points to adjust the text-free area around the item.

HOW TO... NAVIGATE LARGE DOCUMENTS WITH EASE

Take that finger off the scroll wheel! Word 2010 has a whole new bag of tricks to help you wade through complex multi-part documents.

Ploughing through lengthy documents – books, reports, academic papers – can be a chore. Word has tried to make it easier with features ranging from Document Map to the more recent Outline and Thumbnail, but these features haven't always been perfectly implemented. In fact, many of us ignore them in favour of the old-fashioned scroll bar or a one-finger workout with the scroll wheel. Neither approach is ideal.

Word 2010 might have the answer. It takes the best bits from the Document Map, Outline and Thumbnail views, and integrates them with search to create the Navigation pane. This gives you almost instant access to any part of your document, and a great set of tools for keeping longer documents in shape.

To find the Navigation pane, click the View tab and then the checkbox in the Show panel. The pane will appear at the left of the Word window, with a search bar at the top and three tabbed windows below. The first lists the sections or chapters in your document, by heading or subheading, as buttons. The various levels of heading are nested, and you can expand or collapse them by clicking the arrows to the left or by right-clicking a heading button

and selecting Expand All or Collapse All. Not only can you click on a heading to move to it instantly, but you can move sections and subsections within the document by clicking and dragging them upwards and downwards here.

The second tab gives a page-by-page thumbnail view; clicking a thumbnail takes you to the relevant page. This view is particularly effective with more graphical documents, showing where you are at a glance.

The final tab is used primarily for search. Type a search term into the search bar and this tab will list all the occasions where it's used, with a snippet of the surrounding text. Again, it's an effective way of searching for key words or phrases through long documents, particularly if you have a rough idea where the text should be. Flick to the first tab while you have an active search, and you'll also see sections and subsections containing your term or phrase highlighted in gold.

In short, the Navigation pane is an invaluable tool for anyone who has to slog away on long documents.

① NAVIGATE BY THUMBNAIL To open the Navigation Pane, click on the View tab in the

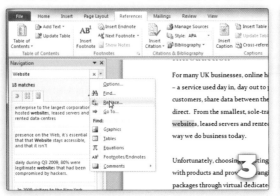

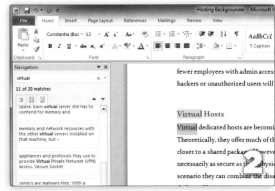

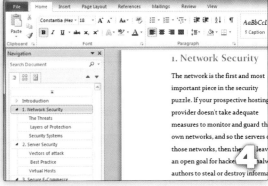

HOW LONG?

A quarter of an hour should be enough to tour the new features.

HOW HARD?

Once you get the hang of it, this is all about making things easier.

ribbon, go to the Show panel and click the Navigation pane checkbox. The middle tab gives you thumbnail views of all the pages in your document in sequential order. Click on the thumbnail to go to the page.

2 **SEARCH AND RESCUE** The right-hand tab is used for searching. Enter a keyword, term or phrase and Word will list every instance of its use in the Navigation pane. Use the arrows to the right of the tab to cycle through the instances, or click on one to see it in the main window. The instance highlighted in the Navigation pane is also highlighted in the editing window in green.

3 **MORE OPTIONS** To see additional search options, click the down arrow to the right of the search box. The topmost Options button takes you to the Search Options dialog, where you can expand or amend your search parameters. The other options give you the power to search for content outside of the main body copy, such as footnotes or graphics.

4 **NAVIGATE BY HEADING** The leftmost tab takes you to arguably the most useful view. The document is divided into sections by analysing your use of Heading styles. Chunks below a Heading 1 style are taken to define the main sections, while Heading 2, 3, 4 and so on are taken as subsections. This only works if the document uses styles – another reason to do so.

5 **CREATE A NEW SECTION** There are two ways of creating a new section. First, just highlight or create a new section heading, then go to the Home tab and apply the Heading 1 style. Alternatively, right-click on a heading in the Navigation Pane and choose the New Heading Before or New Heading After options. You may have to move your heading manually into place, however: just click and drag.

6 **CREATE A NEW SUBSECTION** Similarly, create a new subsection by applying the Heading 2, Heading 3 or subsequent styles, or right-clicking on an existing heading and selecting New Subheading.

7 **RE-ORGANISE YOUR DOCUMENT** Moving sections or subsections around is easy: just click and drag the section from its old place to wherever you want it. All its subsections will move with it, and page numbers will be updated automatically.

8 **TABLE OF CONTENTS** Here's another good reason to maintain structure and style. Insert a new page at the start of your document, then click the References tab. Now click the "Table of Contents" button and Word automatically creates a table of contents from your headings, subheadings and sections. If you make changes or move sections, you'll need to click Update Table to keep everything in the correct order.

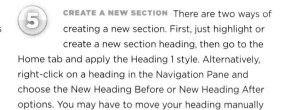

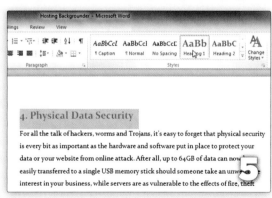

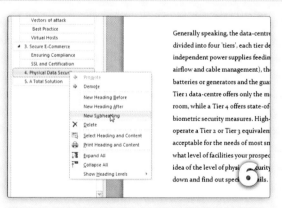

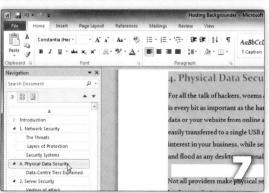

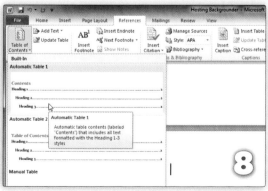

Tip

At times you might want to move a subsection or promote it to being a section in its own right; at other times you might want to move a section to become a subsection within another. Nothing could be simpler. Right-click on the item in question in the Navigation pane, then select the Promote or Demote option. Then just click and drag as needed to the appropriate place.

HOW TO... ADD SCREENSHOTS AND TRANSLATE TEXT

Word's feature list has expanded to accommodate some handy new tools that could make a surprising difference to your home and working life.

HOW LONG?
Give yourself time to explore all the features here – they're worth it.

HOW HARD?
Sometimes a bit fiddly, never difficult.

Every new version of Word brings a few features that won't make headlines, but will save certain people an awful lot of time. Word 2010 is no different. Alongside more obvious additions, you'll find two neat little time-savers: a built-in screen grabber and an improved version of Word 2007's translation services.

The Screenshot tool will be particularly welcome to anyone who needs to include grabs from websites or applications in Word documents. You might be working on a guide or manual that explains how to do things onscreen, or you may need to use images from a website in a report. In the past, this might have meant hitting PrintScreen, opening or pasting the image into an editing program, saving it, then inserting it into your Word document. Now, thanks to Screenshot and the enhanced built-in image-editing tools, you can do it all in Word.

Cleverly, the Screenshot tool gives you two options. Click the button (Insert | Illustrations | Screenshot) and you'll see a thumbnail list of open windows. Click the one you want and it's instantly copied into your document, where you can resize, reposition, crop and adjust it. Select the Screen Clipping option below, however, and Word minimises, giving you a crosshair pointer with which you can select any area.

GAINED IN TRANSLATION Word 2007 had translation capabilities, but the process was a little confusing. The new Translate features are easier to use straight from the taskbar, and Microsoft has also integrated the Mini Translator, which you'll find across most Office applications (see Tip, opposite). It works in conjunction with Microsoft's online Translator service.

Machine translation is no replacement for human language skills, but it can give you the gist of foreign text or produce a rough translation of your English document.

(1) **TAKE A SCREENSHOT** This example is a report analysing the success of recent video games in Europe. To make our point, we need to quote from various online media outlets across the continent. Our first website is already open, so we click the Insert tab, then go to the Illustrations panel and click Screenshot. Select the open browser window from the Available Windows section of the menu.

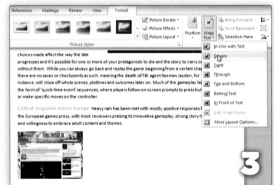

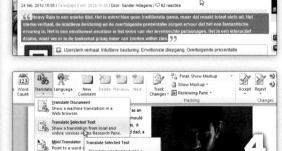

CROP THE SHOT The screen grab is inserted on a new page, as it's too big for the existing one. Let's cut it down. Go to Picture Tools | Format and in the Size panel click Crop. Use the crop marks inside the image to trim any extraneous elements (the browser window, for example). Press Enter when you're finished.

RESIZE AND WRAP Use the corner handles to resize the image, then drag it into position below the body text. Initially Word will wrap text above and below the image, so click on the Picture Tools | Format tab, then on Wrap Text, and select Square.

QUICK TRANSLATE Next we want to cut a snippet of text and translate it as a quote. Switch to the web browser, select some text and hit Ctrl-C to copy it. Return to Word and paste the text in. Here the text is in Dutch; we need it in English. Select the text, click the Review tab, then go to the Language panel and click Translate. Choose Translate Selected Text.

SET LANGUAGES Use the From and To dropdowns in the Translation section of the Research pane to set the source and target languages. Once you select the target, the translated text will appear in the results area of the panel, below the line. Click the Insert button and the translated text is pasted over the original. If you don't see an Insert button, the translator is using a different engine – probably WorldLingo (to check, click "Translation options" in the Research pane).

SCREEN CLIPPING Let's repeat this for a second source, but with a twist: we want to give readers a flavour of what each site says. This time, when you take your screenshot (Insert | Illustrations | Screenshot) select the Screen Clipping option. Word disappears, revealing the desktop, greyed-out. To select the area you want, click at the top-left corner and drag out a rectangular selection. The area appears in full colour. Release the mouse button to insert the new screen grab.

REPEAT THE STEPS Resize this grab, drag it into place and set the Wrap Text option, as in steps 2 and 3. Then follow steps 4 and 5 to copy, paste and translate a snippet of text. Cut and paste more than you need if you're not sure what's relevant yet.

TRANSLATE WHOLE DOCUMENTS To translate a document from English into another language, click the Translate button (Review | Language | Translate), pick Choose Translation Language and select a source and target. Click OK. Click Translate again, but now pick Translate Document. Click OK. If it's set to use Microsoft Translator, a website will load with your original and translated versions, and you can cut and paste from the right-hand window into a new Word document.

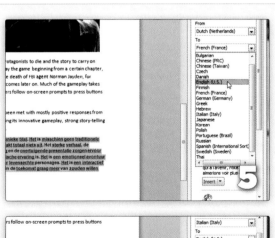

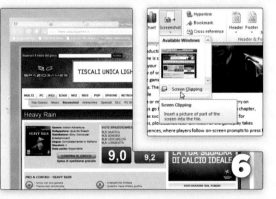

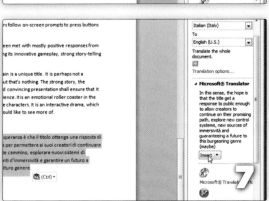

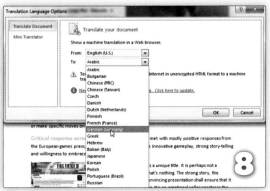

Tip

If you work with a lot of foreign language documents, Word's Mini Translator will be invaluable. Open a document and go to Review | Language | Translate, then switch on the Mini Translator (a gold border around the option shows it's on). Click Choose Translation Language, click Mini Translator, and set the target language to English. Now hover over any word or highlighted phrase: a ghostly Mini Translator window appears. Move the mouse over it to bring it into focus and get an English translation of the word or phrase.

HOW LONG?

Could take as little as half an hour, depending on your document.

HOW HARD?

Much easier than it's ever been before.

HOW TO... ADD BIBLIOGRAPHIES, FOOTNOTES AND CITATIONS

Referencing is always the boring bit. If you have to write essays, reports or academic papers, let Microsoft Word handle the duller side of authorship.

Writing lengthy reports or even simple essays is hard enough at times without having to worry about all the "housekeeping" that comes with it. Tying facts and opinions together and moulding them into a persuasive argument can be absorbing, but marking citations and creating a bibliography is just a chore. Like most housekeeping, it's better done by someone else.

Luckily, Word is happy to bear the burden. Word 2007 introduced new tools for tracking references, sources and citations, and Word 2010 carries on the good work, making the process as pain-free and automated as possible. A few bugbears have been cleared up – it's now possible to add a citation inside a footnote, for example – and you can turn a list of citations into a formatted bibliography with one click. If you've been doing this stuff manually, you'll know what a time-saver that is.

The correct form of a citation or bibliography depends on the standards of the field you work in. By default, Word follows the rules set down by the American Psychological Association, but it's also possible to switch to the Chicago Manual of Style, the Modern Language Association or the ISO690 or Turabian schemes. One advantage of using Word to handle your citations and bibliography is that you can switch styles in an instant. So there's no need to panic if you've been working to Chicago and your journal, examining board or client wants MLA. The only disappointment is that some styles used widely in the UK, including that of the Modern Humanities Research Association (MHRA), aren't supported – although the MLA style is broadly similar.

As well as tracking citations, Word is well-equipped to handle footnotes and endnotes, inserting them at the end of the page or document, and tracking positioning and numbering to ensure they show on the right page, with the right number and in the right order.

1 **THE ARTICLE IN QUESTION** This article might be short, but it's full of references, quotes and other material in need of citation. If our author had been organised he might have added sources as he went (References | Manage Sources), but he wasn't.

2 **INSERT A CITATION** Find the first reference that needs a citation and click just after it, then click

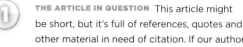

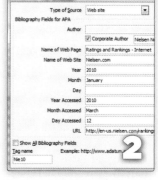

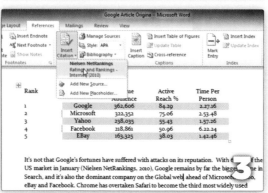

the References tab. Go to the Citations & Bibliography panel and click the Insert Citation button. Here, you can either add a new source or – if you haven't got the information to hand – a placeholder for editing later. In this case, select "Add New Source...". Choose the Source Type (the information needed depends on whether you're referencing a website, a book, journal, film or whatever). Type the relevant details into the boxes, then click OK.

3 REPEAT AS NECESSARY The citation will appear in your document in the current citation style format. Now for the good bit. Having added a source once, you don't need to add it again. If you need to make a second reference, simply click Insert Citation and choose your source from the menu. Be aware, however, that for books, magazines and other printed material, you'll still need to add page numbers for references by hand. Click on the citation in the document, click on the down arrow that appears and select Edit Citation.

4 INSERT A FOOTNOTE Footnotes work in a similar way. Click on the point where you need to insert one, then go to References and click the Insert Footnote button. A number will appear in the document, and the cursor will be whisked off to a section at the end of the page where you type it in. Handily, if you hover over the reference number in the text, a small tip window appears with the relevant text.

5 KEEP WORD ON ITS TOES Now try entering a footnote somewhere in the text above the first (repeat Step 4). Word will change the number of the first footnote and insert the new one on the correct page. You don't have to do a thing. If you add text and push the reference over the page, the footnote follows it.

6 USE PLACEHOLDERS If you're stuck for details when inserting a citation, use the "References | Insert Citation | Add New Placeholder..." option. To insert the source information and turn the placeholder into a citation, click on the placeholder, then on the down arrow that appears next to it, then select Edit Source. Type in the details, click OK and it's done.

7 CREATE A BIBLIOGRAPHY With all the information in, creating a bibliography is easy. Click to set the text insert point at the end of your document, then go to References and click on the down arrow next to Bibliography. Select from the two presets (Bibliography and Works Cited), and the complete bibliography duly appears.

8 SWITCH STYLE If you're faced with a last-minute change of citation style, don't worry. Go to References and click the Style dropdown in the Citations & Bibliography panel. Select a style and your citations and bibliography automatically change to suit.

Tip

The great thing about using Word to track your sources is that you can move them easily from document to document. If, for example, you're working on a series of articles or essays that will regularly reference the same source, go to References and click on the Manage Sources button. You'll see a master list of sources that you can copy over to the current document by highlighting items and clicking Copy. Add new sources as you do your initial research and you'll save yourself lots of time later on.

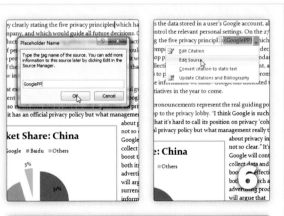

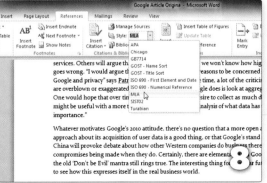

FOUR MORE GREAT FEATURES
IN WORD 2010

Here's our selection of the finest features in Word to help you create the most professional documents with the fewest possible mistakes.

1 **RECOVER UNSAVED VERSIONS** Word offered a recovery option before, but couldn't recover files if you closed the document and accidentally clicked "Don't Save". Word 2010 always saves your latest version, allowing you to reopen the document, pop into Backstage view, and then preview, compare and restore different versions of a file.

2 **CONTEXTUAL SPELLING CHECKER** If you constantly type "their" when you really mean "they're", or "it's" when you should be typing "its", Word's contextual spellcheck could become your new best friend (while saving your grammar blushes). It will highlight your potential error with a blue squiggly line underneath the disputed word; you just right-click on the word to choose the alternative.

3 **LINKED NOTES** A 100-page report lands in your inbox with an electronic thump. You need to read it and make notes as you go along. Now, Word can work in tandem with OneNote (which is bundled with all the Office suites apart from Starter) to let you write comments as you're scrolling through the document, and it cleverly marks where you made them too. Find out more in Chapter 7.

4 **ANYWHERE ACCESS** Want to read your Word documents while you're on somebody else's computer? And what's that, you also want to make changes? Well, now you can. Simply load the document onto a SharePoint server or your Windows Live SkyDrive (see p126 and p148 respectively) and you can fiddle as much as you like from wherever you are.

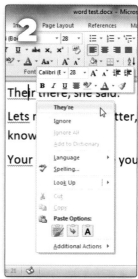

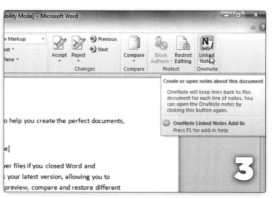

Features we love in Word 2010 include the career-saving ability to recover files you foolishly closed without saving; contextual spellcheck, which helps to spot words that are real words but not the right ones in the right place; linked notes, which attach to the point in a document they refer to; and online access.

Microsoft

Microsoft® Office 2010
MAKE IT GREAT

I want to make it great because my personal assistant's name is ME.

I'm Minreet and I should add personal assistant to the two jobs I have, three if you count being a mum. With new Outlook® 2010 I can easily sync my calendar with my husband's so our crazy schedules are always on the same page. I should give myself a pay rise!

> See how you can make it great with new Office 2010 at
office.com/2010

IN THIS CHAPTER

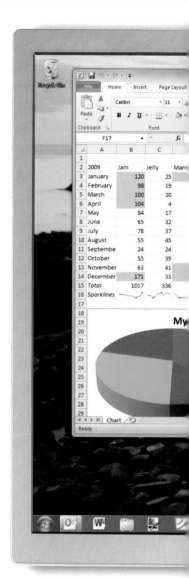

Excel 2010

EXCEL 2010

Excel is an immensely powerful program, and this chapter helps you tap into that power. We start by introducing the fundamental terms, the simplest functions and how to print successfully; all the basics you must grasp to get started with a spreadsheet. You don't need to be a genius to use Excel to take control of your household finances, with templates ready and

waiting to be adjusted to your needs. And our guide
to using formulae will tell you everything you need to
know – all within half an hour. Then, if you're looking
for more of a challenge, we reveal how to dive deep
into your data; how to present complicated results in
a simple manner; how to link to external sources; and
how to use Microsoft's famous PivotTables.

4
Excel 2010

HOW LONG?

Allow a few minutes if you've never used Excel before.

HOW HARD?

Just follow our simple introduction to the basics of a spreadsheet.

HOW TO... GET STARTED WITH SPREADSHEETS

Excel is Microsoft's hugely popular spreadsheet package, widely used to crunch numbers in homes and businesses. So what can it actually do?

The spreadsheet was the first so-called "killer application" for personal computers. At its most basic, it can be thought of as an intelligent ledger where your numbers always add up correctly down the columns and across the rows – a kind of magic when it was first invented. Everyone could see its value, and it was often the reason people bought a computer. By the early 1980s, Lotus 1-2-3 and Quattro Pro ruled the roost; ten years on, Excel was beginning to make its name, and by the mid-1990s it was the product of choice – a position it retains today.

So what can this killer app do for you? Many different things. If you sell produce from your allotment, you can keep records of sales and expenditure, and over time you can see what proportion of your running costs (such as seeds and rent) are offset by garden-gate sales. If you run a car, you can record mileage and fuel and get a very accurate idea of the miles per gallon your vehicle returns. If you're renovating the kitchen, you can keep an eye on costs as the project progresses.

Any task that involves numbers and requires them to be manipulated – even simply adding them up – is almost bound to be easier using a spreadsheet.

ANATOMY OF A SPREADSHEET When you launch Excel, you see a gridded area with columns labelled A, B, C and so on, plus rows numbered from 1 onwards. This is a worksheet. Each intersection of column and row is called a cell, and is identified by the column it occupies and the row it intersects. Cell A1 is in the top-left corner, B1 is to its right, and B2 is immediately below B1.

At the bottom of the sheet is a row of tabs labelled Sheet1, Sheet2 and Sheet3 (you can add more by pressing the small icon to the right of Sheet3). These are for accessing other worksheets within the same "workbook" – Excel's name for the spreadsheet file.

Numbers can be copied and pasted between worksheets, and you can even make calculations that take numbers from several worksheets. If you were upgrading the kitchen and landscaping the garden, you might have a worksheet for each project and bring the total costs together to a single value labelled "What it all cost".

Our example here uses the default blank template, but there are many more. Go to File | New to find examples such as a personal budget (in "Sample templates") and access others online via www.office.com.

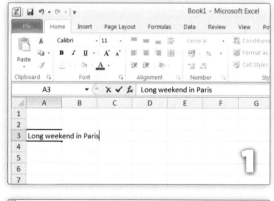

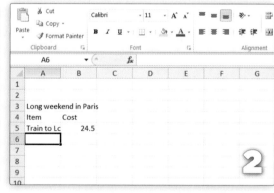

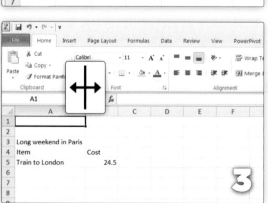

① FIRST STEPS Launch Excel and you get a blank worksheet. We'll work out our expenditure on a weekend away. Start a couple of rows from the top, in case you later need a title or other information. So put your cursor in cell A3 and type a description.

② ENTER DATA In cell A4, type "Item"; enter "Cost" into B4 (without the quotation marks). In cell A5, enter a description of your cost, in this case "Train to London". If you type something wider than a column, the words overlap the column to the right so the whole entry is visible. Now click in B5 and enter "24.50". You'll notice a couple of things. The "-ndon" of London disappears, and Excel ignores the final zero of 24.50, showing 24.5. (We'll add the missing pound sign shortly.)

③ COLUMN WIDTH To see the missing text, mouse to the column header row on the line between columns A and B: once the cursor changes to a vertical bar with a double-headed arrow, double-click. The column will expand to the width of its widest entry.

④ NUMBER FORMAT We want to show costs with a currency symbol and two decimal places, so we'll change the cell format to Currency. Since we want cells below B5 to show currency too, we'll alter the whole column. Click on B5 and drag down to highlight as many cells as you need, or click "B5" to select them all. Right-click the highlighted block and select Format Cells.

⑤ CUSTOMISABLE CURRENCY Select Currency from the category list. The symbol, decimal places and negative value options are shown to the right: all are customisable, but the defaults are usually OK.

⑥ ADD IT UP Click OK. Your value gets a £ symbol and trailing zero. Save your worksheet (either by pressing Ctrl-S or clicking the floppy disk icon, second from left at the top). Now add another row of information, complete with its price in the B column, and that should display properly too. When all your numbers are in, put the cursor in the cell below the last one and click the AutoSum button – the Sigma (Σ) symbol towards the right of the ribbon.

⑦ SUM TOTAL On the sheet, the cells to be added up get a dashed outline and the formula is also shown: =SUM(B5:B11). Hit the Enter key to accept what's shown and voilà, the total is generated.

⑧ PRINT IT To print your worksheet, go to File | Print. The default settings are probably fine (one copy, A4, and so on), so just click the big Print button. To print part of a larger worksheet, you'd click and drag to outline it, then click File | Print | Print.

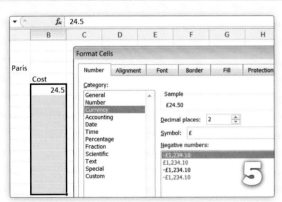

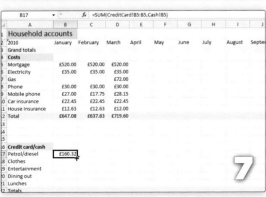

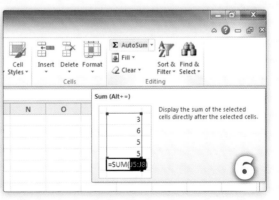

Q&A

Q: I've made a spelling error in one of my cells. How can I edit it?
A: There are two ways. Click on the offending cell and its contents are displayed in the formula bar immediately below the ribbon (to the right of the "fx" symbol). Put your cursor anywhere in the formula bar and edit. Alternatively, double-click in the offending cell and edit the contents there.

HOW TO...
WRITE FORMULAE IN EXCEL

To release Excel's true power you need to use formulae. Writing a basic formula is straightforward, and there's also a range of built-in formulae at your command.

HOW LONG?

Half an hour should be enough to get the hang of the basic principles.

HOW HARD?

Excel makes it easy to write a working formula, and there's built-in help.

You've entered a series of numbers into a worksheet and now you want to do something with those numbers. It's time to write a formula.

In Excel, a formula is written into a cell on the worksheet, but the formula isn't visible in that cell. Instead, it's displayed in the formula bar immediately above the worksheet. What you see in the cell is the result of the calculation set out in the formula.

Adding up numbers is one formula that everybody uses, so Excel makes it very easy: to sum the numbers in cells B6, B7, B8 and B9, put the cursor in B10, click the AutoSum button and push Enter (as we saw on p48). You could also write this formula from scratch into the formula bar: put the cursor in cell B11 and type "=SUM(B6:B9)". It will give the same answer as AutoSum.

Let's take this formula apart. The equals sign tells Excel that what's coming is a formula. SUM is a function for adding values to give a total; it takes "arguments" (the values a function is to work with) inside brackets. Here, the values are in cells B6, B7, B8 and B9.

It would be a pain to have to list all the cells whenever we sum values, so there's a shortcut that lets you specify the first and last cells in the list you want to add up. The argument for the SUM function starts with the first cell to be included, B6; then you put a colon, which tells Excel to include all cells between B6 and the next cell reference in the argument, B9.

A series of values such as this is called a range, and the colon is the range operator. Excel uses operators that are very familiar, including plus (+), minus (-), divide (/) and multiply (*), plus some that may initially be unfamiliar, such as range (:).

A formula can be placed in any empty cell: it doesn't have to be adjacent to the cells holding the numbers it manipulates. You can add up numbers from different locations on a sheet by specifying the cells individually rather than using a range: for instance, "=SUM(C14,G28)" adds values in two non-contiguous cells.

Once you've calculated a value with a formula, you can use it in other formulae: for instance, the total in B10 can be added to or subtracted from a value in another cell, which may itself be generated by a formula.

Things become a little more complicated when you want to use values from more than one worksheet

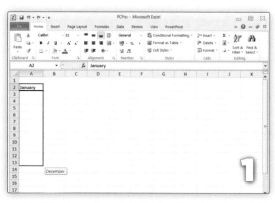

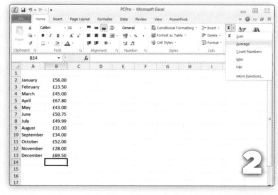

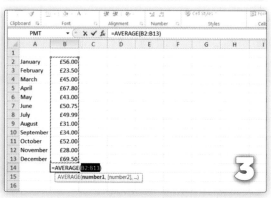

in a formula. For example, "=SUM(C6,Sheet2!C5)" adds the value in C6 on the sheet where the formula is being created to the value in cell C5 on Sheet2.

 BUILT-IN FUNCTIONS Excel's many functions can be inspected by category on the Formulas tab in the Function Library group. However, some of the most popular are also accessible from the AutoSum button, including Average. Here, we'll find our average travel cost over a year. First we need months and values. Type "January" in a cell and click the bottom-right corner with the cursor showing as a cross. Drag downwards, watching the small "hover help" box that appears until you see December, then release the mouse button.

 AVERAGE Excel inserts the month names. Now enter some values. Then place the cursor in the cell where you want the formula, and on the Home tab click the down arrow alongside the AutoSum button and select Average (if you don't see the AutoSum label, just look for the Σ symbol and the down arrow).

③ SET RANGE In the sheet, the values to be averaged are outlined and the formula shown.

④ BLANK CELLS Press Enter. The average appears. The function adds the values in the range and divides by the number of values (12 in this case).

If there's a gap in your values – for example, you missed out a figure by mistake – the formula will outline only those immediately above the cell containing the formula. To include other values, click in a corner of the outline and drag it to expand. If there's a blank cell in the range, the total will be divided by 11, so if any value is zero, enter "0" rather than leaving it blank, or the result will differ.

⑤ COUNT The Count Numbers function (=COUNT) lets us check there are 12 values. As above, you can drag the outline to change the range.

⑥ MAX AND MIN The =MAX and =MIN functions find the largest and smallest value in a range.

⑦ SORTING... Sorting values is easy too: here we can sort expenditure to find the priciest month. Highlight the month names and their values. Click the Sort & Filter button, pick Custom Sort and set Column to the one containing the values (in our case, Column B) and Order to "Largest to Smallest". Click OK.

⑧ AND RE-SORTING To return to calendar order later, change the Custom Sort. Highlight the entries again, and this time set the Column to the one containing the months (here, A). Pop down the Order list, pick Custom List, choose the one starting "January, February," click OK and OK again. Sorted.

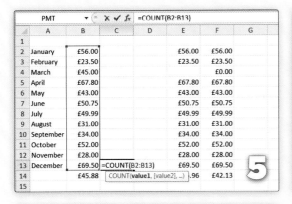

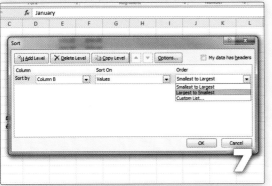

4
Excel 2010

HOW TO...
DISPLAY DATA GRAPHICALLY

A picture tells a thousand words – and it's certainly true for Excel graphics, where a chart can instantly convey an overview of your data

Graphical representations of data are unbeatable for giving rapidly understandable insight into a mass of figures. A bar chart can tell you instantly that last month sales of WhizzClean were half those of ZoomWash, and you can investigate further - is the supply chain broken or has WhizzClean been heavily discounted recently?

Excel offers a wide range of graphs, from bar and pie charts through line, area and scatter graphs to the more exotic bubble, radar and doughnut. While the more glamorous options are tempting, displaying unfamiliar data in an unfamiliar graph type will detract from your message: bar and pie charts are what everyone uses because readers understand them and can concentrate on the message without having to interpret the graph.

Here, we'll chart some sales figures in Excel. We have a year's worth of monthly sales results for a range of products. How can we best display these graphically? To plot data about discrete items, it's best to use a bar, column or pie chart. Data such as this can be described as discontinuous. (If you were plotting the speed of a train over time, your data would be continuous and you'd plot it as a line or area graph.) We'll also introduce Sparklines,

new in Excel 2010. These owe much to the innovative work of Edward Tufte, an acknowledged master of brilliant data displays. A sparkline is a little graphic that encapsulates the behaviour of a set of values: one can show, for instance, monthly sales over the year, and you can quickly see that sales peak in the summer or in December. The new Excel implementation is excellent, and we'll show you how to create these graphics in the steps.

Finally, we'll look at conditional formatting. This is a great way of making important values stand out on your worksheet. You can add conditional formatting to the sales figures for a product so that if the sales exceed 85 units in a month, for example, the figure is shown in red.

(1) SELECT DATA Here's our sales data with yearly totals at the bottom (you can download the worksheet from www.pcpro.co.uk/links/chart). With just a sea of numbers in front of us, it isn't easy to see any trends or anomalies. Let's try a graph. Outline all the cells except the totals, then click the Insert tab. Now click Column in the Charts group to see the available column chart types.

HOW LONG?
Allow half an hour for attractive and informative results.

HOW HARD?
Charts can be tricky to get exactly right, but perseverance pays.

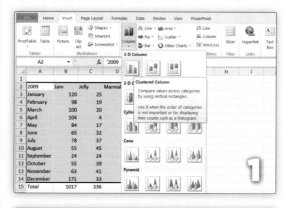

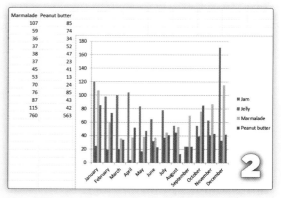

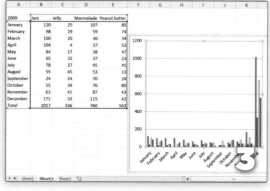

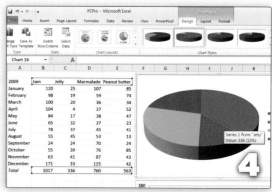

② COLUMN CHART Click the first 2D Column type, a so-called clustered column. Almost instantly Excel creates a colourful graph, labelled with months on the X axis (across the bottom) and sales figures on the Y axis (up the left side). The legend indicates which colour is used for which product. We can now see that jam sales went through the roof in December, with marmalade not far behind, and that marmalade also did well in January.

③ CHANGE THE DATA RANGE Click the chart and the data it displays is outlined in blue on the sheet. Drag this outline to include the totals and the chart updates. Hmm, suddenly the chart isn't so clear.

④ PIE CHART Undo that (press Ctrl-Z) and instead highlight the four product names, then – keeping the Ctrl key pressed – click on the jam total and drag to highlight the other three totals. On the Insert tab, click Pie and pick the first 3D pie chart. That's a much clearer representation of yearly totals. Hover over each segment and Excel even shows its value and the percentage of the total. You can place the graphs wherever you want on a sheet, or copy and paste them into Word documents or PowerPoint presentations.

⑤ ADD TITLES Click on the pie chart and add a title by clicking the Layout tab under Chart Tools, clicking Chart Title and selecting a type. Click in the textbox to add a title.

⑥ ADD SPARKLINES Click in B16, click Insert, find the Sparklines group and select Line. In the Data Range box type "B3:B14". The Location Range – where you want the sparklines placed – is shown as B16. The dollar symbols make this an "absolute" reference, so if you move the cell containing the sparkline, it continues to show the same data. Type in B16 instead.

⑦ CUSTOMISE SPARKLINES Click OK and a tiny line displays a thumbnail sketch of jam sales. Simply drag across to add sparklines for all the products. You should now see the Design tab of Sparkline Tools. In the Show group, you can select Markers to put one in at each end and each angle change, or tick High Point and Low Point to show just these. You can change the marker and sparkline colours by choosing the Marker Color and Sparkline Color dropdowns in the Style group.

⑧ CONDITIONAL FORMATTING Highlight all the monthly sales figures and click Conditional Formatting on the Home tab. Click Highlight Cells Rules and then Greater Than. Under "Format cells that are GREATER THAN", enter a value and pick a colour scheme, or design one with Custom Format, available from the dropdown menu.

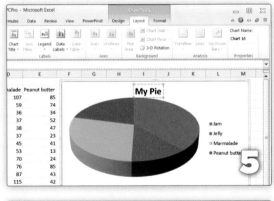

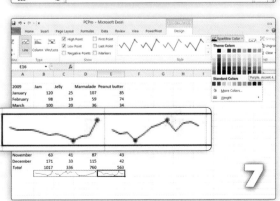

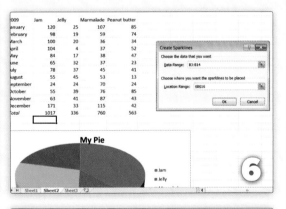

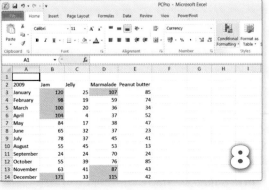

Q&A

Q: How can I find out which chart type will best show off my data?
A: Buttons for the most popular chart types can be found on the Insert tab in the Charts group. Hovering the cursor over one will display information about that type, including a brief description of the type of data it's best suited to. Click Other Charts and the information is shown for each type as you hover.

4

Excel 2010

HOW LONG?

Allow three-quarters of an hour or so to set up your workbook.

HOW HARD?

Quite straightforward. You can develop your accounting sheets as the need arises.

HOW TO...
MANAGE YOUR FINANCES

While Excel can't tell you how to spend or save your money, keeping good records in a spreadsheet can certainly leave you better informed about where it all goes.

A workbook to help manage your household accounts doesn't have to be particularly complicated. The hardest part is entering all the figures at the end of the month.

There are various personal budget templates downloadable from Office Online (go to File | New and pick Budgets), but they're far from perfect. One problem is localisation: if you don't live in America, the dollar signs and references to state taxes aren't much help. It can also be hard to work out what's going on in a worksheet built by somebody else. That said, if you find one that's a good match to your needs, it can be a useful starting point.

If you create your own sheets, you can build them up gradually. From the start, you know you'll want figures for rent or mortgage, heating and so on. As time goes on you can add items such as servicing the car. Using multiple worksheets can work well: in our example, downloadable from www.pcpro.co.uk/links/accounts, the first sheet has all the fixed costs: mortgage, mobile phone contract, insurance, plus things like electricity and gas. The second sheet holds expenditure on a credit card, in categories such as petrol/diesel, clothes and entertainment. Our third sheet is similar, but for cash.

We'll display all the totals for each of these categories on the first sheet, so we can see our costs at a glance but can drill down into the detail when we need to.

If you have a workbook you want to share with others, you can publish it to a website (go to File | Save & Send, then click Save to Web). It can then be viewed from a computer running a web browser without Excel, and we cover this in more detail in the introduction to the Excel Web App (p150). If you're part of a business that's running SharePoint, you can also publish there (see Chapter 10). Whether on the web or SharePoint, other users can sort and filter the data, add formulae and basic formatting.

If you have a Windows Mobile phone, you can use Excel Mobile 2010 to view and edit workbooks emailed as attachments or hosted via SharePoint Workspace Mobile 2010, so you can enter data on the move.

(1) **BUDGET TEMPLATE** Here's an example template from Office Online (go to File | New, then click Budgets; this template is called "Personal monthly budget spreadsheet"). We've changed some cell formatting to display pounds rather than dollars. For

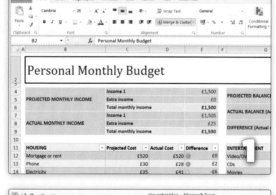

each category of expenditure, such as Housing on the left, you can enter projected and actual costs; the difference is calculated automatically. "Traffic light" symbols have been added using conditional formatting (see p53): a red diamond means the actual is more than £20 above the predicted; a yellow triangle means the difference is up to £20; and a green circle means it's on or below target.

2 **CONDITIONAL SYMBOLS** To see the conditions applied to the values in the Difference column, highlight one of the cells and click Conditional Formatting on the Home tab. Select Manage Rules, click Edit Rule and the conditions for the various icons appear.

3 **FIRST STEPS** Click Cancel, then Close. We'll design our own sheet instead (download it from www.pcpro.co.uk/links/accounts). You can add conditional formatting to your own sheets too, but let's start with a simple approach. Our first sheet is called "Totals" and contains basic outgoings per month.

4 **CATEGORIES** We've named Sheet2 and Sheet3 "CreditCard" and "Cash". They record expenditure per month under categories such as Entertainment and Clothes. Using the same categories on both sheets lets us copy them straight into the Totals sheet. To generate a total for the month, summing all expenditure on Petrol/diesel in both cash and cards, put

the cursor in the cell for January's petrol/diesel costs, click in the formula bar, type "=SU" and pick SUM in the list.

5 **ADD UP TOTALS** The opening bracket is already in place. Go to the CreditCard sheet and click the January fuel total and the cell reference is added (CreditCard!B5). Type a comma.

6 **JUMP SHEETS** On the Cash sheet, click the January fuel total, then type a closing bracket. Hit Enter. Back in Totals, the formula totals up.

7 **COMPLETE THE FORMULAE** To copy the formula to all the other expenditure headings, move the cursor to the bottom of B17 so a cross appears, then click and drag across the remaining months. The formula collects all the figures into the totals. You can also drag the cross down so the formula is copied across all the categories. Then add monthly totals with AutoSum. Coloured backgrounds help totals stand out.

8 **NAME YOUR CELLS** A monthly grand total can be calculated from the two totals, such as "=SUM(B22,B12)". But to improve your sheet's readability, first name the cells. Click on B22, type a name into the Name box (left of the formula bar) and press Enter. Repeat for B12. Create the formula in cell B3 to get something like "=SUM(CardAndCashTotal,JanCostsTotal)".

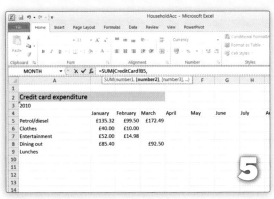

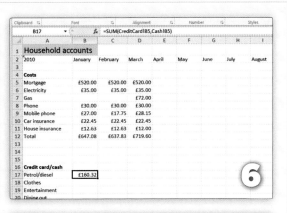

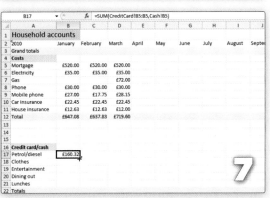

Q&A

Q: I can't always remember what my formulae do – help!
A: As well as naming cells, it's easy to add notes to cells as reminders of what's going on. Highlight a cell and click the New Comment button on the Review tab, then type your reminder. Click away from the note when you've finished. A tiny red triangle in the top-right corner of the cell indicates an attached comment; click to see it.

4

60
55 · 5
50 · 10
45 · 15
40 · 20
35 · 25
30

HOW LONG?

Half an hour should see you pivoting a table.

HOW HARD?

A tricky concept to grasp, but not difficult to use once you get your head around the idea of multi-dimensional data!

HOW TO...
USE A PIVOTTABLE

Excel's PivotTables let you look at your data in a new and interactive way, giving a multi-dimensional perspective that makes it easier to draw conclusions.

Excel can be used to store data, and over time this can add up to quite a large store, especially in a business. We usually store data because we hope it's going to tell us something later, like which is our slowest selling line or who are the most successful sales people.

Typically, we store numeric values, such as the number of items sold. We also store categories that describe the data, like the types of item. The numerical vales can be manipulated mathematically; for instance, we might sum the Unit Sales for all types of item. Time periods or dates are often stored, as are customers, sales people, manufacturers – so we could also sum the sales for different items month by month.

In more formal terminology, the numeric values are "measures" and the categories are "dimensions". Often the questions we want to ask are "multi-dimensional". For example, we might want to know the June sales of products that weren't being promoted. To answer this we need the measure Unit Sales, a dimension that can tell us the month, another dimension that identifies the product, and a third to indicate whether a promotion was ongoing. It's possible, if taxing, to create complex formulae to pull

this information out of the workbook – but there's an easier way, and that, as you might guess, is a PivotTable.

A PivotTable gives you a graphical view of your measures and dimensions, and you can move them about onscreen to produce a view that shows, say, Unit Sales by Product, Month and Promotion. If you want to see this data for all months, that view is just a few clicks away. If you're interested in who sold the most each month, the Sales Person dimension can be pulled in and the data inspected. With PivotTables, the dimensions can be moved around to produce exactly the view you want.

In Excel 2010, PivotTables have become even easier to use with the introduction of "slicers", which show a particular slice of your data. For instance, if you have a slicer based on the Promotion dimension, the slicer interface gives you a button for each promotion, so you can see the figures for sales during the summer special.

When you create a PivotTable, you decide which dimensions to use as columns and rows in a task pane. You can also specify a dimension for use as a filter to show subsets of data. However, slicers act as filters too, and their user interface is simpler and easier to use.

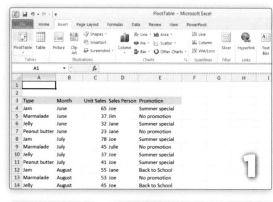

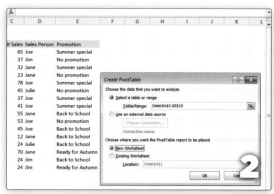

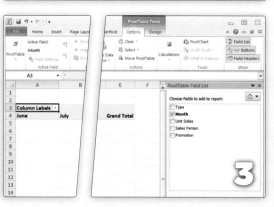

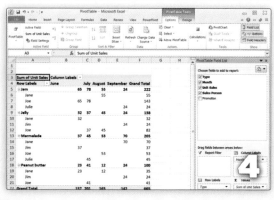

① LOAD DATA This is our dataset: our measure is Unit Sales and the dimensions are Type, Month, Sales Person and Promotion. (You can download this file from www.pcpro.co.uk/links/pivot1.) On the Insert tab, in the leftmost group, click PivotTable | PivotTable.

② CREATE A PIVOTTABLE In the Create PivotTable dialog box, specify the range containing your data: click on the worksheet, then drag from the top left to the bottom right of the range you want, including headers (for example, Type, Month). Select New Worksheet as the location for the PivotTable and click OK.

③ ADD COLUMNS To the right is the task pane titled PivotTable Field List. The fields correspond to the column headers in the data, and below are four boxes. Drag the Month field into the Column Labels box. On the worksheet, the PivotTable begins to take shape: month names and a Grand Total header appear. This last is added automatically by the PivotTable.

④ ADD ROWS Drag Type into the Row Labels box, then Unit Sales into the Values box. You can click on the arrowhead buttons to access sorting and filtering, as when working with an Excel table. Drag the Sales Person field into the Row Labels box. Now the PivotTable shows the top-performing person for sales in each month: here, it's easy to spot that it's Joe.

⑤ ADD A SLICER Collapse the sales person data by clicking the minus button alongside each product name. Let's try a slicer. With the cursor in any cell in the PivotTable, click Insert Slicer in the Sort & Filter group on the Options tab under PivotTable Tools. Tick Promotion and click OK. The slicer, which can be moved around the sheet, has a button for each promotion.

⑥ VIEW SLICES OF DATA Click the "Back to School" button to see the products discounted under this offer; clicking "Summer special" shows these promoted products. By clicking the plus box next to each product, we can see Joe did a good job.

⑦ USE FORMATTING To see the data unsliced, click the crossed-out funnel icon on the slicer's top-right corner. Adding formatting to a PivotTable makes it even easier to read: click in the PivotTable and then on the Design tab under PivotTable Tools, and select a style from the PivotTable Styles group. In the PivotTable Style Options group, Banded Columns can be useful too.

⑧ A FLEXIBLE VIEW To move a row so it becomes a column, click and drag the field from the Row Labels box (in the PivotTable Field List pane) to the Column Labels box. You can have more than one slicer per PivotTable, and on the Options tab under Slicer Tools you'll find styles to apply to slicers too.

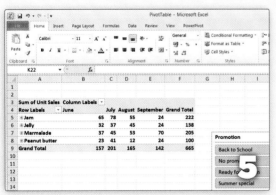

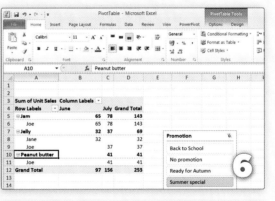

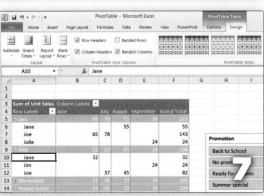

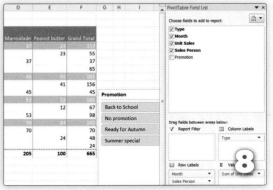

Q&A

Q: Can the grand total row and column on the PivotTable be something other than just a sum?

A: Yes: under Options in PivotTable Tools, clicking the Calculations button reveals a Summarize Values By option. Clicking this shows further options. Select Average to display the average sales per product in the Grand Total column to the right, and the average of all product sales per month in the last row.

4
Excel 2010

HOW LONG?
45 minutes should be enough for some experiments with importing.

HOW HARD?
One of the toughest tasks in this guide, but painless if you follow each step carefully.

HOW TO...
WORK WITH EXTERNAL DATA

Excel can do more for your business if you take advantage of its excellent tools for importing data from external sources, including the web.

Many small businesses hold some data in Excel and some in a database such as Microsoft Access, so there are times when it would be very convenient to bring data in from an external source. Importing data can be as easy as selecting, copying and pasting: you don't have to use the other methods described here unless you want the additional benefits they bring.

Excel has an easy-to-use tool for importing data from Access, and the data is formatted automatically as an Excel table with sorting and filtering buttons already in place. An entire table of data can be imported, or just what's in an answer table generated by an Access query.

The table is linked to the original source, so if more data is added in Access you can update the table in Excel simply by using the Refresh options. Click in the imported table, pop down the options under the Refresh All button on the Data tab, select Refresh and the data is updated to reflect any changes. (Clicking Refresh All will update all linked imported data in your sheet.)

Data in a text file can also be imported: a wizard, as described in the steps below, takes you through the process and lets you control how the data will be formatted in Excel. Text files hold almost no formatting information, so dates in a text file are just text strings. (Incidentally, it's the lack of formatting that makes text files so useful for moving data between programs. Usually it's the formatting, not the data, that the receiving software can't interpret and which causes imports to fail.)

During the import setup, you can identify dates, for instance, and ensure they will be formatted as dates in Excel. The text import process can also be refreshed if the data in the source text file changes: proceed in the same way as refreshing an imported table above, and on selecting Refresh you'll be asked to point to the file again, but you won't see the Import wizard.

The web is a vast source of data, and it's quite possible to import from it. We'll demonstrate bringing in currency exchange rate data using one of the built-in connections supplied with Excel. When we choose this, Excel opens a web query file. This is a text file, with the extension IQV, which contains the path to the data source and the required connection formation. (You can inspect the contents of the file using Notepad if you right-click on it in Windows Explorer – but don't edit it. The file path

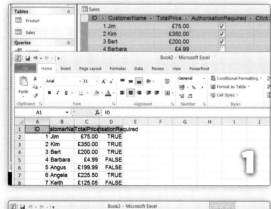

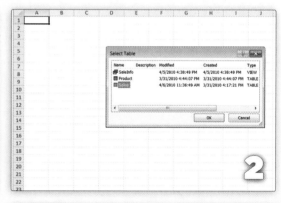

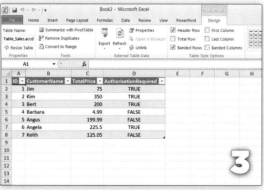

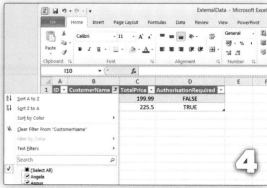

is displayed as a "hover help" tip in the list of Existing Connections.) Data from the website is imported with formatting and hyperlinks, and is refreshable as above.

 CUT AND PASTE Download and unzip the files from www.pcpro.co.uk/links/externaldata. Open the SALES.ACCDB database and double-click the Sales table to open it. Select everything using Ctrl-A, copy it to the Clipboard with Ctrl-C, move to the Excel worksheet where you want the data and use Ctrl-V to paste it. It looks a bit messy, but could easily be tidied up.

 IMPORT FROM ACCESS Or try Excel's built-in importer. Close Access. In a new Excel sheet, highlight the cell which is to be the top-left corner of the imported table and click From Access on the Get External Data group on the Data tab. Navigate to the SALES.ACCDB file and click Open. Select the Sales table.

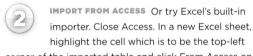 **TABLE FORMATTING** Click OK and OK in the next dialog. There's a tidily formatted Excel table.

 SORT AND FILTER Click the arrowhead alongside CustomerName and data can be sorted. You can also filter it to show just Angela and Angus by deselecting the other names. A funnel symbol appears on the CustomerName header to indicate the data is filtered. To see all the records again, tick "(Select All)".

 IMPORT TEXT Create a new Excel file. Click From Text on the Get External Data group on the Data tab. Select ORDERS.TXT and click Import. Step 1 of the wizard shows the data in the lower window. It's correctly identified as Delimited (there are commas or tabs between items), so click Next. Deselect Tab as the Delimiter and tick Comma: the data goes into columns. Click Next. In step 3, you control formatting. Click the Order Date data to highlight it, and under "Column data format" select Date. Choose the correct format (in this case DMY – date, month, year). Do the same for the Dispatch Date column.

 IMPORT Click Finish, pick the top-left location for the data and click OK. 200 rows are imported.

 DATE FORMATS You can tidy up the dates by selecting them and using the list beside the Format box on the Home tab in the Number group. The commonly used Long Date and Short Date formats can be applied with a further click.

 WEB IMPORT To get currency data, click Existing Connections on the Data tab and double-click MSN MoneyCentral Investor Currency Rates. Enter the cell for the top corner or click OK if already in place. Wait a while… and there's the data. MSN quotes dollar rates, but the dollar/pound rate is listed too.

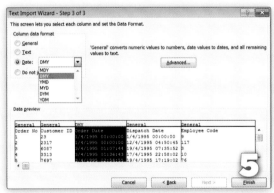

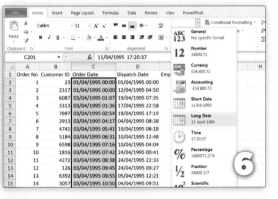

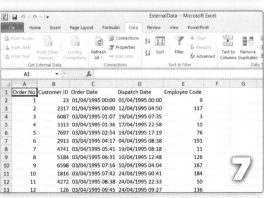

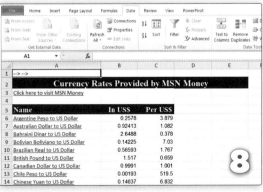

Q&A

Q: People talk about importing CSV files. What are these?
A: CSV stands for comma-separated values, and a CSV file is a type of text file that has no formatting except for commas between pieces of information. The data in a CSV file is, in fact, exactly like the data in the TXT file described in the steps here. Sometimes, a file holding data in this format is saved as a TXT file, sometimes as CSV; both can be handled with Excel's Text Import tool.

FOUR MORE GREAT FEATURES
IN EXCEL 2010

Excel is packed with so many powers we can't possibly cover them all, but here's our pick of four other superb features to give you a taste.

 PROTECT YOUR WORKBOOK You may be sharing an Excel worksheet with colleagues, either via email or over a network, but you don't necessarily want everyone to be able to change its content. If you head to the Review tab, you'll see a group called Changes, which allows you to set certain ranges that can be edited by others, or indeed set the whole workbook to be view-only.

 PASTE WITH LIVE PREVIEW When you copy a table of figures from an email, website or document, you may not want its formatting to be applied as well. To make sure you get the desired result, copy the figures as normal and then right-click in Excel: underneath Paste Options you'll see two choices, Keep Source Formatting and Match Destination

Formatting. What's particularly great is that a live preview shows you how each choice will look.

 SIMULTANEOUS WORKING Excel's Web App is unique in allowing several people to edit a worksheet simultaneously. Save your sheet to SharePoint (see p126) or SkyDrive (see p146), and this public version can then be worked on by colleagues, friends or family to create a collaborative piece of work.

 POWERPIVOT We've touched on Excel's data handling, but a Microsoft plugin now takes this to a new level. PowerPivot, downloadable from www.powerpivot.com, allows businesses to manipulate millions of lines of data and then analyse it in a way that previously required expensive third-party software.

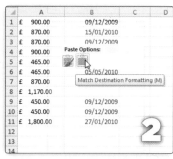

Among our favourite features of Excel 2010 are the ability to prevent changes to your sheets (a feature sadly missing from Excel Starter); live preview for Paste; co-authoring via the Web App (but not in Excel proper – the opposite way round to Word); and the free PowerPivot plugin, a scarily potent tool for data analysis.

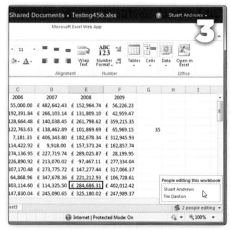

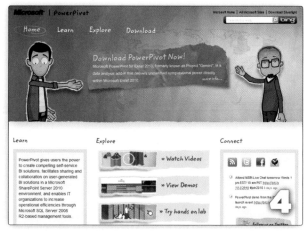

Microsoft

Microsoft® Office 2010

MAKE IT GREAT

I want to make it great so I can get my boyfriend out of the HOUSE.

I'm Shan and my boyfriend hasn't been on holiday since Istanbul was Constantinople. So to persuade him to take me to Turkey, I put text, photos, links, info from the web – everything there is to see and do – into OneNote® 2010. It's like a digital notebook. Can't wait to see how my boyfriend looks in a fez.

> See how you can make it great with new Office 2010 at
office.com/2010

IN THIS CHAPTER

5 PowerPoint 2010

POWERPOINT

With PowerPoint 2010 in your armoury, there's no excuse for creating dull presentations. Whether you're aiming for an all-singing, all-dancing affair packed with video and bizarre effects or you're searching for a classy and understated look, PowerPoint gives you the tools you need. In particular, this edition adds brilliant new features such as the ability to trim videos without

2010

needing a video-editing program: just mark your start and end points and the software will do the rest. In a similar vein, PowerPoint 2010 offers all the photo-editing power we've already seen in Word 2010, so you can add interesting effects to even the dullest of original photos. Read on to discover how to make the right sort of impact with your presentations.

60
55 · 5
50 · 10
45 · 15
40 · 20
35 · 25
30

HOW LONG?

Play around and you'll soon be impressed by what you can do.

HOW HARD?

Mastering the basics is easy, honest.

HOW TO... FORMAT TEXT FOR A PROFESSIONAL PRESENTATION

Formatting your text doesn't have to be a challenge. Themes, the Slide Master view and text effects can give you great results with minimum effort.

While text should never be allowed to dominate a presentation, you'll almost always need a range of headlines, bullet points, quotes, captions and textboxes. The challenge is to give these impact and make them legible on whatever screen you'll be using. Producing beautiful text is an art, but good-looking text is relatively easy to pull off – especially with PowerPoint 2010.

As with all Office 2010 applications, using the ready-built themes and designs is a speedy shortcut, giving you layouts, fonts and colours that work well together, and enabling you to get the bare bones of a design within a matter of seconds. If there are elements you want to change, familiarising yourself with the Slide Master view will save you time and effort.

Each Slide Master works as a kind of boss slide, setting the basic styles and formatting for the actual slides in your presentation. In PowerPoint 2010, a single document or template will have several slide masters that control specific layouts, and a "big boss" slide that oversees all of them. A change made to a boss slide will roll out across every slide created with that layout; a change made to the big boss will affect every slide

in the presentation. So you can change, say, a heading used across the whole presentation with a few clicks, but you can also make more specific changes where they're needed without having to edit every slide by hand.

Slide masters work hand-in-hand with Office's themes. This means changing the theme will override any changes you've made to the Slide Master, but it's possible to save your amendments to a new theme. You can then apply your custom designs to future presentations.

All this is great, but when you first try PowerPoint 2010 you might feel disappointed by its text handling capabilities – particularly once you see the new flashy text features in Publisher, Excel and Word. However, many of the same features are available within PowerPoint if you know where to look, so if you want to create titles with a little extra oomph, there's no reason not to.

(1) **BARE BONES** Create a new Blank Presentation (File | New | Blank Presentation | Create) with nothing formatted. All slides after the initial title slide are created using the basic template: right-click in the Slides pane on the left and select New Slide.

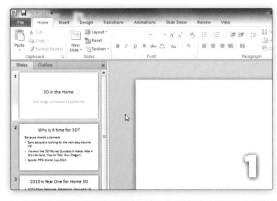

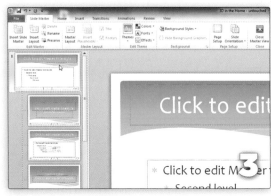

② APPLY A THEME We can make improvements in moments. Click the Design tab, then look at the Themes panel that dominates the ribbon. Hover over a theme and you'll see how the current slide will look with it applied. Or click the down arrow to the right of the panel to expand the selection. We've picked Waveform.

③ SWITCH TO SLIDE MASTER VIEW Click on the View tab of the ribbon and mouse your way over to the Master Views panel. Click the Slide Master button to switch to the Slide Master view. In the Slides pane to the left you'll now see the slide masters set up for the current template and theme. The big one at the top is the overall Slide Master. Click on it to edit.

④ PIMP YOUR TITLE Drag and click over the title text (or left-click multiple times) to highlight it, then right-click on the highlighted text and select Format Text Effects. This gives you easy access to many of the same text effects you'll find in the new editions of Word and Excel. First, we'll apply a drop shadow. Select Shadow on the left, then click on the Presets and click on the Offset Diagonal Top Right option.

⑤ 2D TO 3D A 3D presentation deserves a 3D effect. Click 3-D Format on the left, then set the Top Bevel to Cool Slant, the Surface Material to Translucent Powder and the Lighting to Freezing (found in the Cool section of the Lighting pop-out). Finally, change the Lighting Angle to 70 degrees. Click Close.

⑥ BULLETS AND COLOURS Any change to a Slide Master will roll out across all the slides under its control. Click on the Home tab, then highlight all five levels of text on the Slide Master. Go to Paragraph on the Home tab, click Bullets and pick Hollow Square. Next, highlight the top level of text, go to the Font section, click Text Color and change it to Dark Blue, Text 2, Lighter 40%.

⑦ TWEAK YOUR TEXT The Slide Master can always be amended or overruled. Click the Slide Master tab and select Close Master View to return to the normal editing view, then browse through your slides. This example is looking crowded. Highlight the top block of text, then right-click on it. Select Font, click on the Character Spacing tab and set the spacing to Expanded by 0.6pt. Click OK. Then right-click again, select Paragraph and set Spacing After to 6pt.

⑧ USE FORMAT PAINTING It's easy to apply the same formatting to other text objects. With the Home tab active and your text block still highlighted, go to the Clipboard panel and left-click on the Format Painter button. Now click and drag to highlight the two blocks of text below, and they'll take on the amended formatting.

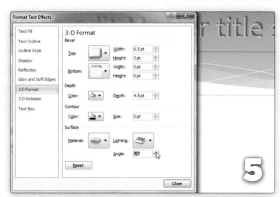

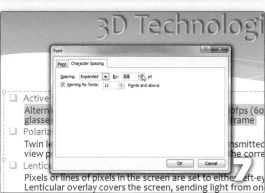

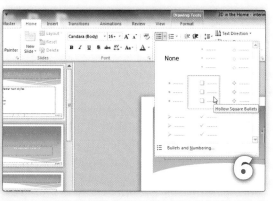

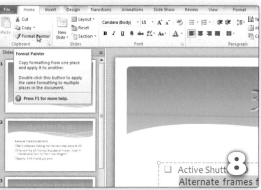

Tip

While the main editing window should be the centre of your design efforts, PowerPoint's Outline pane can be the most effective place to work with your text. Simply click on the Outline tab in the left-hand Slides pane to switch to it. Not only can you type text directly into the Outline pane, you can also right-click on lines or blocks of text and promote them or demote them from one level to another (for example, changing a list item into a heading or a heading into a title).

HOW LONG?
It takes a little time to get to grips with the tools, but it's worth it!

HOW HARD?
We'll tackle some advanced effects here, but step by step.

HOW TO... TAP POWERPOINT'S IMAGE-EDITING POWER

You don't need Photoshop skills to make your slides look great. Thanks to new photo manipulation features, you can do it all within PowerPoint.

PowerPoint 2010 benefits from the much-improved image-editing tools that are now integrated into the whole Office 2010 suite. In Word, Publisher and Excel these are a major time-saver, but with PowerPoint they're potentially revolutionary. After all, PowerPoint slides are visual by their nature, and when creating a presentation you may not have the time or desire to switch to an image editor.

These features are found in the Picture Tools | Format tab that appears whenever you insert or select an image on a slide. For instance, Remove Background can instantly separate a foreground object from the background in the image, as long as there's reasonable contrast between the two (for example, a head shot of someone standing against a painted wall), while Corrections offers a selection of quick and dirty brightness and contrast adjustments to choose from.

Color provides saturation and colour temperature adjustments along with quick colourisation options, and the Artistic Effects panel leads you to a collection of simple Photoshop-style filters, such as blur. Combine these with the Crop tool on the right, and you can cover most of your image-editing tasks right here.

Along with these tools, PowerPoint has a gallery of customisable effects ranging from simple frames to glows, pseudo 3D treatments and reflections. You'll find a gallery of presets in the central Picture Styles panel, while using the Picture Border, Picture Effects and Picture Layout dropdown to the right will enable you to dig deeper and create your own custom versions. Experiment with combinations to create your own knockout styles.

1 **INSERT AN IMAGE** We'll use various Picture Tools to add excitement to a set of slides for a lecture on the legendary Catalan architect Antoni Gaudí. To put the first image in place, click the Insert tab, then go to the Images group and click Picture. Navigate to your chosen image, then click Insert. For our purposes we only want the building in the foreground, so, with the Picture Tools tab active we click Remove Background.

2 **REMOVE THE BACKGROUND** PowerPoint marks the area to remove in purple, so anything we want to keep should appear in full colour. First, use the bounding box as a kind of rough selection to

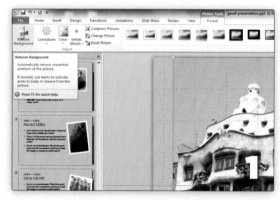

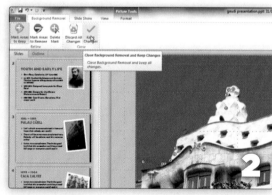

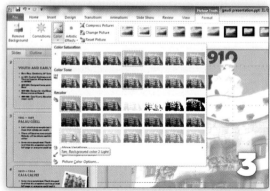

ensure everything you want to keep is encompassed. Next, click the "Mark Areas to Keep" button, and click on any portions of the image you want to include in your selection. Conversely, use the "Mark Areas to Remove" button to remove them. If you make a mistake, use the Delete Mark button and click on the mark in question. When you're happy, click the Keep Changes tick.

3 COLOURISE, RESIZE AND POSITION We only want to use this image in the background, so click on the Color button and, under the Recolor options, choose "Background color 2 Light" (note: that these options change depending on the current theme). Now move the image downwards and use the lower right-corner handle on the bounding box to stretch it out so it fills the bottom of the screen (it doesn't matter if it overlaps). Finally, click Send Backward in the Arrange section of the Picture Tools tab, and the image will sit behind the text.

4 CROP THE IMAGE Now for a second image. Use Insert | Picture, then, with the Picture Tools tab active, click the Crop button (in Size) and select Crop. Use the thick black marks to select the area you want to keep – the rest is shaded grey – then click Crop.

5 FRAME AND ENHANCE Click and drag inside the image to move it, then resize it to fit

your design. To polish this one off, add a basic frame by clicking on the "Simple Frame, White" option in the Picture Styles gallery, then go to Corrections and give both Brightness and Contrast a 20% boost.

6 ARTISTIC EFFECTS Our next image (added using Insert | Picture) needs some help. After cropping, moving and resizing, we use the Corrections tool and pick "Brightness: -20%, Contrast: +40%", then click the Color button and boost Saturation to 200%. This seems like overkill until we click the Artistic Effects button and choose the Film Grain option.

7 FRAME AND TWIST Add "Simple Frame, White", as in step 5, before adding one final twist. We want the look of carelessly tossed photographs, so click the rotate handle at the top of the bounding box and drag left to rotate the image slightly anti-clockwise.

8 ONE LAST SHOT Our final image is cropped, resized, moved and framed as in steps 3 to 5, but with a few differences. Click Corrections, then pick the "Brightness: 0% (Normal), Contrast: +40%" thumbnail to add some extra punch. Next, click Color, go to the Color Tone section and click on the "Temperature: 5300 K" thumbnail. Finally, apply the frame as before, but this time use the rotate handle at the top of the bounding box and drag it slightly to the right (clockwise).

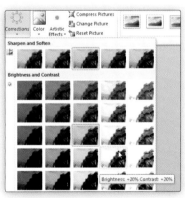

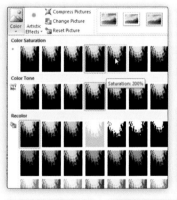

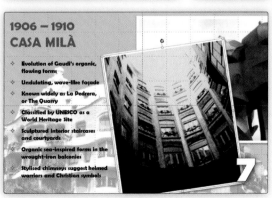
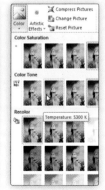

1906 – 1910 CASA MILÀ

- Evolution of Gaudi's organic, flowing forms
- Undulating, wave-like façade
- Known widely as La Pedrera, or The Quarry
- Classified by UNESCO as a World Heritage Site
- Sculptured interior staircases and courtyards
- Organic sea-inspired form in the wrought-iron balconies
- Stylised chimneys suggest helmed warriors and Christian symbols

Q&A

Q: What do you mean by "bounding box"?
A: When you select an image, a rectangular box appears around it with nine square markers in its corners and halfway along each axis. There's also a small green circle at the top. This box (unseen in your finished work) is the bounding box: use it to make the image larger or smaller, or to reposition it on the slide. Click and drag the green circle and you can also rotate the image to any angle.

5
PowerPoint 2010

HOW LONG?
Allow half an hour to jazz up your slides, or more to play around.

HOW HARD?
Probably the easiest mistake to make is to overdo the effects.

HOW TO... ADD ANIMATIONS AND TRANSITIONS

With PowerPoint 2010, it's simple to add slick animations and classy transitions to make your presentations more engaging. Let's get those slides moving!

PowerPoint 2010 is capable of producing stunning presentations. It's even possible to create the kind of smooth transitions and animations you'd expect on TV. You don't need to be a pro: the combination of the ribbon interface, effects galleries and real-time previews makes it ludicrously easy. Inevitably, some PowerPoint users will abuse these new-found powers, but use animation with a little restraint and you can build slides that hold attention from the beginning to end of your presentation.

The average PowerPoint show will contain three sorts of movement. First, animations: text elements, photos, diagrams and illustrations that move in or out of the slide, or undergo some visual change while the slide is on display. Second come transitions, with the old fades, wipes, dissolves and miscellaneous effects that smooth the shift from one slide to the next now joined by some exciting new options that are guaranteed to impress (at least until they become the new clichés). Finally, we have video. We're going to look at that in detail later on.

The beauty of PowerPoint's animation system is that Microsoft has kept it deliberately simple. Click on either the Transitions or Animations tab and the majority

of the ribbon will be dedicated to a gallery of ready-made effects, which you can apply to objects or pages straight away. If you can't see the one you want, click the down arrow to the right of the gallery to expand the options.

Hover over an animation, and you'll even see it applied to the selected object or page as a real-time preview. By default, animations on the same page will run in the order you originally applied them, and you can quickly change the order or the timing using the Timing panel towards the right of the Animations tab. And that's all many users will need. But if you need more control, you have it. Activate the Animation pane and you get a simplified timeline view that you can use to orchestrate more complex animations and get exactly the result you're looking for.

① ADD TRANSITIONS Some people like the same transition throughout a presentation, others prefer to mix and match, but as a rule it's best to stick to one or two effects, with the occasional new one for emphasis. To apply a transition to a specific slide, click on the slide in the Slides pane, then on the Transitions

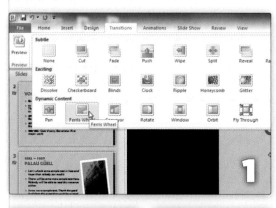

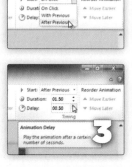

tab, and select from the gallery. Here, we've opted for the Ferris Wheel slide from the Dynamic Content selection.

(2) TWEAK YOUR TRANSITION It looks good, but we have a couple of tweaks to make. First, go to the Timing area of the Transitions tab and increase the Duration. To preview the effect again, you can always click the Preview button on the left-hand side of the ribbon. Now click the Effect Options button, and set the new slide to come in From Left.

(3) APPLY A FADE-IN We want the background image to gently fade in. Click on the image, then click the Animations tab and select the Fade effect from the Animation Styles gallery. Now go to the Timing panel. Set Start to After Previous, Duration to 1.50 and Delay to 0.50. This gives us a nice, smooth fade-in.

(4) FLYING PHOTOS We want our photo objects to fly in from the edge of the screen, so click on the photo at the bottom of the "pile", then select the Fly In animation. Click on Effect Options and set the Direction to From Top. Preview the effect, and you'll see that we want to slow it down. Go to the Timing panel and boost the Duration to 2.00.

(5) RE-USE THE ANIMATION Next, we copy the basic animation across to the other two photos. Just

click on the Animation Painter button in the Advanced Animation panel, then click on first the middle photo, then the top. They'll adopt the same slowed-down fly-in effect.

(6) CHANGE DIRECTION We don't want each photo coming in from the same direction, so select each one in turn and click on Effects Options to change the direction. For the middle photo we'll use From Bottom, and for the top photo we'll opt for From Right.

(7) PULSING TEXT Finally, we're going to add a subtle animation to specific lines of text, so that they pulse when the relevant photo appears. For this we'll need finer control over timing. Go to the Advanced Animation panel and click on the Animation Pane button. The Animation Pane lists the different animations on the slide in order, with the bar indicating delay and duration. Now we highlight the text block shown, and apply a Pulse animation from the gallery.

(8) CHANGE THE TIMINGS We also apply the Pulse to the final block of text. By clicking on the text animation in the Animation pane and dragging it beneath the relevant photo animation, we can quickly change the order. Then set the Start setting in the Timing panel to After Previous. Repeat for the second block of text. When the slide plays, the photo will now fly in, and the block of text will pulse immediately afterwards.

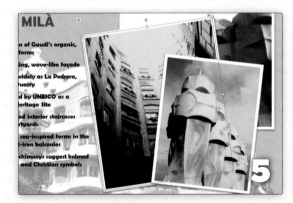

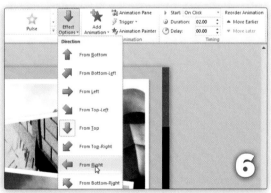

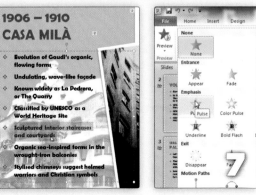

Tip

There's no need to laboriously apply transitions to each slide in your presentation. First, clicking the Apply To All button in the Timing section of the Transitions tab will copy the transition and settings from the current slide to every slide in the presentation. Second, you can organise slides into sections (using Home | Section | Add Section) and apply a transition to a whole section. Finally, you can use the Ctrl-Click and Shift-Click shortcuts to select multiple slides and apply transitions across all of them.

HOW TO...
ANIMATE SMARTART

PowerPoint's SmartArt produces good-looking graphics in seconds.
That's a decent start, but add animation and you're really onto a winner.

Introduced to Word and PowerPoint in Office 2007, SmartArt becomes an even more potent feature in PowerPoint 2010. Having a collection of ready-made customisable graphic elements, diagrams and business-focused illustrations to hand is useful, but when you combine that with PowerPoint's new focus on animation, the results can be fantastic. Effectively, Office 2010 gives you the tools to create your own animated graphics to use in your presentations, without any need to buy and learn a vector-drawing or animation package, or get to grips with technologies such as Microsoft Silverlight or Adobe Flash.

There are two ways of using animation in conjunction with SmartArt; one easy, one not so easy. PowerPoint's animation features can work with the different "levels" of a given SmartArt object, with the options depending on the SmartArt being used. In brief, if you insert a piece of SmartArt and apply an animation to it, you'll find settings in the Effects Options menu to animate your SmartArt level by level, component by component or all at once (see Tip, opposite). If you simply want, say, the blocks in a process diagram to appear in order, this should be all you need.

However, there are limitations. While you can set up Effects Options for the object as a whole, you can't define them for specific components, or change timing settings such as Duration or Delay. Which is where the second way of tackling SmartArt animation comes in.

All SmartArt objects are a collection of grouped shapes and text paths. By selecting and ungrouping the SmartArt, you can break it down into its components and animate each individually, giving you control over what's animated, when and how. It's best to make changes to text or formatting before you ungroup your SmartArt, otherwise you'll have to tackle each component individually, making it harder to maintain a consistent look.

We'll use both approaches in this example, but try inserting some SmartArt and playing around with animation; you never know what you might come up with.

1 **ADD SMARTART** Our business presentation is ripe for illustration. Click the Insert tab, go to the Illustrations section and select SmartArt. Here, we're using the Gear SmartArt. You can find it from the Relationship or Cycle categories on the left.

HOW LONG?
Around 30-40 minutes, depending on the level of complexity.

HOW HARD?
Nowhere near as difficult as it sounds.

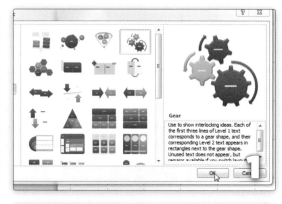

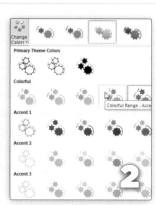

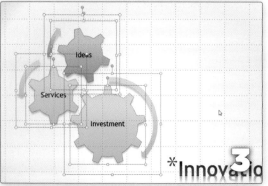

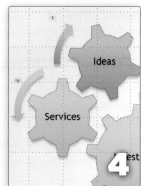

② **DEFINE THE LOOK** Type your text into the SmartArt, either by clicking on the sample text and amending it or by using the flyout text-entry box on the left (click the arrow on the bounding box if you can't see it). Now apply a Style and a Color Scheme to the SmartArt before moving it into position. In our example, we're using the Subtle Effect style and the "Colorful Range – Accent Colors 4 to 5" scheme.

③ **SEPARATE AND ANIMATE** Each gear will eventually revolve, but for that to happen properly we need to break the SmartArt down into its parts. Click the SmartArt object to select it, then right-click and use Group | Ungroup. You may need to do this twice before you see each gear within its own bounding box. Now select the top gear, click on the Animations tab and pick Spin from the gallery.

④ **ANIMATE THE SECOND GEAR…** Click the middle gear and apply the same animation, using either the gallery or the Add Animation button. We have a couple of changes to make this time, however. First, click on Effect Options and set the direction to counterclockwise. Then go to the Timing section and set the Start option to With Previous and the Delay to 00.25.

⑤ **…AND THE THIRD** Now click on the third gear and apply Spin again. This time there's no need to change the direction, but in the Timing section set Start to With Previous and Delay to 00.50. Now click the Preview button on the left of the ribbon and you should see all three gears revolve nicely.

⑥ **INSERT A PROCESS DIAGRAM** Not every SmartArt animation is so complex. Go to a new slide and insert the Vertical Chevron List SmartArt (you'll find it in the Process category). The preset object has only three levels, but we can add another just by clicking in the last item in the text-entry box and typing Enter, then Backspace to start a new top-level item, then Return followed by Tab to type in the subsequent bullet points.

⑦ **STYLE AND ANIMATE** Apply a style and a colour scheme as you did in the last example, and then move the diagram into position. Now, with the SmartArt object still selected, click on the Animations tab and apply the Fade animation.

⑧ **SEQUENCED ANIMATIONS** Now click the Effect Options button. PowerPoint recognises you're animating a multilevel object and offers options to control whether its elements animate together or in sequence. In this case, picking One by One will make the chevrons and text labels fade in one by one in sequence.

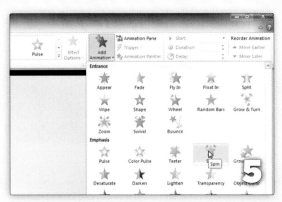

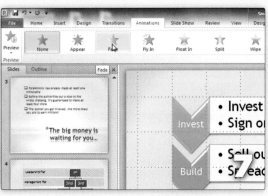

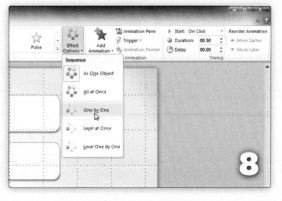

60
55   5
50   10
45   15
40   20
35   25
30

HOW LONG?

Not long to add video, but customising it will take a bit more time.

HOW HARD?

It's surprisingly easy to produce advanced video effects.

HOW TO...
ADD IMPACT WITH VIDEO

PowerPoint 2010 has finally caught up with the need for dynamic content, and now makes video as easy to work with as text and still images.

Over the past decade, video content has become a crucial part of many PowerPoint presentations, yet Microsoft has never quite given it the same welcome as text or still images. With PowerPoint 2010 that finally changes. At last, you can embed video directly into your documents, edit it from within PowerPoint, make adjustments and apply effects, and combine video with text and animation in a range of appealing ways.

You can add video to your presentation in much the same way as any content; by clicking on the Insert tab, mousing over to the right-hand side of the ribbon, and clicking the Video button in the Media panel. Once you've inserted a clip, you'll see two new tabs appear within the banner of Video Tools. The first, Format, gives you the tools to correct, recolour, crop, arrange and apply shapes, borders and effects to your clip, along with a gallery of preset Video Styles – most of these will be familiar from the Picture Tools (see p66).

The second tab, Playback, is more specific to video. If you're using an already edited clip, you can simply apply a Fade In and Fade Out effect to it, but it's also possible to trim longer clips down to size,

meaning that rough footage pulled directly from a digital camcorder can be taken into your presentation.

You'll also find settings for soundtrack volume and choosing full-screen playback, and a facility to add bookmarks. This last feature can be powerful. By setting animations, for example, to trigger when a specific clip reaches a specific bookmark, you can set a relevant bit of text to appear or pulse when that point is reached, or a second clip to appear and start playing.

PowerPoint welcomes a range of video formats, including MPEG2, MP4, WMV, Adobe Flash and QuickTime files (although in practice support may vary from file to file). It's also possible to embed video directly from a website such as YouTube, should you wish.

In this example, we're going to give some of PowerPoint's new video features a workout, but we're only scratching the surface. Embrace the moving image, and you can build presentations that engage your audience in ways that static presentations can't match.

(1) **INSERT VIDEO** One blank slide, ready for the insertion of video. Click the Insert tab, go to the

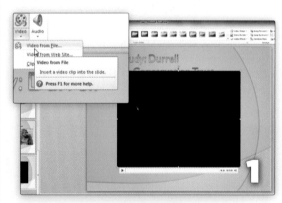

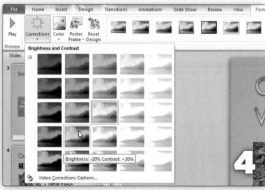

Media section on the right-hand side and click the Video button. Navigate to your video file and click Insert. The clip appears in the middle of your slide at its native size.

2 TRIM TO LENGTH In this case, our clip is a short amateur video captured during a trip to the Durrell Wildlife Conservation Trust in Jersey. We need something short and to the point, so click on the Video Tools | Playback tab, then the Trim Video button. You can watch your clip through, then move the green and red sliders to select new Start and End points. When you're ready, click OK. PowerPoint won't actually cut your clip at this point, so you can always re-edit later.

3 CROP TO FIT Those big black bars are wasted space. On the Video Tools | Format tab, click Crop. Move the bottom and top crop marks so the black bars are greyed out, then click Crop once again. Now resize and reposition the cropped clip as shown.

4 COLOUR CORRECTION The colours look slightly washed-out. To give the footage extra punch, click the Corrections button, then the "Brightness -20%, Contrast +20%" thumbnail.

5 STYLISE THE CLIP For added impact, we're going to apply a Style to the clip. Click on the down arrow to the right of the Video Styles gallery to expand the selection, then go down to the Intense category and choose the Reflected Perspective Right preset.

6 ADD A BOOKMARK That's the video in place, but it's only one part of this slide. To make the second part work, we need to add a bookmark. Either press the Play button beneath the clip and wait, or click/drag the progress bar until you're a second or so away from the end of the clip. Now click on the Video Tools | Playback tab and hit the Add Bookmark button.

7 INSERT A QUOTE Our bookmark will trigger the appearance of a quote, which is just a textbox added and styled using a nice serif font, with the quote itself italicised and the attribution resized and made bold. Now select the quote, click on the Animations tab, and choose the Shape entrance animation.

8 SET THE TRIGGER Go to Effect Options and set Direction to Out, then set Duration (in Timings) to 1.50. Click the Trigger button in Advanced Animation and select On Bookmark, then the bookmark we created earlier. Now, when playback reaches this point, the quote will appear with a nifty iris-in effect. You can use this feature in a number of ways: for example, when a video supports a list of bullet points, have each bullet point "pulse" as the video reaches the relevant point.

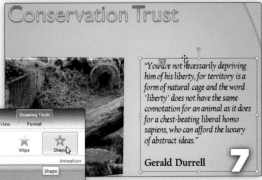

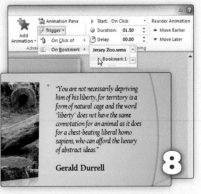

Tip

Adding video to a presentation will have a dramatic effect on file size, which could be a problem if you're moving it around a network or sending it via email. Luckily, PowerPoint can take care of this for you. Click on File to go to the Backstage view and you'll see the Compress Media button. Clicking on this will give you options to save the file in one of three quality settings: Presentation Quality, Internet Quality, or Low Quality for email. Choose one and PowerPoint does all the hard work for you, removing trimmed bits of video, compressing images and video clips down to size, and making the file as lean as possible. In our tests, compressing one file with just three video clips for Presentation Quality cut nearly 60MB of unwanted baggage, so it's well worth doing.

HOW TO...
CO-AUTHOR IN POWERPOINT

Simple online collaboration is another strength of the new and improved PowerPoint 2010. Here's how you and your colleagues can take advantage.

HOW LONG?
It takes just a few minutes to see how co-authoring works.

HOW HARD?
Once the file is shared, co-authoring is easy.

Tip

You can also see who's at work on a given document by clicking File to go to the Backstage view and looking at the Info section. Click on the Send a Message button to email or IM your co-author before you start work on the document. You don't want to end up fighting over the same page!

Few of us work entirely alone. A presentation will usually need input from others, quite likely as part of a team. Before Office 2010, this wasn't always easy; you'd often be swapping files with others, running through comments, and accepting or rejecting amendments.

PowerPoint 2010 brings real-time co-authoring. Two or more can work on the same file at the same moment, with PowerPoint tracking each user's changes and synchronising them when you save; your changes are uploaded to the version on the server, and others' changes are downloaded to the version on your PC.

To co-author you'll need access to a SharePoint server (mostly in large businesses) or a Windows Live account, which lets you upload your file to Microsoft's SkyDrive online storage service, share its folder with your collaborators, and go from there. Your collaborators don't even have to use PowerPoint, as long as they have access to the Office Web Apps version from a web browser.

1 **FIRST STEPS** Open a document online (see p147), and if someone else is editing it you get a notification in the bottom left corner of the

screen. A small icon on slides in the left-hand pane tells you a slide is being edited by one of your co-authors.

2 **MEET THE AUTHORS** Clicking the co-author icon at the bottom left of the screen will list people currently working on the document. Clicking on one of the names or profile pictures gives you contact details plus options to email them, schedule a meeting, or message them if you both have instant messaging open.

3 **MAKING CHANGES** PowerPoint's existing review tools still work. In this case, adding a comment to the SmartArt object and clicking Save will post the comment to the collaborator's version of the document when he or she next saves, along with any changes to the text or the design you've made.

4 **TO AND FRO** Our co-author reads our comment, changes the SmartArt and text, and adds a reply. They then save their version. We save ours, and the server syncs the files, updating our file with the new SmartArt and comment. Real-time collaboration!

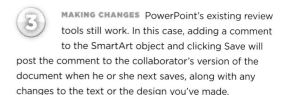
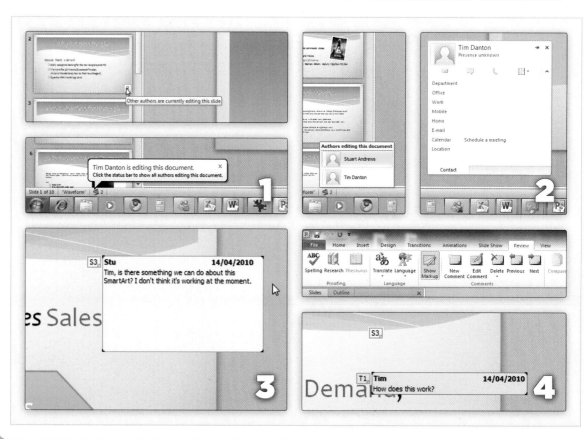

HOW TO... BROADCAST YOUR PRESENTATION

It isn't always possible to give a presentation in person, but the impact is lost if your audience can only download the PowerPoint file or use an online sharing service such as SlideShare (www.slideshare.net). The new Broadcast Slideshow feature is the answer. You still give the presentation live, and can even provide a spoken commentary while your audience, anywhere in the world, views the show through a web browser. There's no need for annoying plugins, and content such as photos and video will still play back (although some fonts, transitions and animations might not appear exactly as designed).

You'll need access to a SharePoint server or a Windows Live account. Your audience needs only a compliant browser (Internet Explorer 8, Google Chrome and Firefox all work fine). Broadcasting is simple, and the great thing is that you control the presentation just as you would normally.

To invite someone to join your virtual audience, you need only email them the link or cut and paste the broadcast URL into an IM, Facebook update or tweet.

① COMPRESS MEDIA So your presentation is ready. Wait: if there's multimedia content in there, you'll need to compress it for internet streaming. Go to File | Info. Click Compress Media and select Internet Quality. Let your files compress, then click OK and save.

② PREPARE FOR BROADCAST Now click on Save & Send, choose the Broadcast Slideshow option and click the Broadcast Slideshow button. PowerPoint assumes by default that you're using the Windows Live-powered PowerPoint broadcast service. Click the Start Broadcast button, then enter your Windows Live login details and click OK.

③ SEND INVITATIONS PowerPoint prepares the presentation for broadcast, then returns with a dialog containing the URL for your broadcast and an option to invite prospective audience members via email. If you want to provide a vocal presentation, using a voice-enabled IM client with chatroom functionality such as Windows Live Messenger makes sense. You can just paste the URL into an IM rather than emailing it.

④ TAKE CONTROL Here's the presentation running in PowerPoint and within a browser. You can click your way through the slides as you would if presenting live. Note that you can send out additional invitations at any time using the Send Invitations button. When you're done, hit the End Broadcast button. The presentation will stop right there, and there's no worry about members of the audience taking the presentation away and re-editing it or pinching elements from it later.

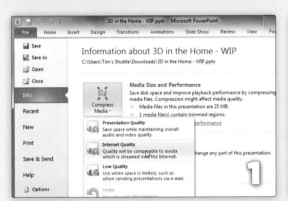

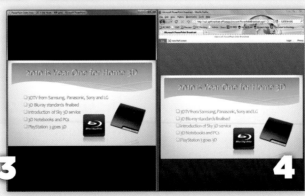

HOW LONG?
The only thing that takes time is compressing video.

HOW HARD?
The basics are simple; adding voice commentary is trickier.

Tip

Font support inside the Broadcast Slideshow option is dependent on the fonts stored on Microsoft's servers. If you want to ensure that your page looks the same on your screen and that of your audience (transitions and animations permitting), try embedding fonts before your broadcast (File | Options | Save | Embed fonts in the file).

IN THIS CHAPTER

6

Outlook 2010

OUTLOOK 2010

While many people are turning to web-based services to handle their email and diary, there's nothing to match the power of Outlook 2010 when it comes to managing your home and professional life. With vastly improved search facilities, the option to ignore irrelevant email chains, and the ability to edit photos copied into messages, Outlook remains the outstanding choice for

email connoisseurs. Outlook's calendaring facilities – which make it easy to share calendars with family and colleagues, local and remote – also make it an essential application for the busy professional, and new features such as Quick Steps only enhance this status. In this chapter, we'll show you how to master all of these features and many more.

6
Outlook 2010

HOW LONG?
You should have your email just how you want it within minutes.

HOW HARD?
Initial setup is easy, but advanced features (such as integrating Hotmail) may present a couple of hurdles.

Tip

Outlook's RSS feed reader is rudimentary compared to many of the services found on the web. Google Reader (www.google.com/reader), for instance, combines the headlines from your various feeds into a single stream, allowing you to see the latest news from different sites in one hit. It also recommends newsfeeds based on your preferences.

HOW TO...
SET UP YOUR EMAIL

When you first install Outlook 2010, you'll be presented with the Email Account Setup wizard. Here's how you go from there to your email up and running.

1 **EMAIL SETTINGS** The wizard will invite you to enter your name, email address and password, and Outlook should download the relevant settings automatically. If Outlook doesn't have your ISP's settings in its database, you'll have to enter these manually. Your ISP should have sent you details of your incoming/outgoing mail server addresses when you signed up; if not, check the help section of its website.

2 **ADD SUBFOLDERS** Email should now arrive in Outlook's Inbox. If you want to keep selected emails separate, create a subfolder. Right-click the Inbox link in the left-hand panel and select New Folder. Give it a name and click OK. You'll now find that folder listed under your Inbox. There are two ways to move messages: first, you can drag and drop them from your Inbox onto the folder's name. Alternatively, open an email, click Move (on the ribbon) and select the folder.

3 **BRING IN HOTMAIL** If you have a Hotmail or Windows Live webmail account, you can view email, calendars and contacts from that within Outlook 2010, as well as your regular email. This requires a small download called the Outlook Connector, available from www.office.com. Type "outlook connector" into the search box and it should be the topmost link. With the Connector installed, you should find your Hotmail or Live account in the left-hand panel of Mail, Calendar and Contacts in Outlook. You can now send and receive email, and create appointments and contacts, without having to go to the Hotmail site. See p88 for instructions on how to share a family calendar in Outlook via Hotmail.

4 **SET UP RSS FEEDS** Outlook 2010 includes an RSS feed reader to keep up with the news from your favourite websites. To find the feed address of a site, look for a little orange RSS button on the homepage. For example, *PC Pro*'s main RSS feed is http://feeds.pcpro.co.uk/pcpro-today. Then, in Outlook 2010, right-click RSS Feeds in the list of folders and select "Add a New RSS Feed". Enter the address and click Add, then Yes. Outlook will now start pulling in the latest headlines and previews from that site, and provide a link to read each full story.

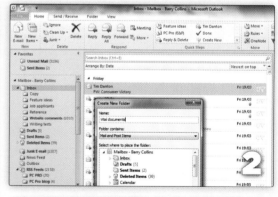

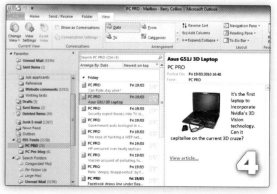

HOW TO...
MANAGE YOUR CONTACTS

① IMPORTING EXISTING CONTACTS Chances are you've already got a stash of contacts, whether in a previous version of Outlook, on a mobile phone or in a webmail system such as Google's Gmail. Outlook can import them in a variety of formats. First, go to File | Open | Import. This launches the Import and Export wizard. Choose "Import from another program or file" (unless you're importing from Outlook Express, Windows Mail or Eudora, in which case select "Import Internet Mail and Addresses").

You'll see a list of contacts formats that Outlook accepts. Go to your existing contacts software or phone and look for an option to export. Try to match the export format to one on Outlook 2010's list; comma-separated values (CSV) is a decent fallback if there are no other matches. Once you've exported your contacts, save the file to your PC's desktop, then go back to Outlook 2010's Import and Export wizard and click Next, then Browse. Navigate to the file you saved, press Next and then Finish.

② ADD NEW CONTACTS To create a new address book entry, click on the Contacts tab in the bottom left corner of Outlook, then click New Contact at the top left. Entering details into the relevant fields is self-explanatory, but if you can't find a particular entry just click the down arrow next to any of the phone number fields and select a suitable heading from the dropdown menu. Click the Details button in the ribbon for the option to insert extra data, such as birthday or nickname. Click Save & Close when you've finished.

③ SUGGESTED CONTACTS Outlook 2010 makes the process of creating contacts even easier. At the top left of the Contacts screen is an option called Suggested Contacts; Outlook automatically creates records for anyone who's been in touch with you recently, with their name and email address filled in. To add this person to your Address Book, drag and drop the business card onto the Contacts folder link below.

④ CREATE CONTACT GROUPS If you regularly email the same bunch of people – members of a club, say, or people on a particular project – it makes sense to create a Group for them in your Contacts folder. Click New Contact Group and give your group a name. Then click the Add Members button and select From Outlook Contacts from the dropdown menu that appears. Double-click on the name of anyone you want to add to the group, and click OK when finished. Finally, click Save & Close. The next time you need to email the group, you can simply enter the group's name into the To field of your email message.

HOW LONG?
The import process may take a little time, but a lot less than typing in all the details manually.

HOW HARD?
If you've never imported a file into Outlook, it may seem scary. We promise it isn't!

Tip
To edit an existing Contact Group, first find them in your Address Book. Open up the details and you'll see an option to edit the list.

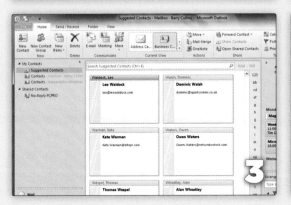

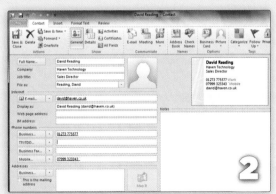

6

Outlook 2010

HOW LONG?

Once you get into the swing of it, a matter of seconds per email.

HOW HARD?

There's nothing difficult about the process, but an eye for design will help.

HOW TO...
MAKE YOUR EMAIL SPARKLE

There's no need to stick to boring old plain text in outgoing messages – Outlook 2010 sports several ways to make your email more attractive.

While many people will spend hours labouring over the presentation of a Word document, most people don't give a second thought to the aesthetic of their email. For day-to-day messages, that's perfectly understandable. But for special occasions – showing off the first photos of a new baby, sending out invites to a party, or producing an email newsletter, for example – it's possible to make your email look magnificent with only a few simple tweaks. And they won't take any more than a few minutes to master, either.

Here are eight ways to give your email more visual impact:

1 ALTERNATIVE FONTS There's no need to stick to the humdrum default typeface when writing email. Create a new message and enter the recipient's name/address in the To field, then select the Format Text tab at the top of the email message. Here you'll find the full range of fonts, styles and typographical effects you're used to from Word 2010. Be aware that unless your recipient is also using Outlook 2010 or 2007, fonts and effects may not show up in their software – especially on a mobile device, such as a BlackBerry.

2 INSERT PHOTOS You don't have to attach photos as a separate file – you can embed the picture into the email message. Click the Insert tab and select Picture, then rifle through the pictures stored on your PC until you find the image you want. The photo will drop into the message, with little square/circle handlebars on the edges and corners; click on these to adjust the photo to the desired size.

3 EDIT PICTURES When you inserted your photo into the email, you'll have noticed a new tab called Picture Tools at the top of the screen. This allows you to make the photo look better before you click the Send button. Click Corrections (in the leftmost Adjust group) and you'll find a pop-up menu that offers a number of options for sharpening or softening the photo and adjusting its brightness. Drag your cursor over the grid of thumbnail previews and you'll see the photo change interactively as you move between the options. Click the left mouse button when you find the one you want to keep. There are other options to adjust the colour of the photo and apply a range of artistic effects.

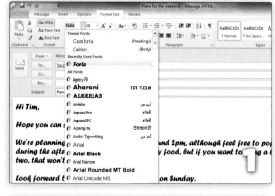

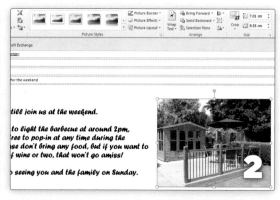

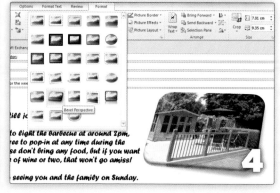

80 THE ULTIMATE GUIDE TO OFFICE 2010

PHOTO FRAMES Now you have the photo looking perfect, how about adding a frame? A small selection of frames appear above the Picture Styles label: hover your cursor over each rectangular thumbnail to see a preview of what the frame will look like, and left-click to select. For a wider selection, click the down arrow next to the frames. Here you'll find some really flamboyant options, such as 3D frames that make the photo appear as if it's bursting out of the screen. Click the Picture Effects button for even finer control over your photo frame.

SMART ART It isn't only photos that can be embedded into emails. There's also the option to include SmartArt – ready-made graphics that can be useful for displaying business information such as workflows or organisation charts. Click Insert | SmartArt and select from the vast library of graphics. You can then enter your own words into the SmartArt graphics by clicking on the textboxes. Don't worry if it looks as if you have too much text for the size of the box, Outlook will automatically adjust the font size to fit.

INSERT CHARTS Need to share news of the company's latest sales figures? You can embed a quick chart directly into your email by clicking Insert | Chart. This opens Excel 2010, and once you've made a choice from the chart styles on offer, you can plug the necessary figures straight into the spreadsheet on the right-hand side of the screen. Changes to the figures are instantly reflected in the chart in the email on the left.

 ADD TABLES Information such as shop opening times or squash club fees is often far clearer in a table than in plain text. Go to Insert | Table and select the number of rows and columns your table will need (don't worry if you miscount, it can be corrected later). Then choose a design from the Table Styles options that appear in the ribbon (click the down arrow for more) and start entering your data. You'll find even more options via the two Table Tools tabs, Design and Layout, that appear in the ribbon when you're working on tables – for example, splitting the table or changing the text direction.

 TAKE A SCREENGRAB Seen something brilliant on a website that you want to share? Or need technical help and want to show someone what's appeared on your screen? Click Insert and select Screenshot, and you can send someone a quick snapshot of whatever is on your screen. This feature lets you take a grab of any open window; if you just need to share a small part of a screen (say, a picture on a web page), select the Screen Clipping option.

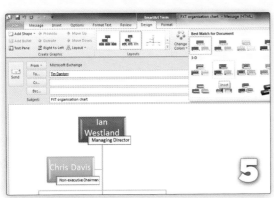

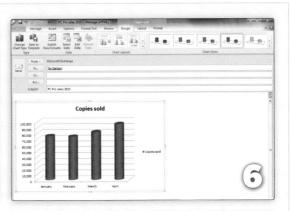

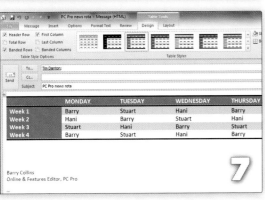

Tip

Don't get too carried away jazzing up your emails with different coloured backgrounds. It's much harder to read light text on a dark background than plain black on white, and those with even mild forms of colour blindness may not be able to read your message. If you use a coloured backdrop, maintain high contrast between the text and the background.

HOW TO...
MANAGE YOUR INBOX

Take control of your inbox – before it takes control of you – with our eight-step guide to the email management tools available in Outlook 2010.

HOW LONG?

It takes a while to explore the options, but it will save time in the long-run.

HOW HARD?

Some of the features are ridiculously easy to use, but others need more serious consideration.

Coping with the sheer volume of email traffic has become such a problem that book-store shelves creak under the weight of email advice manuals. Whether you're dealing with junk mail (p86) or merely an avalanche of genuine messages, information overload can become a time-sink.

Fortunately, Outlook now contains more tools than ever before to help you deal swiftly with important email and disregard the rest.

1 CONVERSATION VIEW New in Office 2010, Conversation View is designed to display all the messages from a particular conversation (the long-running sequence of messages about your wedding arrangements, say) in one thread, so when you click on the latest message on that topic you'll find the previous ones beneath. We have reservations about its effectiveness. For a start, it doesn't always do a brilliant job of working out which messages are part of the same conversation – it can be fooled by other messages having the same subject, for instance. You can turn this feature on and off by clicking the View tab and then ticking (or unticking) "Show as Conversations".

2 CLEAN UP INBOX If you do decide to persevere with Conversation View, the Clean Up option in the Home tab makes it notably better. This feature bins redundant messages – those where the content has been repeated in subsequent emails and there's no longer any need to keep a copy of the original. The Clean Up tool can be applied to individual conversations or your entire Inbox folder. We suggest you start by cleaning up a couple of long conversations, to see if it works for you, before attempting to clean up everything.

3 IGNORE CONVERSATION Fed up of getting messages about the bowling night you're not going to? Click on one in the Inbox and select Ignore from the Home tab in the ribbon. All subsequent messages on that topic will go straight to Deleted Items.

4 QUICK STEPS Quick Steps are Outlook 2010's best time-saver. If you're performing the same actions – forwarding messages to your boss, say, or moving messages to a folder – then you can set

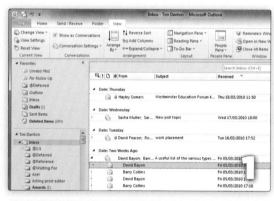

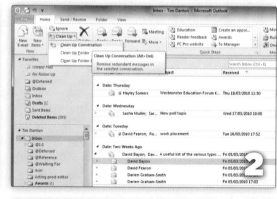

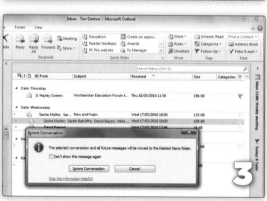

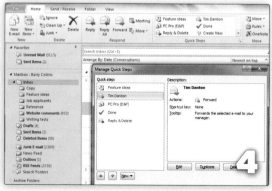

up a shortcut. In the Home tab, you'll find the Quick Steps group. You may need to expand it before the Create New icon (a lightning bolt) appears; then click it and give your new Quick Step a name (such as "Forward to Steven"). Choose the type of action from the dropdown list and follow the instructions, then click Finish. Now, when a new email arrives, click on the Quick Step to deal with it.

5 **COLOUR-CODE MESSAGES** Categorising email is a deft way to keep on top of your inbox, especially if you're managing multiple projects. On the Home tab, click Categorize | All Categories. You can now assign a different colour to each project by picking a colour and selecting Rename. When a new message arrives about a project, click the Categorize button and pick the appropriate colour/category from the dropdown menu. To quickly view all the messages on a given project, click Filter E-mail on the far right-hand side of the Home tab (assuming you're currently viewing the Inbox), select Categorized and pick the relevant category.

6 **FLAG MESSAGES** Got an important message, but haven't got time to deal with it now? Click the red flag Follow Up icon and choose from the list of predefined times. Back in your Inbox screen, you'll notice the email has been added to your list of tasks on the right-hand side (if the list isn't there, click the small left-pointing arrow at the right, below the ribbon).

7 **INBOX SEARCH** The search tools in previous versions of Outlook were so patchy that hunting down an email in a large inbox could take five or ten minutes. The vastly improved search facility in Office 2010 should reduce that to seconds. At the top of the Inbox is a Search Inbox bar: use this to search for a specific name or subject line, or a keyword or phrase you recall. Once you've clicked in the search box, a Search Tools menu appears at the top of the screen. This is invaluable for narrowing down your search. Say you want to find a spreadsheet that you remember Tim emailed you last month: select From in the Refine menu and type "Tim", then click the Has Attachment button and you should be able to swiftly find the relevant message from the date-ordered list that appears below. Click the Close Search button to return to the normal Inbox view.

8 **ESTABLISH RULES** Another means of taking control of your inbox is to set up rules for emails arriving. You could, for example, move all messages from a certain sender into a specific folder: go to File | Manage Rules & Alerts | New Rule, select "Move messages from someone to a folder" and follow the instructions. Among dozens of other rules, you can also set messages from your boss, say, to be flagged as urgent.

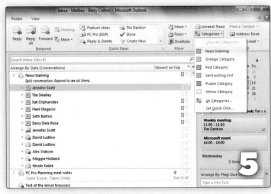

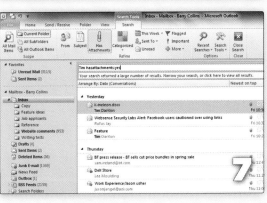

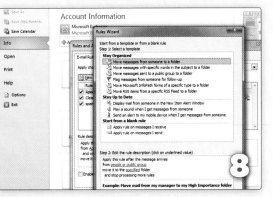

Tip

If you find yourself repeatedly using the same search on your inbox, you don't have to retype those keywords every time. Simply press ‹Ctrl-E7› to enter the Search menu, click on the Recent Searches button, then select your search from the dropdown list that appears.

HOW TO...
EMAIL LIKE A PRO

Outlook is the professional's choice of email software for a reason – it's packed with business-friendly features. Find out how to put them to good use.

HOW LONG?
Take time to explore these features – you'll find something you'll end up using every day.

HOW HARD?
So long as your office uses Microsoft Exchange Server, nothing here should trip you up.

Tip

Ever sent an email to the wrong person only to realise after it's too late? Or replied instantly to someone when angry and regretted it? By default, Outlook sends emails as soon as you press Send (if you're online). But you can add an automatic delay: go to File | Options | Advanced and untick "Send immediately when connected".

Outlook is primarily a business tool, and an immensely powerful one. Used correctly, it will not only make your business email look professional, but also make your working life easier. Use it poorly, however, and your communications will feel amateurish and you'll waste time on housekeeping tasks such as adding your name to the foot of every message.

Here we'll show you how to take advantage of Outlook's many work-orientated features. Note that some of the options depend on the software being used in an office environment with a full Exchange Server setup. If you're running Outlook at work this will almost certainly apply, but it's worth checking with your IT department beforehand if in doubt.

① CREATE A SIGNATURE Let's start by creating a signature – the standard piece of text added to the end of every message, normally containing your name, position, and contact details. Go to File | Options, select Mail from the list down the left-hand side, then click the Signatures button. Click New and give your signature a name. In the blank Edit Signature box at the

bottom, enter the text you want to appear at the foot of every message. Click OK. Use the dropdown menus at the top right to choose if you want the signature added to both new messages and replies.

② MAKE NOTES Want to make notes about an email you've been sent? Outlook integrates with Office's underrated OneNote application, which allows you to edit, highlight or even scrawl handwritten notes (if you have a tablet PC) on the text of email messages. To pass an email to OneNote, open the message and click the OneNote icon in the Move group on the email's ribbon. (See Chapter 7 for more on OneNote.)

③ PEOPLE PANE A new feature in Outlook 2010, People Pane is a convenient way to keep track of email. At the foot of every message you'll see a thin strip with the sender's name in it. Click the little up arrow on the far right of the strip and it will unveil a pane showing all your recent correspondence with that person, including email and appointments in your calendar. It's a terrific way to review long-running discussions.

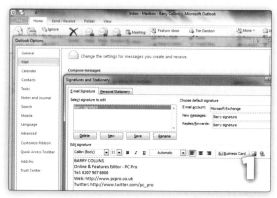

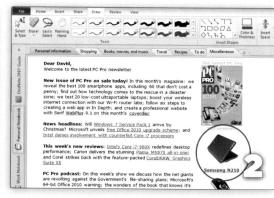

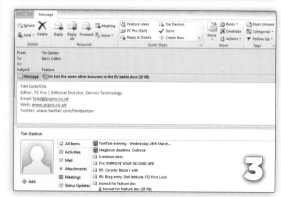

OUT OF OFFICE If you're leaving the office for a few days, don't leave colleagues and clients in the dark. Setting up an automatic Out Of Office reply is easier than ever: click File and hit the Automatic Replies button in the centre pane. Click "I am currently Out of the Office" and fill in a brief message (providing an email address for a colleague, for example). When you're finished, click OK. Out Of Office messages will only work if your office is running an Exchange server, or you leave your PC on and connected to the internet while away.

 RECEIPT REQUEST How often have you phoned someone to check they've received an email? Avoid this by requesting email receipts: delivery receipts tell you the email has arrived in the recipient's inbox, and read receipts show you they've opened it. Either or both can be switched on by clicking the Options tab in a new message window and ticking the appropriate boxes. Be warned: read receipts aren't infallible. They rely on the goodwill of the recipient, who'll be asked if they want to notify you the message has been read; and they don't work with every email system, especially webmail. Use receipts sparingly: correspondents will resent the Big Brother checks on every message they receive from you.

VOTING BUTTONS Sometimes, emails just need a yes/no answer: should we move the planning meetings to Mondays? Shall we buy this present? For such occasions, Outlook has voting buttons that allow your recipients to reply with no more effort than a click of the mouse. In a new message, click the Options tab and select Use Voting Buttons. There are three predefined options – Approve/Reject; Yes/No; Yes/No/Maybe – or you can customise the buttons with your own answers. Once you're done, type your question into the body of the email and select your recipients as normal. Note that voting buttons will only work with other Outlook users.

 DIVERT REPLIES If you have a PA or deputy, you may want them to deal with replies to a particular email: an invite to a team meal, for instance. To divert replies to them, click the Options tab in a new message and click the Direct Replies To button. Enter their name or email address into the "Have replies sent to" field and click Close.

 SHARE YOUR INBOX To give a PA access to your inbox, or let a colleague get your messages while you're away, you can share access to your email. In the Inbox, click the Folder tab and select Folder Permissions. Click Add, double-click a name in the Address List and click OK. Select Full Details and click OK. On the receiving PC, your colleague should go to File | Open | Other User's Folder and enter your name. They should then have access to all your incoming messages.

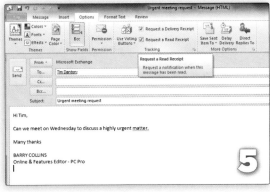

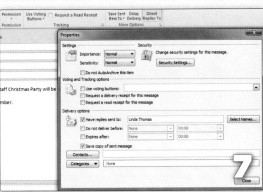

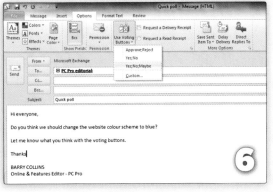

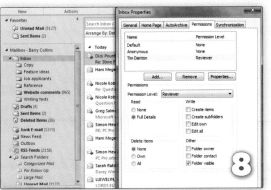

HOW TO...
DEAL WITH JUNK MAIL

Don't waste your precious time reading about pills you never wanted to buy, or inheritances that will never be yours. Junk them automatically instead.

HOW LONG?
About ten minutes to set up, but it's an ongoing process.

HOW HARD?
Blissfully simple both to set up and tweak.

① SET FILTERING LEVEL Junk mail – or "spam" – remains one of the biggest irritants of the digital world. Given that well in excess of nine out of every ten emails sent is spam, it's a miracle so few junk messages actually trickle through. In addition to the junk mail filtering applied by your broadband provider and security software, Outlook 2010 has its own methods for dealing with spam. Its junk email filter is running from the moment you install Office 2010, but you can tweak its settings by clicking Junk in the Home tab and selecting Junk E-mail Options. Here you can pick the level of protection, ranging from no automatic filtering to only allowing messages from approved senders. We suggest you start with the Low setting, moving up to High if you find too much junk email is seeping through the net.

② FALSE POSITIVES As you start to receive email, Outlook will alert you if it's decided a message is spam. It isn't infallible, so from time to time check your Junk E-mail folder (in the list of folders down the left-hand side of the Inbox screen); if it's blocked a genuine message, click on that message, click Junk in the

ribbon's Home tab and select Not Junk. The message will be returned to your inbox, and you'll have the option to allow all future messages from that sender. Likewise, if an iffy message slips through, click Junk | Block Sender to prevent a recurrence. Keep an eye on your blocked/safe senders list from the Junk E-mail Options menu.

③ SAFE SENDERS Sometimes, Outlook blocks a message from someone you've sent a message to, leaving you wondering why they've not replied. You can prevent this by entering the Junk E-mail Options menu, clicking the Safe Senders tab and ticking the box that says "Automatically add people I e-mail to the Safe Senders List".

④ BLOCK HIGH-RISK NATIONS A good deal of spam emanates from countries such as China, Nigeria and Russia. If you have no regular dealings with anyone in these countries, you can block all email from those shores: select the International tab in Junk E-mail Options and click "Blocked Top-Level Domain List". China is CN, Nigeria is NG and Russia is RU.

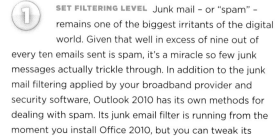

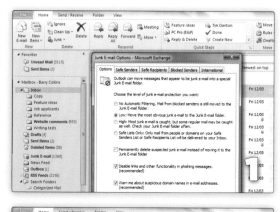
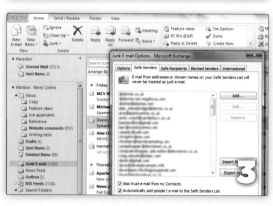

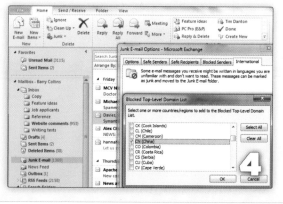

HOW TO...
ORGANISE YOUR DIARY

1 **ADD APPOINTMENTS** Outlook's Calendar is ideal for keeping both your work and personal life organised. It's also the best tool for arranging meetings with friends, colleagues and clients. We'll kick off by adding a new appointment. Click the Calendar tab at the bottom left of the screen, then New Appointment at the top left. Enter the subject and location of the event, and use the dropdown menus to select start and end times. If it's an all-day appointment, or spans several days (like a holiday), tick "All day event".

At the top of the screen is a Show As option: this lets you determine the nature of the appointment. Select Busy or Out of Office if you'll be unavailable during the appointment, since this alerts colleagues that you're off limits if they're trying to find a meeting slot in your diary. Finally, you can set a reminder for anything between five minutes and two weeks before the meeting using the dropdown menu. Click Save & Close when you're done.

2 **SCHEDULE MEETINGS WITH OTHERS** Outlook really comes into its own when you're trying to arrange meetings. To create a meeting request, add a new appointment and fill in all the details as in step 1, but when you're finished click on Scheduling. If you're arranging a meeting with colleagues in the same office, type their names into the slots below and (assuming your company runs a Microsoft Exchange server) you should be able to see if they're free for the meeting. If there's a diary clash, try pressing AutoPick Next at the foot of the screen to find the next available slot in all your diaries. It's also possible to invite people from outside your office by typing their name and email address into the slots, but you won't be able to preview their diaries. When you click Send, meeting invitations are sent out to all attendees, who can accept or decline, or even suggest a new time and/or date. You'll get an email confirming each response.

3 **CALENDAR VIEWS** The appointments are in; now it's time to scan your diary. Several calendar views are available, including a single day (Day), working week (Work Week, Monday to Friday by default), full week (Week) or a month (Month). Switch between these using the buttons at the top of the Calendar screen.

4 **TAKE MEETING NOTES** Want to prepare notes ahead of a meeting, or take notes during one? Open the appointment and click the OneNote button at the left of the Appointment ribbon: this creates a notes page for this meeting. You can even record audio or video. The notes will remain tied to this appointment, so to go back and review later, just find the meeting in your diary and click the OneNote button again.

HOW LONG?
It only takes a few minutes to discover Outlook's key diary-making abilities.

HOW HARD?
The basic stuff is easy, but integrating with OneNote takes a little longer to master.

Tip

If an appointment takes place at the same time every week or month, you don't need to create a fresh calendar entry each time. Make a new appointment for the first instance, then click the Recurrence button in the ribbon (in the Options group). Here you can choose to run the meeting on the same day every week or, say, the second Monday of each month.

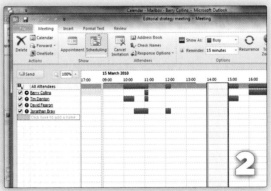

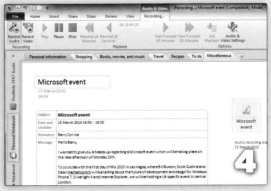

HOW TO...
SHARE OUTLOOK CALENDARS

Avoid diary clashes by sharing your Outlook calendar with friends, family and colleagues, and never miss a crucial date again.

It's all well and good having your personal calendar in order, but how do you know when it's your turn to pick the kids up from school, or whether your colleagues are going to be in the office this week? Shared and public calendars are the solution, allowing you to view the dates in your own diary alongside those of friends, family and colleagues. Office 2010 has a selection of calendar-sharing features. Here, we'll show you how to pick the appropriate calendar-sharing option for both home and office needs.

1 **SHARE CALENDARS WITH FRIENDS AND FAMILY** Outlook allows you to share calendars over the internet by publishing them online at Office.com. In our tests, however, we found this to be cumbersome. A cleaner way to share calendars via Outlook is to go to http://login.live.com, which is Windows Live Hotmail's homepage. Create an account if you don't have one, then select Calendar (which may be tucked away on the topmost menu, underneath More) and click "Add a new calendar". Give it a name and a description, then click Edit Sharing and insert the email addresses of your friends and family. Finally, click Save. If you've

already followed the instructions for adding a Hotmail account to Outlook on p78, you'll now find your newly created diary in the list under Calendars. Tick the box next to its name to view the calendar and add appointments.

2 **ACCESS COLLEAGUES' CALENDARS** If you're using Outlook in an office running Exchange Server, it's a doddle to find out what your colleagues are up to. Click the Calendar box at the bottom left of the screen, then – making sure you're in the Home tab – click Open Calendar. Choose "From Address Book..." in the dropdown list and double-click on the name of the person whose calendar you wish to view. Click OK. That person will be added to your Shared Calendars list on the left of the screen. Tick the box next to their name and you can view their diary – although you'll only see appointments blocked out, not the details of those appointments. If you need that extra information...

3 **GET FULL DETAILS** Seeing full details of another user's calendar requires their permission. Click the Home tab and select the Share Calendar

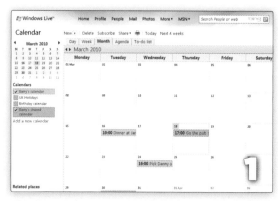

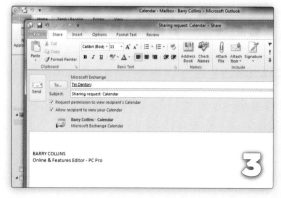

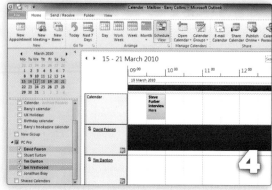

button. Enter the name(s) of your colleague(s) into the "To..." field and tick the box labelled "Request permission to view recipient's Calendar". If your colleague agrees, you'll now also find their calendar listed under Shared Calendars on the left-hand side of the screen, but this time with complete appointment details.

 SCHEDULE VIEW The Schedule View is a new feature in Office 2010 that allows you to see what you and your colleagues are doing today on a single screen. Click the Home tab and select Schedule View, then tick the names of the calendars you want to see side-by-side from the menu down the left-hand side. You can view both personal and shared calendars in Schedule View.

 CALENDAR GROUPS If you're sharing calendars with several friends or colleagues, you might want to organise them into dedicated groups (one for each project you're involved with, for example). Click the Home tab and select Calendar Groups | Create New Calendar Group. Give the group a name and click OK. You'll then be asked to add the names of people you wish to add to the group.

 EMAIL CALENDARS If you're trying to book a meeting with someone but don't want to give them full access to your calendar, you can email them a snapshot of your diary so they can find a free time slot. Select the E-mail Calendar option from the Home tab, and use the dropdown menus to select which calendar you want to send them and the date range (the next 30 days, for example).

It is also possible to select the level of detail you wish to divulge: if you only want them to see the available time slots, not the details of your appointments, leave this set to the default option of Availability Only. Click OK and the calendar details will be embedded into a new email message. Simply enter the recipient's name into the "To..." field and the calendar will be sent.

 PUBLIC HOLIDAYS Want to add Bank Holidays to your calendar, as well as notable dates such as St Patrick's Day? Click File | Options | Calendar and, under the "Calendar options" section, click "Add Holidays...". Make sure the UK box is ticked (select other countries if you wish) and click OK.

 WEBMAIL ACCESS If your company runs an Exchange server, you should be able to access your calendar at any time through a web browser (as well as your email inbox). Ask your IT department for the details of your webmail server – the login details should be the same as the ones you use for Outlook on your PC.

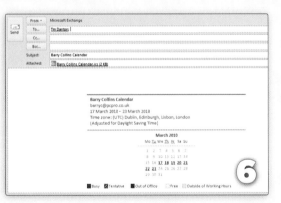

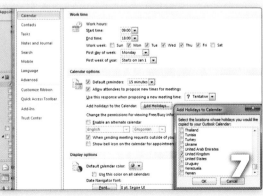

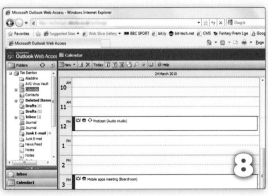

Tip

Microsoft provides a series of templates for calendars that can be printed out and used in the home and office. These include photo calendars, wall planners and academic calendars. You can choose from dozens of extra calendar designs at www.pcpro.co.uk/links/calendars.

HOW LONG?

Seconds to enter a new task; minutes if you need to add more detail.

HOW HARD?

One of the easiest things to do in Outlook.

HOW TO...
CREATE TO-DO LISTS

Outlook 2010 makes it quick and simple to create to-do lists that efficiently remind you – and your colleagues – of the tasks you need to get through.

With email arriving, the phone ringing and the litany of other interruptions to a working day, it's easy to lose track of what you're meant to be doing. Instead of jotting on an easily misplaced sticky, use Outlook to keep up to speed.

1 **CREATE TASKS** To add an item to your to-do list, click Tasks at the bottom left of the Outlook screen and then New Task, which will appear at the left-hand side of the ribbon. It's possible to create a task simply by typing its name into the panel in the middle of the screen, but you'll get more control over its settings if you use the New Task button. Give your task a name and set the due date (and start date, if any). If you tick the box next to the Reminder field, Outlook can send you a prompt a day or so before the task is due, avoiding last-minute surprises. You can also categorise a task, using the same project headings as for your email (see p83).

2 **ASSIGN TASKS** Managers can assign tasks to team members. Fill out the task form as normal, then click Assign Task in the ribbon. Enter the employee's name/email address into the "To..." field. You'll

notice Outlook has pre-ticked two other boxes that will ensure an updated copy of the task is kept on your to-do list, and that you're sent a status report when the job is finished. Untick these if necessary. Click Send.

3 **SEND A STATUS REPORT** Conversely, if your manager has sent you a task, you can keep the boss updated on its progress. Double-click on the task in your to-do list and, as you progress with the job, alter the status and percentage complete settings. To give a written update on the task, you can tap out a message in the blank box at the bottom of the window.

4 **MONITOR TASKS** There are several ways to keep on top of your to-do list. Tasks will be inserted into your calendar on their due date. A small window at the foot of the To-Do bar lists tasks (if the To-Do bar isn't visible, click the left arrow next to the search box). For more detail, click Tasks at the bottom left and select Detailed from the Current View box in the ribbon. This lets you sort tasks by due date, status or category, by clicking the headings at the top of the table.

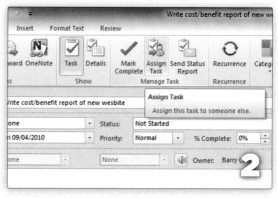

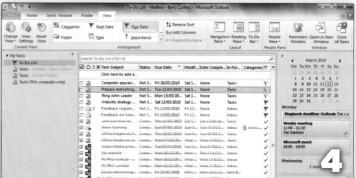

THE ONLY WINDOWS 7 MAGAZINE YOU'LL EVER NEED TO BUY

MAGBOOK

THE ULTIMATE GUIDE TO
Windows
7

OVER
150
PAGES
OF EXPERT
ADVICE

ONLY £7.99

What's new
Every feature explained

Stay secure for free
Block viruses & spyware

Sky+ power on your PC
How to watch, record & share TV

Easy upgrades
How to transfer files
from XP and Vista

Secret extras
From Movie Maker
to parental controls

Laptop boost
Tips and tricks for
better battery life

From the
experts at
PC Pro
magazine

PC PRO

7

OneNote 2010

ONENOTE 2010

It's far too easy to dismiss OneNote as a makeweight application, thrown into the various Office suites to make up the numbers. Certainly, Microsoft doesn't see it like that: it's one of the first apps to have been converted into an Office Web App (see chapter 12) and has been cleverly designed for use in conjunction with Word, Internet Explorer and PowerPoint. And,

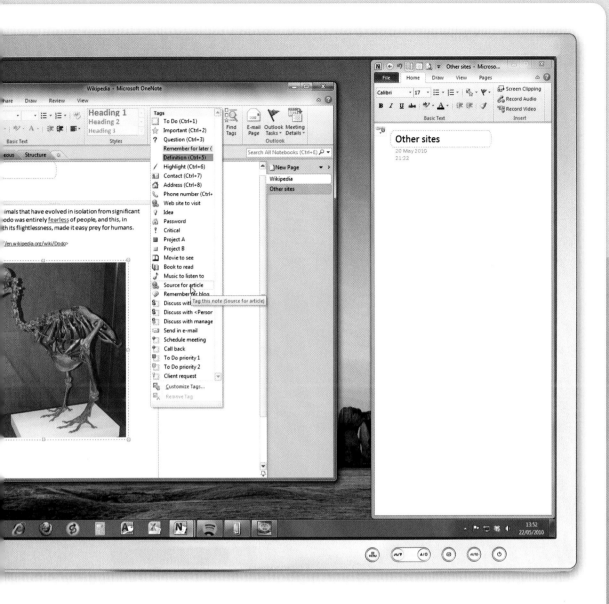

as we'll see in this chapter, if you choose to embrace its abilities OneNote could make your life a lot easier and more organised. You can use it to take notes in meetings, to draw up action points, to analyse Word documents sent to you by colleagues, to research and create in-depth projects... if you use your imagination, there's very little it can't do.

Getting started with OneNote

OneNote is a fascinating little application that tends to split opinion down the middle. Some people are left bemused, wondering what it's for – after all, they can fire up Word and make some rough notes, so why bother with a separate app? Others absolutely love it and keep OneNote open all day, at the ready to record their every passing thought.

And in essence, that's OneNote's purpose. To give you a place to write three quick lines relating to nothing in particular when they happen to occur to you. To sit docked on the side of your screen while you trawl the web researching the perfect wallpaper for your dining room. To group together all your thoughts on the various aspects of the project you're currently working on.

ONENOTE'S ANATOMY The simplest way of understanding OneNote is to see it as a series of paper notebooks. You might have a work notebook, a personal notebook, a project notebook, a notebook where you store all your story ideas. If you were particularly organised, you might even break those notebooks into sections. For work, that could be Project Aardvark, Project Beaver, and so on.

In essence, that's how OneNote is structured as well, except all your notebooks happen to be electronic and searchable. You'll find all the notebooks you've created arranged in tabs down the left-hand side of the screen, so it's easy to flick between them.

All the sections sit at the top of the writing area, below the ribbon. At the right of the existing sections sits a small tab marked with a star; press this to create a new

section. Finally, down the right-hand side you'll find all the pages the current section contains.

MEETING OF MINDS One of the most common uses of OneNote is to scrawl down notes in a meeting. There are a number of reasons why it's better than Word for this task. The first is that it's less structured. In Word, you start at the top and keep on typing until you reach a new page, and so on. The structure of OneNote means you can take notes in this way if you like, but it also offers more flexibility.

Click on an empty area of the page, for instance, and you can start typing. Want to make a comment on a related topic? Easy: just start a new text box to the right. If you've begun a new topic, you can create a new subpage linked to the page you started on. While this may all sound a little chaotic, it actually suits the flow of meetings much more than Word ever will.

What's more, Microsoft throws in a number of helpful tools. One of our favourites is the ability to record a meeting as it happens (both in video and audio, although audio is more likely to be used). Then, if you need to clarify what someone said when you're typing up your notes, you can jump straight to that clip in the proceedings.

Finally, it allows you to email all the notes you've made to your fellow attendees.

ACTION STATIONS The tools don't stop there. On the Home ribbon you'll find a series of tags; things such as Important, To Do and Question. You can also customise tags to your

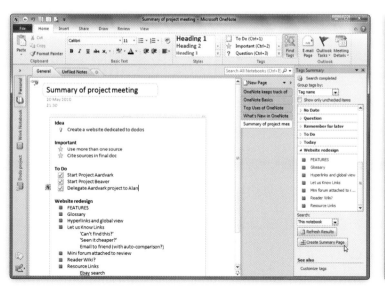

Far left: you can instantly create a page summarising the highlights of a meeting from your notes, then send it on to the other attendees by clicking E-mail Page.

Left: Give some order to your notes by tagging them as you go along. Microsoft has provided an extensive list of tags, but you can also create your own custom tags.

INSIDE ONENOTE 2010

This is the **Dock to Desktop** button: press it and a new OneNote window will dock to the right-hand edge of the screen. The rest of the space can then be dedicated to other apps, and they won't be allowed to overlap the OneNote area. Pressing the icon to its right switches to full-screen view, minimising the ribbons and other "furniture".

OneNote 2010 features some neat integration with **Outlook**, including the ability to email a page of notes from within the app, to assign Tasks from within OneNote that will then appear in Outlook, and to paste any details from a meeting (that are held in the appointment) straight into the current page.

Enter a **search** term here and OneNote will trawl through all your notebooks for mentions. The results are shown in a dropdown display. You just click on a match and you'll be taken to the right page.

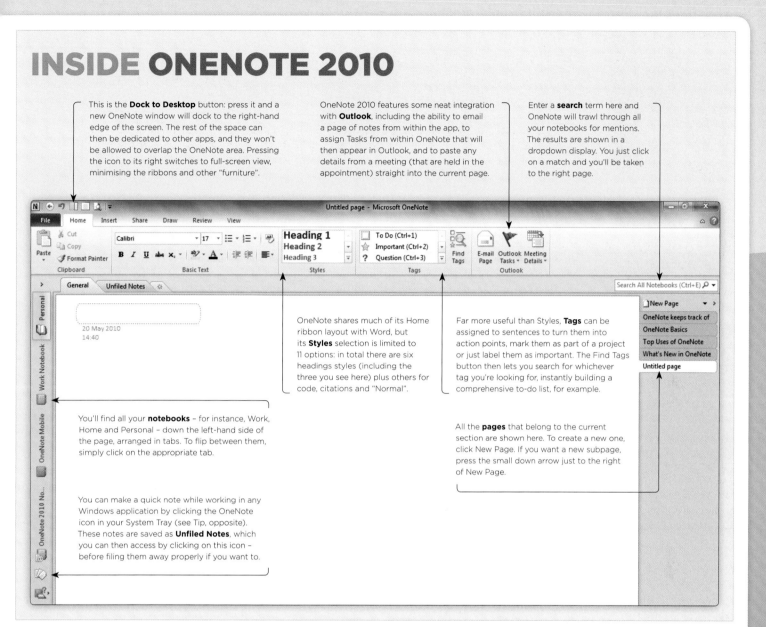

OneNote shares much of its Home ribbon layout with Word, but its **Styles** selection is limited to 11 options: in total there are six headings styles (including the three you see here) plus others for code, citations and "Normal".

Far more useful than Styles, **Tags** can be assigned to sentences to turn them into action points, mark them as part of a project or just label them as important. The Find Tags button then lets you search for whichever tag you're looking for, instantly building a comprehensive to-do list, for example.

You'll find all your **notebooks** – for instance, Work, Home and Personal – down the left-hand side of the page, arranged in tabs. To flip between them, simply click on the appropriate tab.

All the **pages** that belong to the current section are shown here. To create a new one, click New Page. If you want a new subpage, press the small down arrow just to the right of New Page.

You can make a quick note while working in any Windows application by clicking the OneNote icon in your System Tray (see Tip, opposite). These notes are saved as **Unfiled Notes**, which you can then access by clicking on this icon – before filing them away properly if you want to.

---

needs, so if you're working on Project Aardvark you simply create a Project Aardvark tag and apply as necessary.

The power of tags becomes more obvious when you press the Find Tags button. By default this searches the current notebook, but you may want to restrict it to a specific section or even just pages you've created this week; this way, you can quickly find all the To Do items and make sure they actually get done.

Then, by pressing Create Summary Page (at the foot of the search results), you can create a new notebook page that contains all the tagged items in your selection. It's never been easier to generate a page of action lists.

HANDS ON With all this talk of notebooks and meetings, it's little wonder that OneNote is also well geared towards people with touchscreen laptops. Click on the Draw tab, and you'll find all sorts of tools available: there are 35 different pens for handwriting notes and drawing, a Lasso

Select button so you can quickly grab the notes you're interested in, and the ability to quickly create preset shapes (such as rectangles).

What's clever about the handwriting approach is that OneNote has handwriting recognition built in, and it's surprisingly effective at working out what your scrawls mean. If you're able to write more quickly than you type, it's an excellent way to take notes in a meeting.

The final piece of good news is you don't need a touchscreen laptop to make this work. Companies such as Wacom produce graphics tablets from around £50 that allow you to add this capability for a very low cost.

BUSINESS LINK Here we've covered all the key features of OneNote, and to put them into practice we're going to embark on a project over the next four pages. To do this, we'll highlight some of OneNote's more advanced tools – such as linking with Internet Explorer and Microsoft Word.

HOW TO... USE ONENOTE TO RESEARCH ON THE WEB

You need never misplace a note or forget a source again, thanks to the clever features built into Microsoft's note-taking software.

HOW LONG?
Our example research project will take only around 20 minutes.

HOW HARD?
Most of this stuff is simple, but a couple of steps could confuse.

OneNote is an excellent research tool, so our first task is going to concentrate on this area. We're preparing a school project about dodos, starting from an empty page.

We'll take advantage of a feature introduced in OneNote 2010: Linked Notes. OneNote will create a link to the web page you were working on when you made a note, ready to jog your memory later. There's only one problem: Linked Notes only works with Internet Explorer (versions 6 and above), Word and PowerPoint.

1 **NEW NOTEBOOK** First, we'll create a new notebook. Click File | New. You're offered three choices of location, and instinctively you might choose Computer rather than Network or Web. However, we'll want other people to pitch in ideas later, so let's pick Network. We enter a name ("Dodo project") and choose a network location. The easiest way is to hit Browse and navigate to a shared network resource – possibly just a folder on another PC in your network. (If you're going to be working with people outside your network, choose Web. This way, they can use the OneNote Web App to make notes.) Click Create Notebook.

2 **TIME TO SHARE** If you chose a network location, you'll be asked if you'd like to email a link. The recipient can then (if they have permission to view the network) work on the notebook simultaneously. This is only true if they're running Office 2010; if not, they won't even be able to view the notebook.

3 **NAMING STRATEGY** By default, a tab appears that says "Section 1". Right-click on it and select Rename. We're splitting our sections into three: Research, Miscellaneous and Structure. Research is where we gather together all our research notes, Miscellaneous for random things that occur to us as we go along, and Structure for working out our presentation's, well, structure. To create new sections, click the small tab with a star just to the right of the existing section. Now click on the Research section and name the page "Wikipedia".

4 **LINKED NOTES** This is where things get clever. Click the Review tab, then Linked Notes. A dialog appears asking you to pick a section or page in which to place the item. In this case, choose

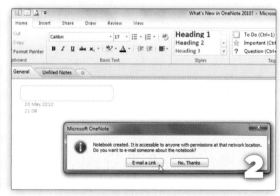

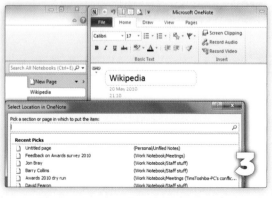

"Wikipedia (current page)" and click OK. You'll notice the OneNote page you named Wikipedia will have docked to the right-hand side of your screen. If you try to drag other windows over it then your efforts will fail: Windows is now treating this area as if it was the edge of the screen.

 START EXPLORING Now fire up Internet Explorer, head to www.wikipedia.org and search for "dodo". We're particularly interested in why the dodo became extinct, so we'll copy a paragraph from this section. Copy it in the normal way, by dragging over it and using Ctrl-C, then right-click in OneNote. As with Word 2010, you're offered a few options when pasting from other applications: Keep Source Formatting, Merge Formatting or Keep Text Only. Unlike in Word, you don't see a live preview of how the formatting will work out, but in general Merge Formatting will be the best choice: the advantage of this is that it adds a link to the page you pasted the paragraph from while getting rid of any unusual formatting (such as large text).

 ADD PICTURES You should take care when using photos from websites, as even copying an image to your PC may infringe copyright, but private study is generally fair dealing. Right-click on a pic and choose Copy, then right-click again in the OneNote notebook. Three choices are on offer: Keep Formatting, Merge Formatting and Picture. We'd generally choose Picture, because this automatically adjusts the size of the photo to the width of your textbox.

ADDING PAGES In OneNote's Docked form, you don't have access to the full ribbon. There are a number of features available, however, if you click on Home, Draw, View or Pages at the top. Home, for instance, offers formatting tools and allows you to start recording video or audio, while Draw gives you highlighters and more. You can also switch to the normal view at any time by clicking the Dock to Desktop icon in the Quick Access Toolbar, at the top left of the OneNote window. In our case, though, all we want to do is start a new page, which we do by clicking Pages, then New Page.

REVIEW YOUR NOTES Name your page, head back to Internet Explorer and browse for other resources on dodos. Copy and paste to your heart's content before calling it a day and closing the OneNote window docked to the side of your display. You can now close OneNote if you so wish, but whenever you reopen it – today, tomorrow or next year – you'll be able to go straight back to the source web page. Hover your mouse over the text or picture until a small Internet Explorer icon appears to its left. Move your mouse over to the icon and click on it: the browser will launch and head back to the precise page you were looking at when you performed your initial research.

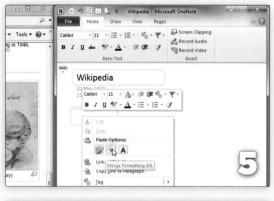

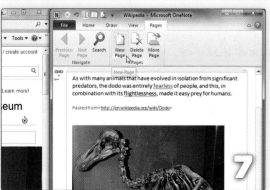

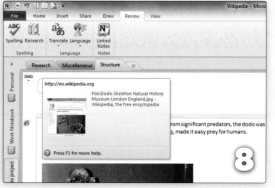

HOW TO... USE ONENOTE WITH WORD AND POWERPOINT

The Linked Notes feature comes into its own if you want to make notes on documents that other people send you. Here's how to take advantage.

Carrying on our project from the previous page, let's start by writing up our findings in Word as a short report. The key here is OneNote's Linked Notes feature.

1 **LINK WORD TO ONENOTE** Launch Word and go to the Review tab (this feature isn't in Word Starter). At the far right is a Linked Notes button. This won't work until you've saved, so name your file – in our example, Dodo Project – then click Linked Notes. You're asked to choose the OneNote page you want to link to, which should be in Recent Picks. Here we want the Miscellaneous section. Click the "+" next to Dodo Project under All Notebooks; click Miscellaneous, then OK.

2 **SCRAWL AS YOU GO** You can now start creating a report in Word. There are bound to be things you want to check while you write, but it makes sense to make a quick note of these for later rather than interrupting your flow. Name the OneNote page "Things to check", then write these down as you go. When you've finished your first draft, you can run through the checklist. Just hover your mouse over the note until the small blue Word icon appears, then click this: you'll be taken to the precise point in the Word document where you were when you made the notes.

3 **LINK A PRESENTATION** Linked Notes works the same way in PowerPoint. Open a presentation, then press the Linked Notes button (again on the Review tab). It's a powerful tool when you want to make notes on a presentation someone else has sent you, especially if you take advantage of tags (see p94). For example, tag something as a question while you review the document, then collate all the questions at the end.

4 **PRINT TO ONENOTE** The other way to share work between PowerPoint, Word and OneNote is via Print to OneNote, in the Backstage view of each program. Go to File | Print, then select Send To OneNote 2010 as your "printer". Once you select a destination within OneNote, for example Dodo Project | Miscellaneous, it will appear in a new page as a print-out. Note that the print-out is effectively a picture object within the OneNote page, but you can choose to extract the text by right-clicking on it and selecting "Copy Text from All the Pages of the Printout".

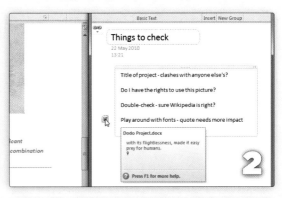

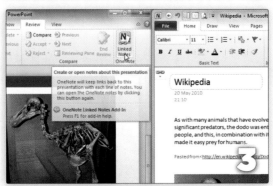

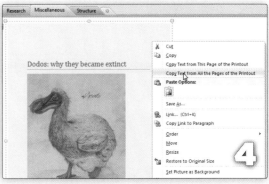

HOW TO...
WORK WITH DOCK TO DESKTOP

If you followed our guide to using OneNote to research on websites (see p96) you'll have encountered the Dock to Desktop feature. Here we go into a little more depth to show what it can and can't do, but first let's examine why you'd want to use it in the first place.

Some people might choose to have OneNote docked permanently, so they can scribble notes as they go along through a day. Others may use it in parallel with the Linked Notes feature (see opposite page) when examining Word or PowerPoint files. Many more people will use it in ways that neither we or Microsoft conceived; it has the potential to be a very versatile tool.

1 SWITCH DOCK TO DESKTOP ON (AND OFF) The quickest way to switch to the Dock to Desktop view in OneNote is by clicking the small icon in the Quick Access Toolbar; by default, it's the third from the left at the very top of the window.

This will immediately shrink your current OneNote page to a fraction of its horizontal size while stretching it from top to bottom of the Windows desktop. It effectively reserves this space, at the right of the screen, as its own: no other windows can be dragged over it, which means OneNote is always available for a quick scribble. To switch back to normal view, simply click the Dock to Desktop icon again or click on the Normal View button in the View tab.

2 ONE SIZE DOESN'T FIT ALL You may want your OneNote dock to consume more or less space. Move your mouse so that it hovers over the window's left-hand edge, and a two-way arrow appears. Left-click and then drag left or right, depending on whether you want to make the OneNote window bigger or smaller.

3 CRAMPED CONDITIONS Microsoft has reduced the number of commands available in the Dock to Desktop view due to the limited space and, in particular, it cuts the number of tabs from six to four: Home, Draw, View and Pages. These tabs also contain fewer commands than the full OneNote versions. You'll note that Insert is one of the tabs that's been dropped, but you can still add screengrabs, audio and video via the Insert group found on the Home tab.

4 ADD YOUR OWN COMMANDS So all the most common choices are still available – but if there's something you want to add then you can. Right-click on an empty space in the ribbon and choose "Customize the Ribbon...". Click on "Home (Narrow)", for example, and click New Group. You can then add any command to the group, and it will appear in the Home tab when in Dock to Desktop view. For more details on customising ribbons, see p20.

HOW LONG?
In five minutes you can become a Dock to Desktop master.

HOW HARD?
Very easy, in fact.

Q&A

Q: I can only see the words Home, Draw, View and Pages at the top of the screen in Dock to Desktop view. How can I make the ribbon appear?
A: This is the default view, to save space; to make the ribbon appear briefly, click on Home (for instance), then select the command you need. To make it appear permanently, double-click on Home, Draw, View or Pages.

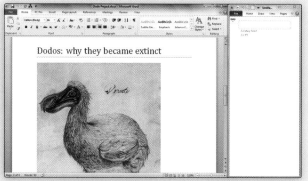

Dodos: why they became extinct

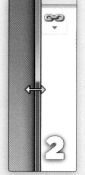

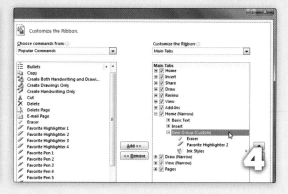

IN THIS CHAPTER

Publisher 2010

PUBLISHER 2010

Unless you're a professional designer hooked on Adobe InDesign and QuarkXPress, you'll be pleasantly surprised by just how much publishing power is packed into Microsoft's oft-forgotten Publisher. In this chapter, we provide an insight into its skills, not only offering a step-by-step guide to creating a personalised invite card from one of Publisher's copious templates, but going far

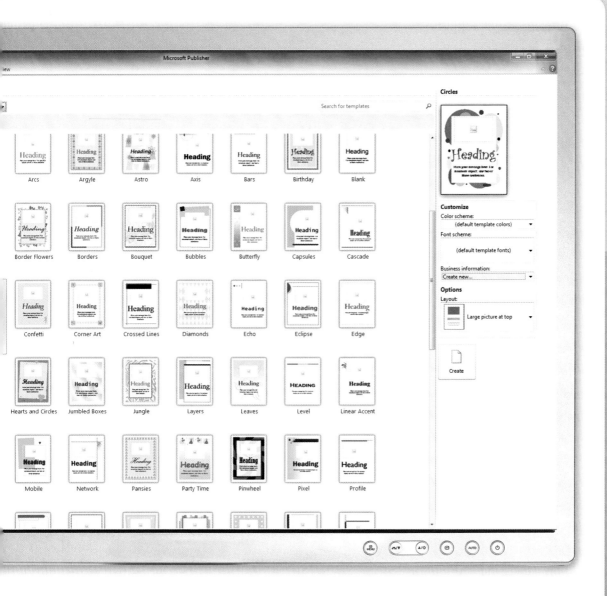

beyond that using advanced tools anyone can pick up. We explain how to use Building Blocks to mould a style that's perfect for your individual use or for a business, then using that style as the basis for a brochure. Finally, we reveal how to avoid some costly mistakes – both in time and financially – by using the new Design Checker tool.

HOW LONG?

Half an hour; longer If
you spend time trying
fonts and colours.

HOW HARD?

Publisher is an easy DTP
package, but precision
work takes practice.

Tip

If you use coloured
page backgrounds,
you'll want to make
your textboxes
transparent; by default
they show as white.
To do this, right-click
on the textbox, select
Format Text Box and
select No Fill using
the dropdown menu
next to "Color:".

HOW TO...
CREATE YOUR OWN INVITATION

The new, more user-friendly Publisher 2010 makes it much easier for non-designers to create polished-looking documents based on ready-made templates.

The idea of Publisher is to enable non-experts to create cards, flyers, newsletters and other publications with a near-professional finish. With Office 2010 that becomes even easier thanks to a mass of new templates, preset colour schemes and font schemes, plus live previews that show you what result options will produce. While it's possible to start documents from scratch, a template provides a solid basis for your work, and you can then personalise each element.

You'll come into contact with templates as soon as you start Publisher or make a new document (File | New). The Backstage view handily puts them in categories, right up front. The trick to using templates well is understanding that they're just a launch pad. While it makes sense to look in, say, the Brochures section if you want to create a brochure, don't feel constrained. If you're doing invitations for a cocktail party, don't just look at the party section: check out the wedding invitations, those for wedding showers, and even the baby shower invitations.

With your template selected, some of Publisher 2010's enhancements come into play. While font schemes and colour schemes – predefined sets of fonts and colours

chosen to work together – aren't new, Live Preview has made them more useful. Click on the Page Design tab in the ribbon, mouse over the schemes in the central section, and you can see instantly which will fit your document and which won't. Click the Fonts button and mouse through the font schemes, and the same applies. It's an effective way of making quick global changes to a document, and the preset schemes will help you steer clear of eyesore colour clashes or those car-crash font combinations beloved of jumble sale organisers.

Playing with the templates also gives you a chance to look at two of Publisher 2010's major new features. First, it will help you produce more attractive text without having to understand ligatures, kerning, leading and tracking. Provided you use specific OpenType fonts, you can flick between different stylistic alternatives and even add exuberant flourishes with ease. Second, Publisher 2010 now offers more sophisticated in-document image-editing capabilities. It doesn't matter if your photo isn't perfect when you add it to the page, as a range of basic colour, contrast and cropping tools will help you get it just right.

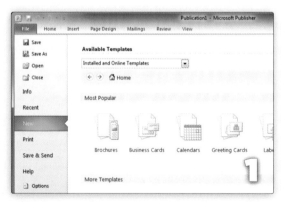

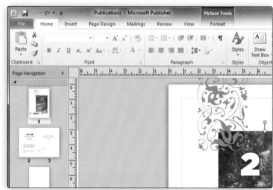

① PICK A CARD Although our card is for a baby event, we'll take our template from Wedding in the Invitation Cards category. From the Backstage view, click Invitation Cards | All Event | Wedding Shower 4. You could delete elements here.

② CHOOSE A PIC We do need to change the picture on the front. Right-click it and choose Change Picture | Change Picture. Navigate to an appropriate image and click Insert. This is a good time to amend the textboxes too. Delete any you don't need.

③ CHANGE FONTS Now click the Page Design tab of the ribbon and click the Fonts button to see the available font schemes. As you hover over one, the live preview shows how it will look applied to the finished card – although discrepancies between font sizes may affect this. Here we've gone for the Monogram font.

④ ADD IMPACT Now for some more customisation. Select the top textbox on page 2, then click and drag it outwards to expand it. Now click on the Text Box Tools tab and select the OpenType Gabriola font, taking the size up to 30 for greater impact.

⑤ STYLISTIC SETS Gabriola is one of a handful of fonts that works with Publisher's new type-handling features. Click the Stylistic Sets dropdown (in the Typography group on the Text Box Tools tab) to see a selection of treatments that add exotic flourishes to the basic letter shapes or "glyphs". Choose the final option. Go back to the opening page, select the textbox, change the font to Gabriola and the size to 22, and apply the same Stylistic Set. You'll need to play around with the blue box element to make the text fit.

⑥ PICTURE EDITING Now we can use Publisher's built-in editing tools to knock the baby image back into the background. Click on the image to select it, then click the Picture Tools Format tab. Click Brightness and set it to +20%, then do the same to Contrast. Resize the image if you'd like to, and – as we've done – delete any unwanted graphics.

⑦ THINK COLOUR Click the Page Design tab and try mousing over some of the schemes. If you need more, click the down arrow in the slider box to the right to expand the list. We've picked Eggplant.

⑧ ONE STEP BEYOND There's no need to stop there. We've applied a background (from the Page Design tab), added a Picture Style to the image (Picture Tools Format | Picture Styles) and changed the colours of our stylised text using Font Color on the Text Box Tools tab. Stick to colours in the same scheme to avoid introducing a jarring element to the finished article.

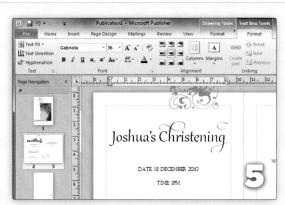

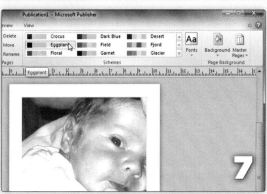

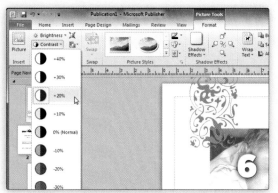

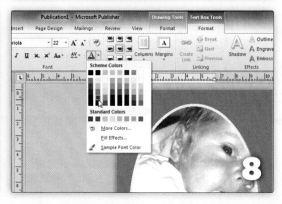

Q&A

Q: Why does my text keep disappearing?
A: If your text gets hidden or lost when you add new objects, you need to get to grips with Wrap Text and the Bring Forward/ Send Backward options. First, the text in a box may be set to repel when a picture object, or other textbox, is placed over it (even if the text itself isn't covered up). Select the textbox, then go to the Drawing Tools Format tab and click Wrap Text. Try setting None or Tight in the options. Alternatively, your text might be hidden by the edge of another box. Select the textbox, then go to Drawing Tools Format, and next to Wrap Text; you'll see the Bring Forward/ Send Backward options. Use these to change the order in which the objects are layered, dictating what's visible when they overlap.

8

Publisher 2010

HOW LONG?

As little as half an hour, but more if you need to track down images.

HOW HARD?

Despite the simple building blocks, there's more hands-on design involved here.

HOW TO... CREATE A BROCHURE USING BUILDING BLOCKS

If the templates don't fit your project, you still don't have to build from scratch. With Publisher's Building Blocks you can quickly create your own layouts.

Publisher ships with a large selection of templates, but it's unlikely you'll always find one to match your needs. Sometimes you'll have to start with a blank canvas, but there's no reason to do all the heavy lifting yourself. Thanks to Publisher's Building Blocks, Font Schemes and Color Schemes, you can put your page together using ready-made components.

You can find the Building Blocks in the Insert tab of the ribbon, and they comprise a range of page parts – headings, pull-quotes and sidebars, a selection of drop-in calendars, a number of decorative borders and accents – and a collection of elements that might be useful if you're putting together marketing materials and adverts. Be warned: some are utterly tasteless, and appear unusable at first glance, but few are without any redeeming values.

The beauty of Building Blocks is that each element can be edited and amended to your taste, either by adjusting each block of text or visual option by hand, or by applying font styles and colour schemes. The latter route makes it easier to stick to a consistent set of fonts and colours, and you can see the result in the live preview while you work. When you have something you're happy

with, you can resave your effort as a new Building Block for later use in your publication or a future project.

The other challenge non-designers face during the layout process is getting those Building Blocks in the right place. Publisher helps via a system of unobtrusive snap-to guides that help to create consistent, professional-looking pages, but that don't prevent you from placing elements off-kilter if that's the effect you're after.

The result? While using templates is still the easiest and most time-efficient way of creating a club newsletter, marketing materials or event invitation, it's quite possible for mere mortals to create something new and personal without them. Here, we're going to create a simple four-page brochure for a holiday firm to prove it.

(1) CREATE BOOKLET We'll start with a blank booklet. Begin a new Publisher document (File | New) and browse to the templates, then the More Blank Page Sizes category. Select the Booklets folder in the Publication Types section and choose the A4 Booklet template. Click the Create button, and select Yes when asked if you want to add additional pages.

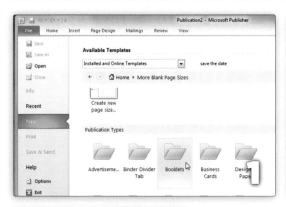

② **COVER** The cover is your first page. Click the Insert tab in the ribbon, then the Picture button in the Illustration section. Choose an image, and drag it to reposition and resize it so that it covers the first page. If you need to rotate it, use the button tucked away in the Arrange group of the Picture Tools Format tab.

③ **ADD A LOGO** The company logo goes on next. Publisher supports the industry-standard EPS and TIFF formats, but you may find you get the best results using a WMF file. Use the resize handle on the bottom right of the frame to reduce the size of the logo, then drag it into position at the top right. Note the way that the margin guides take on a subtle highlight when you hit the edge of the printable area.

④ **BUILDING BLOCKS** Here comes our first Building Block. Click the Insert tab, mouse to the Building Blocks section and click on the Page Parts button. Browse down to Pull Quotes and select Brackets. Resize the new text block and move it down to the bottom-left corner, watching for the margin guides to make sure it doesn't go over. Retype your text, and feel free to change the font scheme at this point. We've gone for the Solstice preset.

⑤ **CHOOSE GUIDES** Now for the middle spread. Click on the thumbnail in the Page Navigation pane on the left to select the double-page spread. First, set up some guides to work with. Click the Page Design tab and select Guides, then choose the simple 3 x 3 Grid.

⑥ **SNAP TO GUIDES** Time for the next Building Block. As before, click the Insert tab, mouse to the Building Blocks section and click Page Parts. This time browse to Stories and the "Convention (Layout 3)" component. Drag the building block into position, using the guides for accurate placement. The box should snap against the guide if you have the Align To Guides option ticked in the Layout section of the Page Design tab (it is by default). Now click and drag the bottom right-hand corner to resize the box until it fills the whole page.

⑦ **TWEAK THE PAGE** Replace the images with your own by right-clicking on each picture and selecting Change Picture | Change Picture. Apply the Solstice font scheme (from Page Design | Fonts), and make any tweaks or amendments necessary to get the page looking as you'd like it.

⑧ **SAVE YOUR BLOCK** Now things get clever. Click and drag around all the elements on page 2, making sure all are selected. Right-click on the group and select Save as Building Block from the menu. Enter a name, and a description if you like, then save. You now have your own building block, ready to be used again.

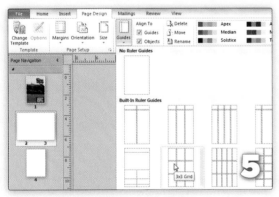

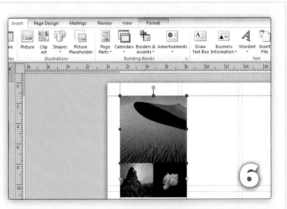

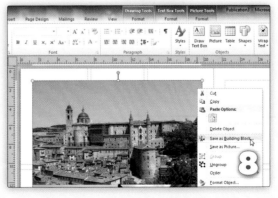

Tip

If an image isn't working well on the page, use Publisher's built-in image-editing tools to bump up its contrast for a punchier approach, or try one of the Recolor options. As well as greyscale and sepia treatments, you'll find dark and light monochrome variations based on the current colour scheme.

HOW LONG?

Allow plenty of time for this; the rewards make it worthwhile.

HOW HARD?

You don't need huge amounts of technical knowledge, just a good deal of patience and attention to detail.

HOW TO... PREPARE YOUR PUBLICATION FOR PRINT

If you're not careful, you can waste a lot of money and time by misprinting your carefully prepared document. We explain how to avoid the traps.

On the previous pages we showed how to create a brochure using Building Blocks. Now we'll finish the job and go through the all-important final pre-press checks.

Even with Publisher's helpful guides, people often struggle to ensure that page elements sit within the margins and all the text is in place on the page. Luckily, Publisher 2010 provides a range of tools to help ensure your publication is ready for print, whether you're having thousands of copies output professionally or just running out a few invitations on your inkjet at home.

Two new features benefit either scenario. First, the old Print Preview option has gone, replaced by a new, more fully featured preview integrated into the Print option of the Backstage view. This gives you a chance to preview your publication exactly as it should appear when output on the currently selected printer. You can carefully check to ensure elements aren't being cropped off, and if you're printing double-sided you can preview the flip from right-hand page to left-hand page to see how it will look.

Second, if you need more than a quick check then the new Design Checker tool, in the Info section of the Backstage view, will run through everything for you.

This finds lost lines of text, images that have crept into the margins, and all sorts of other common errors. Clicking through the error messages in the Design Checker pane to the right of the Publisher window, you'll get details of each error, explanations of causes and effects, and in some cases quick-fix options to sort out the problem in seconds. Bug-checking publications is no picnic, but it's better to do it before a large print-run than after.

The Commercial Print Settings panel will be more useful if you're preparing your work for professional reproduction, where mistakes or missing fonts can be costly. This allows you to change the colour mode to CMYK (usually required, but check with your printer), embed or replace the fonts used and – for more advanced users – set up trapping, overprinting and spot colours. (Don't worry about these unless you know you need them; again, if you do, it's wise to talk to your printer.)

If you prefer to deliver your work paperlessly, Publisher has finally developed an affinity for Adobe's PDF format. Not only is there a Save as PDF option, but clicking Save & Send in the Backstage view will enable you to send your publication via email in HTML format,

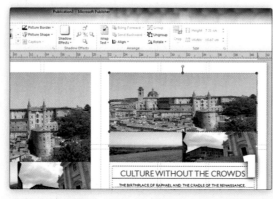

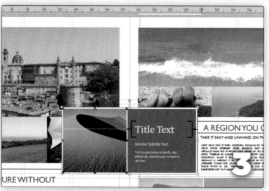

or as an attached PDF or XPS document. Publisher also shares Word's Mailings tab, so it's easy to set up mailing lists to get your publication into the right hands.

(1) FINISHING TIME First, it's time to finish off the brochure we started. Click on the right-hand page and go to the Insert tab, then Building Blocks and Page Parts. You'll see your new building block listed. Click on it to place it on the right-hand page.

(2) FINE-TUNE POSITIONING Reposition and rescale the new building block so it occupies the top two-thirds of the page. Again, use the guides to help. Now just replace your images and text as required.

(3) BOTTOMS UP We'll complete this page with another pre-designed building block. Go back to the Building Blocks section of the Insert tab and click on Page Parts. Browse down to the Sidebars category and select the "Brackets (Layout 2)" component. Reposition and resize it so that it sits neatly on the right-hand page beneath the main story section.

(4) SWITCH SCHEMES Again, just change the words and pictures: we've picked a map and some appropriate text. This is also a good time to see how the document will look with different colour schemes. Click the Page Design tab and look through the options.

(5) FINAL TOUCHES Click on the final page in the Page Navigation panel to select it, choose the 3 x 3 guide as before and insert a photo object (Insert | Picture). Reposition and resize it to occupy the top left two-thirds of the page. We've added the logo we used earlier, the "Brackets (Layout 1)" sidebar Building Block, and two basic text boxes in the right-hand column.

(6) VISUAL CHECK Now to proof the brochure before printing. First, a quick visual check. Click File | Print for the new print preview. Zoom in using the zoom control at the bottom right, and take a good look at each page to spot any basic layout issues. Here, the boxout at the bottom right of the page will lose its bottom border when printed. Press Escape and fix it.

(7) DESIGN CHECKER Don't trust your eyes: use Design Checker too. Click File for the Backstage view, select Info, and click Run Design Checker to pick up any obvious errors. Note the options at the top: pick "Run commercial printing checks" for press output.

(8) FIX ERRORS Click any error that appears in the pane to highlight it, then click the arrow to the right for options. Select "Go to this item" to highlight the problem object, or "Explain" for online help. If you're lucky, Publisher may be able to sort out the problem automatically; select the fix and the job is done.

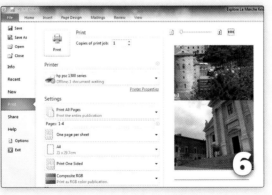

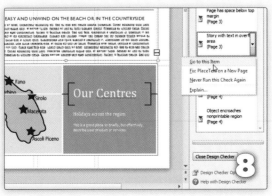

IN THIS CHAPTER

Access 2010

ACCESS 2010

Office's database has been criticised in the past for being too difficult to use, but in Access 2010 Microsoft has made a big effort to help, with pre-built templates that don't need a lot of customisation to make them work. We explain not only how to create a basic database, but also how to transform it into something that looks professional and better reflects your needs. If

you want to go in deeper, Access will reward you with tremendous analytical tools, and we then explore the more complicated worlds of data macros and linking with other sources of data at the end of the chapter. First of all, though, we recommend newcomers read our simple two-page guide to why they should care about databases in the first place.

9

Access 2010

A beginner's guide to Access

Data: it can be untidy stuff. Many an address book has crossings out, semi-legible numbers in crayon, sticky notes here and there, old Christmas cards tucked inside the cover, and umpteen expired mobile numbers for your friends. Wouldn't it be nice if all your addresses and numbers were up-to-date, easy to find and easy to read? What you need is a database.

"Can't I use a spreadsheet?" comes the plaintive cry. Yes, but you don't get all the benefits. Excel excels at calculations and Access excels at storing, retrieving and manipulating data. Simple projects such as address lists can certainly be achieved with Excel, and there are ways of finding the information you want.

The problems arise because Excel has little rigour or structure: you can enter data onto any part of any enormous sheet. It's common for people to return to a worksheet they created several months previously and find it baffling. Excel also runs out of steam once you want to do anything more complex, like run a home-based business. Access is adaptable, flexible, and more than capable of running databases for home and small-business use.

So, databases bring order to data. A well-designed database stores data in a rigorous way, so you can always find the information you need. You can look for Sam Spade under S as you would with your battered book, and it's also easy to find all your contacts in Glasgow if you're planning a few days there. Databases have other benefits over books: if you can't recall Ermintrude's last name, you're not stuck until it comes to you at four in the morning. You'd simply look for anyone called Ermintrude and then pick the one you want to call (presuming you know multiple Ermintrudes – admittedly, an unlikely scenario).

A database can contain one table (for instance, an address/phone book) or multiple tables with relationships set up between them (a small business selling to customers). We'll start with the fundamentals of Access and introduce its four key elements: tables, queries, forms and reports.

TABLES Tables are the basic structures for holding data. When you look at a table in Access, it typically looks like a grid of intersecting rows and columns. In database terminology, columns are often called fields and rows are called records. Fields in a contact table are likely to include FirstName, LastName, PhoneNo and so on. Each row will contain the data about one contact.

One of the rules of thumb for good database design is that a table should contain data about one real-world object. A table could contain data about your contacts:

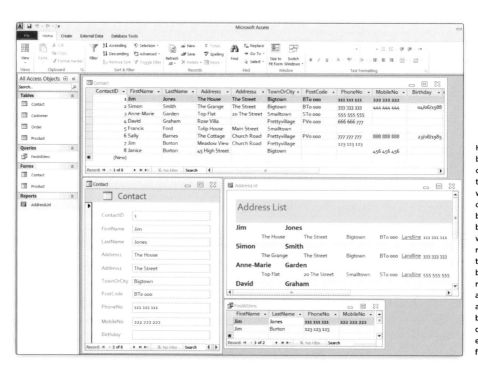

Here you can see the big four elements of Access. At the top left is a table in which many records can be seen, and below it is a form based on that table which shows the records one at a time. To the right, below the table is a report that produces an alphabetical address list, and below that is a query that finds everyone with the first name of Jim.

names, addresses, phone numbers, birthdays, allergies – anything that's particular to a contact. (This doesn't mean you have to know all these details about every contact.) If you also wanted to computerise your film collection, you'd have entries for title, year, whether it's on Blu-ray and so on.

Keeping records of like objects in separate tables means we only store those details once. If we have a Customer, a Product and an Order table in our business database, we only have to enter a record for each customer/product/order once, which reduces the likelihood of errors creeping in. Repetitive entering of the same data is almost bound to produce typos and other inaccuracies.

QUERIES Queries are Access' powerhouse, the means of reaching all the data you've stored in your tables. Access has a graphical query builder that lets you pick the fields you want to see in the result, perhaps all the names and addresses in the table, without birthdays and so on. You can also pick the records you want, so you can find everyone who lives in Suffolk. These two requirements can be combined into a single query to produce an address list for all Suffolk-dwellers.

Queries can be saved and reused many times. A query returns an answer table containing its results, and this looks just like a table of data. The answer table is generated afresh every time you run the query, so the answers are always bang up to date.

FORMS A form lets you present a table of data in a user-friendly way to anyone using the database. They usually show you the records one at a time, and they automatically provide controls for moving backwards and forwards through records. Forms can be colourful and decorated with graphics or photographs. You can build several forms based on the same table. You might even create a form that showed all the fields for a record and use it for entering data. You might design another to inspect basic address data, with just names and addresses. Forms are very versatile.

REPORTS You can present data from your database in a structured way using a report. They're printable, and they too can be embellished with colour and artwork. In a report, records can be set out as you wish and grouped so that like records are displayed together: contacts could be grouped by city, for instance.

KEYS Each table should have a primary key. This is a column (or columns) that contain an entry that uniquely identifies each record. Access offers a neat way of generating unique numbers for each record, called AutoNumber. The first record you enter will be number 1, the next 2 and so on.

Keys are one of Access' ways of introducing rigour into data storage. They become more important when your database comprises multiple tables (see Relationships, below). If we have tables of customers, products and orders – all real-world objects – keys let us keep track of who bought what. Linda's primary key value of 4 in the Customer

table is used as what's called a foreign key in the Order table: once we see 4 in the Order table we can tell what she bought. Similarly, each product has a primary key and following it to the Order table, where it appears as a foreign key, identifies any purchase of tuna and tomato sandwiches.

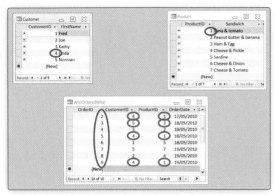

■ Primary key ■ Foreign key

RELATIONSHIPS Once we've stored data about different objects in separate tables, we use relationships to help those tables work together. There is a one-to-many relationship between the Customer table and the Order table: one customer can place many orders. There is also a one-to-many relationship between the Product table and the Order table: one product can be ordered many times.

Access' Relationships tool (found on the Database Tools tab) lets you put relationships in place. The primary key field – identified with a key symbol – in the Customer table is joined to the foreign key field of the same name in the Order table. At the Customer end of the line representing the relationship is a 1 and at the other end is an infinity symbol (∞): one customer can place many orders. The second relationship is between the primary key field in the Product table and the foreign key field in Order.

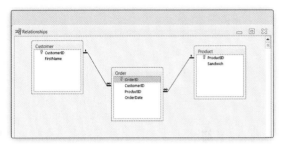

CUSTOMISING Databases don't have to look dull. Access 2010 has introduced a range of colour schemes that can be applied to forms and reports with a few clicks of the mouse (see How to customise your Access database, p114) but customisation doesn't stop there. You can put a text label on a form and format the font, its colour, the background colour of the label – there's a wide range of artistic decisions to make. A company logo can appear on a form, or a photograph or a piece of clip-art.

You can even design forms for different users: you could create one for your partner that displayed a favourite picture from your last holiday, and one for yourself showing the Citroën DS you've always wanted. Adding labels to help make entering a new record easier can also be good: for example, one saying "Please just ignore this field if you don't know his or her birthday."

Keys (top) identify data between tables, and relationships (centre) represent logical connections between them. You can customise your database (bottom) to present information clearly and attractively to users.

HOW TO... CREATE A DATABASE FROM A TEMPLATE

Using a predefined template when building a new database saves hours of time and effort. You can use it as is or tweak it to suit your requirements better.

HOW LONG?

About three-quarters of an hour; more to explore the database fully.

HOW HARD?

Quite straightforward, even for a database novice.

Load up Microsoft Access 2010 for the first time and it may not be obvious where to start. It's tempting to click straight on Blank database, the default, but to get going we suggest heading to Sample templates first.

There are seven client database templates for use on a standalone PC or sharing over a network, and five web databases that are primarily intended for publishing on the web with SharePoint (see p126). The templates contain tables to hold your data, plus a range of forms, reports and queries, ready for you to enter data.

We'll use the Tasks client database template: it has two tables, Contacts and Tasks. Details of the people who work for you can be recorded in the Contacts table (name, address, phone number) and the Tasks table holds details about jobs. A relationship is in place between the two tables, so a job can be assigned to a person, and each person can be assigned many jobs. Relationships such as this are known as one-to-many relationships.

Within the Tasks database you can store the basic data about people and jobs, and add photos (useful for identification at meetings). Attachments can be added to tasks, such as spreadsheets, pictures, video and music.

There's some scope to modify a database built from a template. For instance, the Contacts table has a column called "Zip/Postal Code", which you might rename "Postcode". Other objects that display the column name (the report that generates an address list of all contacts, say) are automatically updated to reflect the change.

Not all changes are so smooth. If you delete the "State/Province" column from the Contacts table, the report that generates an address list will complain. This is because the column name forms part of the report definition: it's expecting to find State/Province and fails when it doesn't. You can edit the report, but finding and fixing dependant objects can be time-consuming.

If the template-derived database needs considerable modification, or you already have data you wish to import, it's likely that the work required to modify a template-based database will be greater than that of creating one to your own design.

Nevertheless, templates demonstrate Access' potential, and simply loading up a couple and browsing around inside them will give you an excellent idea of what can be achieved.

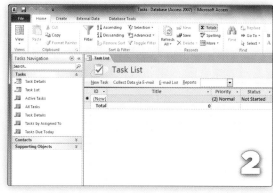

① LOADING A TEMPLATE Launch Access 2010 and you'll see the File menu open. New is already selected; under Available Templates, select Sample templates. Click the one called Tasks and, on the right, name your database and choose a location for it (click the folder icon to browse). Click Create.

② EXPLORING THE CONTENTS The template is prepared and the database opens, displaying the Task List form showing a default entry in its first row. If the Security Warning bar appears, click the Enable Content button. Expand the Navigation pane on the left to see the objects in the database. The Tasks section has two forms and five reports; pop down the Contacts and Supporting Objects sections to see the rest.

③ ADD A CONTACT Double-click the Contact Details form and enter some (or all) of the information for Joe Bloggs.

④ ADD A PICTURE Double-click the placeholder picture; in the Attachments dialog, click Add. Double-click an image file, click OK and the picture is displayed in the record. Click Close, top right, to finish the record. Or, to add another, click Save and New.

⑤ ADD A TASK Double-click the Task Details form (not the green report) and add a task. Select Joe from the "Assigned To" list. Complete the record. Double-clicking on the paperclip by Attachments opens the dialog from step 3. Find an attachment as before.

⑥ INSPECTING ATTACHMENTS Click OK to add the attachment. Attachments won't be immediately visible but are readily accessible. Click Close to save the task. If the Task List is still open you can display the new record by going to the Records group (on the Home tab) and clicking Refresh All. Re-open the Contact Details form and inspect the Tasks tab for Joe's record to see he now has a task. To inspect attachments, double-click in the Attachments column and double-click the attachment you want. When finished, close the form.

⑦ REPORTS Enter a few more records, then try running the various reports: click the dropdown arrow next to Reports in the Task List view. As their names suggest, these show a list of all tasks or those due today, or phone and address lists of your contacts.

⑧ MAKE CHANGES Close any open forms or reports. Right-click on the Contacts table (in Supporting Objects) and select Design View. In the list of Field Names, change "Zip/Postal Code" to "Postcode". Click the Save icon (top left) and close the table. Inspect the Contact Address Book report to see that the change is implemented.

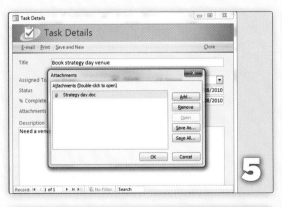

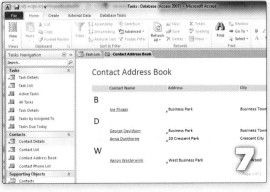

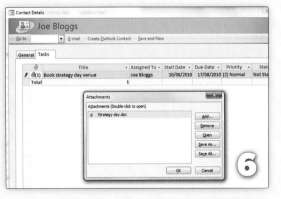

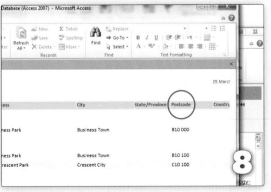

Q&A

Q: Those form controls really are difficult to read. Can I change them?

A: Yes, the Design View lets you change the appearance of a form and move objects to different positions. In the Tasks Navigation pane, right-click the form and select Design View. You can now make changes and inspect the result by clicking Form View (click View, found on the far left of the ribbon). When you've finished, save the form.

HOW TO... CUSTOMISE YOUR ACCESS DATABASE

The best databases both work well and look good – and applying colours and fonts to forms and reports is no longer a chore thanks to Access 2010's themes.

You've built a database, designed its tables and created the queries, forms and reports that work with the data. The forms may contain labels with text to guide users and helpful buttons with macros attached; and perhaps the form uses tabs to reduce the overcrowding that's sometimes unavoidable if there are many fields and controls displayed on a single form. Everything works. Who could wish for anything more?

Well, the users of your database will mainly interact with forms and reports; and their perception of the entire application will be influenced by the appearance of these elements. Give your database a smart, coherent, professional look and users are more likely to be happy. Natty colour schemes won't mask poor design, but if you're confident the design is sound, making it look attractive as well is a huge bonus. Even if the database is for your personal use only, why settle for a run-of-the-mill look when you could have something more appealing?

Access 2010 has a number of customisation features to enhance the look of a database, but here we'll concentrate on themes. These are design schemes that can be applied to forms and reports. In Access 2007,

it was possible to apply an AutoFormat to forms and reports, but the chosen format had to be applied to each object individually.

The process is much slicker now: choose a scheme and it takes just a click to apply it to all the reports and forms in a database. You still have the option of applying a theme to a single object, or to all objects of a particular type (for example, all forms or all reports). You can also design and save your own themes.

You can make subtle alterations to the colours used in a form/report using the palette of theme colours: the basic colours for a theme are displayed along with variations on each. For instance, the colour for the text in a report header might be red; if you deem this bright colour unsuitable for a report to the board, you can alter it to a more sober shade.

Themes can be applied in other Office applications too. So, for example, if you're writing a business plan in Word, you can give it the same look as the database, and if you're preparing a PowerPoint presentation you can do the same. It all adds up to a more professional look and feel to your output.

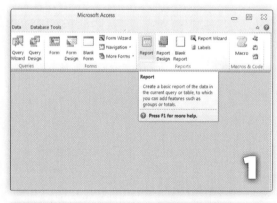

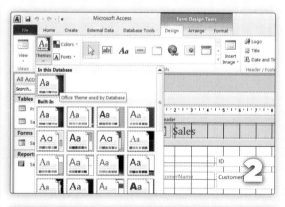

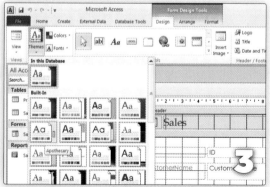

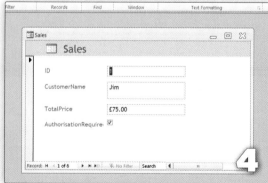

① GETTING STARTED Open a database, highlight an existing table in the Navigation pane and, in the Create tab, click Form in the Forms group. Access generates a form based on the data in the selected table. Save the form and repeat the operation, but this time create a report (click Report in the Reports group).

② THE THEMES GROUP Right-click on the new form in the Navigation pane and choose Design View; this takes you to the Design tab under Form Design Tools. In the Themes group, click the Themes button. A box pops out displaying the theme used in the current database.

③ CHOOSE A THEME Below, under Built-In, are 40 predefined themes from which to choose. Hover the mouse over one to display its name and you'll see the appearance of the form automatically update as you move from theme to theme (assuming your PC is fast enough to refresh it before you move on).

④ APPLY A THEME Click a theme to select it; move to Form View (Home | Views) to see the effect.

⑤ FORMS AND REPORTS TOO If you don't like your new look, go back into Design View and try another. You can also return to the Office default, the top-left theme in the pop-down list (the rest are in alphabetical order). We've swapped from Opulent (too pink) to Essential (bold and bright). Open the report and the Essential theme has been applied here too.

⑥ TWEAK THE THEME... This report is for the board: let's tone down that bright red Sales label. Open the report in Design View, click to select the Sales label, click the Home tab, and in the Text Formatting group click the arrowhead by the Font Color control. The top row in Theme Colors shows those associated with the current theme. Fourth from left is the offending red, with a column of alternative colours below. How about the last but one, a red that's 25% darker? Click to select it.

⑦ ...FOR INDIVIDUAL OBJECTS The label is now a sober dark red, and that colour is set to be the current default for the Font Color control, making it quick to apply it to the date and time textboxes too. That looks more businesslike. These changes are applied only to this report; the Sales form retains its cheerful red, as do any other forms and reports.

⑧ MULTIPLE THEMES If you create new forms and reports, they'll use the chosen theme. If you want a different theme for a single report, find a theme you like, right-click on it and select Apply Theme to This Object Only. Alternatively, pick Apply Theme to All Matching Objects so all reports use the theme.

Q&A

Q: Do I have to stick with the default icons in the headers of my forms and reports?
A: No, try some more customising. Highlight the icon in Design View, click Logo in the Header/Footer group (making sure you're viewing the Design tab) and navigate to a preferred image. Double-click to select the image. It may not display properly, so in the Property Sheet (found in the Tools group), find the Size Mode and change it to Zoom to adjust the image to the largest possible size without affecting its aspect ratio (proportions).

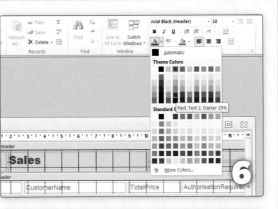

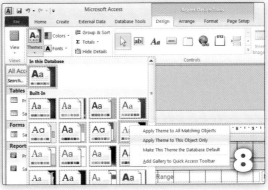

HOW TO...
WRITE A DATA MACRO

Microsoft has introduced the data macro feature into Access 2010 to give you more control over what goes into your tables. We explain how to build one.

HOW LONG?

Half an hour; more if you experiment with the Macro Designer.

HOW HARD?

Not for the computing novice, but if you're familiar with macros the transition isn't too tough.

Access lets you build a lot into a database application using the interface (forms, buttons, reports), but there are limitations. In most database management systems the next step is to learn a programming language, but Access offers macros as an alternative. A macro is a tiny program triggered by an action such as clicking a button.

The ability to write macros has been part of Access for years, but in Access 2010 the way macros are built has changed thanks to the new Macro Designer. You can create a macro just as before – for example, you could build one to ensure your data-entry form always displays the last record entered. Entirely new, however, is a type of macro called a data macro, and the arrival fills a hole in Access' feature list that has previously been gaping.

Macros wait for something to happen (such as the opening of a form) before they carry out their job (say, moving to the last record). The difference with a data macro is it's attached to a table action, rather than to objects in the user interface. You can't attach one to a button, or use one to open a form. Their role is to manage the data in the tables and to ensure the data conforms to what are termed "business rules". These sound rather

serious, but in fact are simply an additional means of making sure you store only accurate data.

A business rule could be, "If a purchase is more than £200 then authorisation is required from the boss." You can write a data macro that checks the sale value when it's entered into the Sales table and if the value is £200 or more, a Yes/No column called AuthorisationRequired is automatically set to Yes.

Data macros can be written to act before or after certain actions, and come in five flavours: BeforeChange, BeforeDelete, AfterInsert, AfterUpdate and AfterDelete. BeforeChange triggers for inserts and updates to the table, such as the sale authorisation above.

A data macro is attached to a table, so any form based on it inherits the macro. Whether data is entered directly into a table or via a form, the rule is applied. And data macros can be named and reused in other tables.

GET STARTED Download our example database from www.pcpro.co.uk/links/salesexample. Open the Sales table in Design View (to follow these steps it must be a table, not a form or report, as

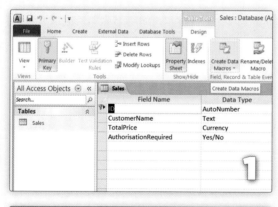

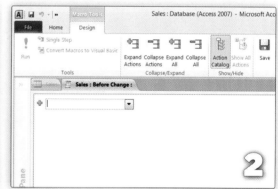

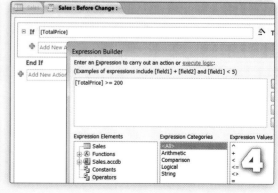

these have different ribbons). In the ribbon, find the Create Data Macros button on the Design tab.

 ENTER MACRO DESIGNER Click the button, select Before Change and the Macro Designer opens. The macro is built in the left pane labelled here, "Sales : Before Change :". The Action Catalog (right) lists all the available actions you can insert into the code.

 ADD AN IF STATEMENT This is how our macro should behave: "If the value in TotalPrice is greater than or equal to 200, then set the value in the AuthorisationRequired field to True". Pop down the Add New Action list (the box top left preceded by a green plus symbol), select "If". An outline appears: the condition for the "if" statement to evaluate is written in the box immediately after. So start typing the field name and an IntelliSense list appears showing various functions and any field names that fit (IntelliSense is Microsoft's auto-complete technology.) We want the TotalPrice field.

 USE EXPRESSION BUILDER Double-click TotalPrice to add it. Now type ">= 200" directly into the box (without the quote marks). Alternatively, click the wizard symbol on the right to open the Expression Builder; select Operators in the list of Expression Elements and >= from Expression Values, then type "200".

 ADD A SETFIELD STATEMENT Click OK to insert the expression into the code. To the right is the word "Then" and below is a second Add New Action box. Here, we tell the macro what to do once it calculates whether the value in TotalPrice is 200 or greater. Select SetField from the list. Against Name enter the field you wish to update: AuthorisationRequired. Again, there's IntelliSense help. Against Value, type "True" (or select it from Constants in the Expression Builder).

TRUE = YES The data macro is complete. The authorisation field is a Yes/No field, so we're telling the macro to put a check in the box ("True") if the condition is met. Save the macro and Close it. Save the table and move to Datasheet View.

TEST IT Add a new record: Jim spends £75. When this is saved, AuthorisationRequired remains unchecked. Fine. Add Kim's £350 purchase. When that's saved, AuthorisationRequired is checked. Add more rows. The data macro is working! Check a purchase of exactly £200: happily, this too is flagged for eyeballing by the boss.

FORMS In a form based on this table, the data macro continues to work. If you need to edit the macro, open the table in Design View, click Create Data Macros and select Before Change.

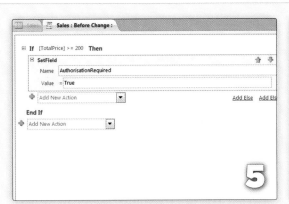

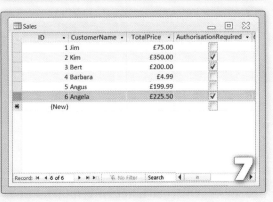

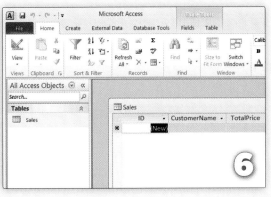

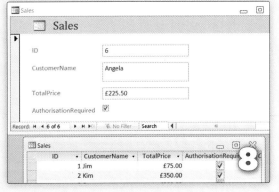

9
Access 2010

HOW LONG?

About an hour if you already have a spreadsheet to link to.

HOW HARD?

The wizards make tasks easier, but this still isn't for the faint-hearted.

HOW TO... USE ACCESS AS A LANDING PAD FOR DATA

Any modern database needs to interact with data from different sources, and Microsoft has adopted the "landing pad" metaphor for Access 2010 – here's why.

Data is usually kept in more than one place. You might have human resources data in an Access database, but staff commission records in an Excel spreadsheet. In general, combining data from different sources is difficult, often involving a lot of tiresome and repetitive work. Access has always had excellent abilities to link to (and import) data from other sources, bringing data together. But these abilities haven't always been easy to use.

The "landing pad for data", new in 2010, is designed to make this whole process much easier. For example, you can use a query to combine data and display it in an Access report. In our example, we can show commission totals for staff members along with other data from the database, such as salary data held in the database. A report could also use "conditional formatting" to show when more than a specified sum has been earned in commission. (We'll demonstrate this with sample data.)

You can combine data from sources other than Excel, including tables in Microsoft SQL Server and other Access databases. And Microsoft has extended the range of sources to include web content and data from web services, accessible from a new Web Browser control.

IMPORTING It's possible to import data into your database: that is, copy it into a table you've made for it or append it to an existing table. However, there may be excellent reasons why you prefer to continue using Excel to store the data, and simply use Access' querying and reporting features. It may also be that you receive spreadsheet data from other organisations and want to make use of it without storing it yourself. Here, you'll use linking.

LINKING From Access you can create a link to data in Excel: links can be made to a particular worksheet or a named range. The data appears as a table in the Navigation pane with an Excel symbol. Although you can see and interact with it, the data remains stored in Excel. Linked data can't be edited from within Access, but you can query and report on it. The spreadsheet data is edited in Excel as usual and, back in Access, the linked table is refreshed with the click of a button and the latest data is ready for querying or populating a report.

① **LINK TO EXCEL** Download our example Excel file from www.pcpro.co.uk/links/landpad. In Access,

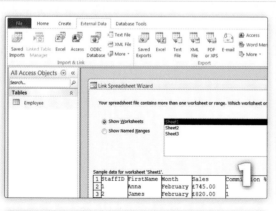

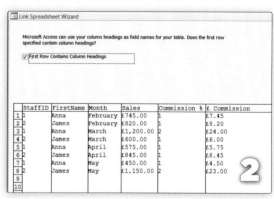

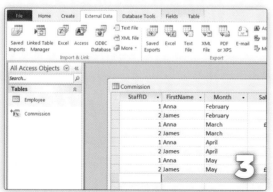

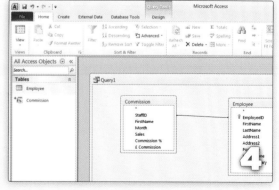

create a new blank database. Click the External Data tab and then the Excel icon in Import & Link. Browse to the Excel file and click Open. Select the third option ("Link to the data source by creating a linked table") and click OK. The wizard shows the Excel data: choose Sheet1.

② **SPECIFY FIELD NAMES** Click Next. Cleverly, Access can use column headings as field names: if the wizard has identified these correctly, check the First Row Contains Column Headings box.

③ **NEW LINKED TABLE** Click Next, name the linked table, click Finish and then OK. The Navigator shows a new table, with an Excel arrow icon, and a normal Access table – in our case, titled Employee. Open both tables by double-clicking. Our staff members have an ID number for all records: it's in the StaffID field in the Commission table and EmployeeID in Employees. If we make a relationship between these columns, Access will know which records refer to which member of staff.

④ **DESIGN A QUERY** We can do so when we create a query. Click the Create tab, then Query Design; highlight the two tables, click Add and close the Show Table dialog. Now we click and drag the EmployeeID column name in the Employee table and drop it onto the StaffID column name in the Commission table. A line indicates the relationship. We add the FirstName

and CurrentSalary columns from Employee and Month and "£ Commission" from Commission.

⑤ **BUILD A REPORT** Click View and pick Datasheet View to see the data the query will provide, then save it. Now we have the data for our report. On the Create tab, click Report Wizard (green square with wand). Under Tables/Queries, choose the new query and select all fields using the double arrow. Click Next. We'll add two grouping levels, FirstName and CurrentSalary.

⑥ **COMPLETE THE REPORT** Click Next. Accept the defaults in the next two screens, name the report and click Finish. There's the basic report, but we can do more using conditional formatting.

⑦ **CONDITIONAL FORMATTING** Close Print Preview View (ribbon button, far right). The report is shown in Design View. In the Detail section, right-click on "£ Commission" and select Conditional Formatting. Click New Rule. Edit the rule to read: "Format only cells where the: Field Value Is | greater than or equal to | 20". Set the background colour to something bright and the text colour to contrast with it.

⑧ **THE RESULTS** Click OK and OK again. In Report View, inspect the result. Any commission more than £20 is now highlighted and easy to spot.

IN THIS CHAPTER

10
Office for business

OFFICE FOR BUS

We've already seen many of the business features included in the Office applications, and there's no doubt you can work faster – and produce better results – using Office 2010. But that isn't the whole story. What if your teams could share documents and even work on the same one at the same time? Or if you could see at a glance whether someone was sitting at their

INESS

desk, talking on the phone or busy in a meeting? This becomes possible thanks to the "presence" features built into Office, while co-authoring and sharing rely on server-based software called SharePoint – which you can now get free of charge. This chapter explores all the Office 2010 features specifically for businesses, and should make it far easier to justify the outlay.

IF YOU RUSH INTO BUYING OFFICE FOR YOUR SMALL BUSINESS, YOU COULD BE PAYING MORE THAN YOU NEED TO – AND MISSING OUT ON SOME KEY FEATURES.

Buying Office for your business

Office 2010 comes in six editions, of which only four are suitable for business use. The free, ad-supported Starter edition (see Chapter 11) provides cut-down versions of Word and Excel and is available only with a new PC. The Home and Student edition is licensed for non-commercial use, so it isn't suitable for businesses. Of the remaining four editions, Standard and Professional Plus are available only to Volume Licence customers. Finally, the Professional and Home and Business editions will be available through retail stores as well as via company licensing agreements.

There are no upgrade prices for customers who already have a previous version of Office. The choice is between the full retail price of the boxed product, the Key Card price (for a licence without physical media), or one of the many different Volume Licence prices available.

There's one other way for a business to get Office 2010: bundled with a new PC. Here, you'll get an "OEM" (original equipment manufacturer) licence, but probably no DVD; if anything goes wrong, you'll have to restore your PC to its factory state to recover your software. If you scrap the PC and buy another one, the licence dies with the machine.

All these restrictions make OEM licences cheaper, and you may see them available for purchase from online retailers as well as supplied with PCs. But, in addition to the above restrictions, if you call Microsoft for support, the company will politely turn you away.

LICENSING You don't have to be a big player to use the Volume Licence programme. The minimum purchase is five licences; that could be five copies of Office, or three new PCs with Windows and Office licences. For organisations with fewer than 250 computers there are two main licence programmes: Open Licence and Open Value. (The various licensing options are summarised in the chart opposite.)

OPEN LICENCE Open Licence is a pay-as-you-go deal, where you buy some licences and add more as you need them. It's a two-year agreement, and the price depends on how many of each licence you buy, through a complicated system of product pools and points. You need 500 points to qualify for an Open Licence agreement, and that equates to licences for 63 computers running Windows and Office when bought with Open Licence and Software Assurance (SA).

Software Assurance is an optional extra that allows you to upgrade to the latest version of the software whenever it's released (within the lifespan of your SA agreement). As you'll gather, Open Licence is a complicated programme, and you'd need to talk in-depth to your retailer or advisor to find out if it would be right for you.

OPEN VALUE The Open Value programme allows you to spread the cost of licences by paying in three equal annual instalments. It includes Software Assurance, and after the third year you get to choose whether or not to continue with the SA payments and again spread these over three years.

The costs from year four onwards, when you're paying only for the SA and not the licence, are usually around one-third as much. If you need more licences within the term, you can start a separate Open Value programme for them or add them to your existing agreement, adjusting the costs to reflect the different timescale.

Another option, Open Value Company-wide, is for organisations standardising all their desktop and laptop PCs and offers greater discounts than the standard option, which applies to only some of your PCs.

Whichever version you choose, Open Value is a good deal for most small businesses: it's much simpler than Open Licence, and spreading the payments over the three-year agreement gives you predictable costs.

Just to make things a little more complicated, there's also Open Value Subscription. This has the lowest annual cost initially, but it remains the same over the life of the agreement rather than reducing from year four. You're effectively renting the software: stop paying, and you lose the right to use it. However, you can convert a subscription into a standard, perpetual licence after the first year, by paying one extra year's subscription.

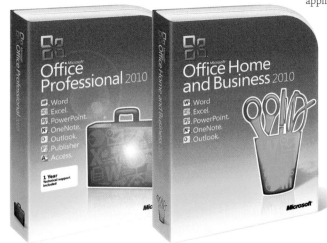

MICROSOFT'S LICENSING SCHEMES

Under 250 computers
- **Open Licence**
  - **Standard**
  - **Company-wide**
  - **Subscription**
- **Open Value**

Over 250 computers
- **Enterprise Agreement**
  - **Subscription**
- **Select Licence**
  - **Select Plus**

As a quick comparison between licensing and retail costs, ten copies of Office Professional Plus on an Open Value non-Company-wide agreement will set you back a total of about £2,825 over three years. That makes the cost per licence £282.50, which is nearly 23% less than the £366 for a retail copy of Professional edition – and it includes more applications, the rights to the next version when it's released, and the benefit of paying £941.60 each year rather than £2,825 up front. The price depends on how many copies you buy, and your retailer may be able to do better than Microsoft's recommended pricing, as quoted here.

LARGER ORGANISATIONS For larger organisations, the Enterprise Agreement has a three-year term, big discounts on retail pricing and Software Assurance. The Subscription version gives even lower annual payments, but again you're renting, not buying. Select and Select Plus are based on forecasts and measurements of the software you use. If you're not sure how many copies of Office you'll need throughout the agreement, this allows you to guess and pay for that, then measure what you actually used and pay extra, if necessary, later. Select Plus lets individual business units manage their own software purchasing while maintaining the price benefits of purchasing as one large organisation. Schools, universities, government departments and charities can all get cheaper licencing terms.

For more information on all aspects of Office 2010 licensing – including the Microsoft Licensing Advisor, which will price and advise on licences to suit your needs – visit www.microsoft.com/licensing.

OFFICE 2010 EDITIONS

	Word	Excel	PowerPoint	OneNote	Outlook	Publisher	Access	InfoPath	Communicator	SharePoint Workspace	Retail	Volume Licensing
Professional Plus	●	●	●	●	●	●	●	●	●	●	✗	✓
Professional	●	●	●	●	●	●	●				✓	✓
Standard	●	●	●	●	●	●					✗	✓
Home and Business	●	●	●	●	●						✓	✓
Home and Student	●	●	●	●							✓	✗
Starter	●	●									On PC ✗	

Recommended retail prices

exc VAT (inc VAT)

Home and Business

Boxed product	Key Card
£204 (£240)	**£162** (£190)

Professional

Boxed product	Key Card
£366 (£430)	**£255** (£300)

✳ UNLESS YOU ENJOY PRESSING "NEXT" REPEATEDLY, TAKE ADVANTAGE OF
THE TOOLS PROVIDED TO MAKE MULTIPLE INSTALLATIONS OF OFFICE EASIER.

Planning to deploy Office 2010

Planning is crucial to a successful roll-out of any software across an organisation, large or small, and never more so than with a complicated and much-used product such as Office. That's why you should take advantage of Microsoft's tools to help assess your current environment, check your existing documents, templates, add-ins and other solutions for compatibility, and customise your deployment of Office.

First stop is the Office Environment Assessment Tool. This helps you see what Office apps and add-ins you already have. It can be run on each workstation or automated across a department or company, and its centralised reporting means you get a single report or Excel workbook to analyse the results. A clever Passive Scan mode lets the tool remain running on clients for several hours, watching for any apps that try to automate Office apps.

The report will show machines that don't meet the specs for Office 2010 or have add-ins or other code that are incompatible. You should also check your own code using the Compatibility Inspector (www.pcpro.co.uk/links/compinsp). This comes in two versions, one for VBA code in Office documents and templates, and one for Visual Studio. Both highlight lines that may cause problems in Office 2010 and offer guidance. This is especially useful if you need to check code for both 32-bit and 64-bit Office.

DEPLOYMENT OPTIONS Unless you have only two PCs, you really don't want to take the DVD round to each in turn to install Office 2010 manually. At a minimum you should be copying the contents of the DVD to a network folder.

You can use a startup script to deploy Office 2010 automatically the next time a computer boots. This requires only Notepad and a working knowledge of group policies. You edit the sample script to point to the network folder where you put your installation files and the config file where you set the installation options, then add that script

to a group policy object that you assign to the computers on which you want to install Office. Always check your group policy and script by assigning it to one computer and seeing that it does the job properly before rolling it out. See www.pcpro.co.uk/links/gpolicy for detailed advice.

OFFICE CUSTOMISATION TOOL To customise your distribution of Office, you run "setup.exe /admin" from the folder where you copied the installation files to launch the Office Customisation Tool (OCT). This lets you accept the licence terms, enter a volume licence key, customise features and settings in Office, and configure options such as how verbose it is while installing. There are many options in OCT, and you should take the time to check each one, since all your Office installations will be based on these settings. OCT writes an MSP file to the setup folder containing your customisations to be used when installing Office on client PCs. You'll also probably need to edit CONFIG.XML if using a setup script.

ACTIVATION OPTIONS In previous versions of Office, the product keys issued under volume licence agreements bypassed the need for activation. Microsoft has fixed this loophole for Office 2010. Your Office installations can activate directly with Microsoft over the internet, like retail copies, using a Multiple Activation Key (MAK), or you can implement a Key Management Service (KMS) on your server and have your installations activate through that.

MAK works well for laptop PCs that are out of the office for a long time. If some computers don't have an internet connection, you can use the Volume Activation Management Tool (VAMT) to do the activation for them and copy back the resulting activation key. KMS activation is recommended if you have more than 50 desktop PCs on your network. The KMS service collects and authorises activation requests from the PCs and you manage them

The 64-bit version of Office can take advantage of the latest processors, but the business benefits aren't clear-cut.

Windows versions compatible with Office 2010

Operating system version	Windows 7	Windows Vista SP1	Windows XP SP3	Server 2008 R2	Server 2008	Server 2003 R2	Office version
32-bit	●	●	●	●	●	●	32-bit
64-bit	●	●		●	●	●	32-bit
64-bit	●	●		●	●		64-bit

through VAMT. You don't need a product key for each copy of Office, but the software will try to reactivate with the KMS Service every 180 days to check it's still licensed.

64-BIT For the first time ever, there's a 64-bit version of Office. Each Office 2010 DVD will ship with both 32-bit and 64-bit versions for you to choose between. 64-bit processing does bring some advantages, but it isn't all plain sailing: there are some disadvantages as well.

First, you have to work out if you can run the 64-bit version, and that depends on whether your machines have a 64-bit operating system. The table opposite shows the OSes on which Office 2010 will run. Note that Windows XP 64-bit isn't supported at all; it can't even run 32-bit Office 2010. Nor can you run 64-bit Office 2010 on 64-bit Windows Server 2003 R2. Any other OS – forget it.

If you want to keep some, or all, of your previous Office installation, you can't use *any* of the 64-bit apps. If you have other MAPI-based messaging applications besides Outlook, you're similarly restricted to the 32-bit version of Office 2010. You can't upgrade from a previous version of Office to 64-bit Office 2010: you have to uninstall first.

The two advantages of 64-bit are that it lets you use additional memory in the computer – for example, Excel 2010 workbooks can be bigger than 2GB and Project 2010 can work with very large projects consisting of many sub-projects. You also get enhanced security through Data Execution Prevention by default. But that's where the advantages stop. The 64-bit applications aren't significantly faster; indeed, they may be slower in certain circumstances, and there are a whole host of other drawbacks.

Not many people actually need Excel workbooks bigger than 2GB. If you ever made one that big you couldn't store it in SharePoint – or share it with anyone who wasn't running 64-bit Office 2010, because they wouldn't be able to open it. Access databases with their code removed (split data and code in separate files) can't be shared between 32-bit and 64-bit versions of Office, and any VBA macros may not be compatible between 32-bit and 64-bit versions.

But the biggest problem by far is that ActiveX controls, add-ins and COM DLLs written for 32-bit Office won't work with the 64-bit version. Microsoft will have to issue new versions of ActiveSync and the Windows Mobile Device Center used to sync Outlook data to a mobile phone. A new VSTO (Visual Studio Tools for Office) runtime will bridge this gap for DLLs and add-ins written using Visual Studio, but other manufacturers will have to test, possibly change, and re-issue their DLLs and add-ins in 64-bit.

Check that all your add-ins, sync software and other solutions will work with Office 2010 64-bit. You don't want to deploy it only to find the chairman's mobile phone will no longer collect his email or synchronise his calendar.

There are tools to help you install Office 2010 on multiple machines, but there are also issues it's vital to investigate first. Take a good look at your environment in the mirror before you take the plunge.

Introducing SharePoint

SharePoint is Microsoft's document collaboration platform. Now coming up to ten years old, it's matured and grown ever closer to Office with each version. SharePoint 2010 sports the same ribbon interface as Office applications, and it's more flexible and powerful than ever.

SharePoint builds websites. These are usually internal, such as departmental or company-wide intranets, but it can be used to build great extranets for providing information to or collaborating with partner companies. It can even build big, public, customer-facing websites, and many international companies use it for just that, including huge names such as Kraft and Ferrari.

SharePoint 2010 runs on Windows Server 2008 or Windows Server 2008 R2 (only the 64-bit versions), and stores its data in Microsoft SQL Server 2005, 2008 or 2008 R2 (again, it must be the 64-bit version). It can even use the free SQL Server Express edition, but if you want a SharePoint database bigger than the 4GB limit of SQL Server Express, you'll need to buy SQL Server Workgroup, Standard or Enterprise edition if you don't already have it.

SHAREPOINT'S ANATOMY The basic unit of information in SharePoint is a list of items. There are many item types built in, such as Announcements and Calendars, and you can customise these by adding, changing or deleting fields. Or you can build your own lists of your own item types.

A specialised type of list is a "document library", which holds virtually any kind of file along with properties about those files. Office documents can be saved to document libraries and the documents' metadata automatically promoted to show as columns of data in SharePoint. You can sort, group, filter or search by the metadata, and invent your own metadata fields to be collected when Office documents are created and published to SharePoint. You can have any number of different views of the data in a list or library, showing different columns or with different sorting, grouping or filtering.

You can instigate check-in/check-out policies, approval workflows or capture new versions of documents as they're revised, and require approval before new versions are published. This content management system means the staff in a department can easily collaborate on revisions to documents and have them approved before the rest of the company (or partners, or the public) get to see them.

Anyone with access to a list or document library can set up a subscription to be notified if a certain item or document is changed, or indeed if anything in the list or library changes. These notifications can be sent immediately or only once a day or once a week.

You can also open any document library in Windows Explorer. This means you can use all the standard Windows Explorer features, most notably drag and drop to move or copy documents. You can connect just about any list or library to Outlook, making the content available in Outlook even if you're not connected to the network.

Occasionally, connected users – such as sales people or consultants – can use SharePoint Workspace, previously known as Groove, to collaborate on documents, lists and projects with other mobile and office-based users.

THE EDITIONS SharePoint Foundation is a free basic version of SharePoint that includes many not-so-basic features you'd think would be reserved for its paid-for big brother. These include the standard lists and document libraries, team workspaces, blogs and wikis. You can also add the Office Web Apps (see Chapter 12) to SharePoint Foundation,

SharePoint's built-in item types include Calendars and Announcements to help keep your teams organised.

Which version of SharePoint do you need?

Size of company	Intranet	Extranet & Internet
Small	SharePoint Foundation 2010 (free)	n/a
Medium	SharePoint Server 2010 + Standard CALs	SharePoint Server 2010 for Internet Sites, Standard
Large	SharePoint Server 2010 + Enterprise CALs	SharePoint Server 2010 for Internet Sites, Enterprise

Search features by size of business

Size of company	Intranet	Extranet & Internet
Small	Search Server Express 2010 (Free)	n/a
Medium	Search Server 2010	n/a
Large	FAST Search for SharePoint 2010	FAST Search for SharePoint 2010 for Internet Sites

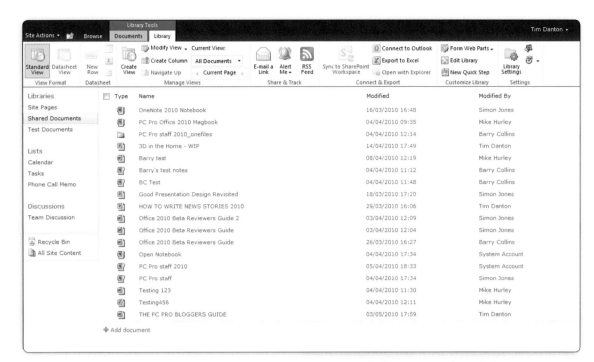

so you can preview and edit Word, Excel, PowerPoint and OneNote documents in a browser without having to open the document in the full desktop application.

The big brother is SharePoint Server, and if you buy this you also need CALs (Client Access Licences) for all the users. The Standard CAL enables the core capabilities, including My Site personal pages for all staff. To the user, their My Site lists items such as their recent documents and what colleagues are working on. To colleagues, it lists the user's areas of expertise, interests and publicly available information such as a blog. My Sites are great for encouraging collaboration and ad hoc team working, and make people more discoverable and approachable.

The Enterprise CAL is required for interacting with external line-of-business data, dashboards, advanced analytics and advanced workflows. You can have a mix of CALs if not all users require the Enterprise facilities.

If you want partners or the general public to be able to interact with your SharePoint site, you'll need to buy SharePoint Server 2010 for Internet Sites. This comes in Standard and Enterprise editions, depending on whether you want the full enterprise capabilities for external users.

For developers, SharePoint Designer 2010 is free; it can be used to customise the look and feel of SharePoint pages and sites, and to create new custom workflows for documents and list items. Visual Studio 2010 adds more capabilities and may be useful for advanced solutions.

The table opposite should help you see at a glance which version is likely to be right for your business.

SEARCHING QUESTIONS You get basic search capabilities in SharePoint Foundation, but if it's crucial to your business you'll want to take a look at Search Server. Search Server Express is free but basic: the emphasis is on ease of use

and quick setup. Upgrading to the full version of Search Server brings scalability and redundancy (Search Server Express can only be installed on one server), but for serious enterprise search abilities you'll need to invest in FAST Search Server for SharePoint 2010. This extends to external-facing websites as well.

HOW LONG?

Allow plenty of
time, especially for
preparation.

HOW HARD?

The wizard stage is
easy, but it takes know-
how to get that far.

Tip

Before installing
SharePoint, you need
a hotfix for Windows
Communication
Foundation (WCF).
Get this for Windows
Server 2008 SP2 from
www.pcpro.co.uk/links/
wcffix1, or for Windows
Server 2008 R2 from
www.pcpro.co.uk/links/
wcffix2.

HOW TO... INSTALL SHAREPOINT FOUNDATION 2010

SharePoint Foundation is a useful tool in its own right and as a way to try before you buy SharePoint 2010. Check the system requirements: SharePoint 2010 requires Windows Server 2008 SP2 or Windows Server 2008 R2. Installation on Windows 7 or Windows Vista is supported only for testing. No 32-bit OSes will work; you need 64-bit. You'll also need four processor cores running at 2.5GHz to get decent performance; fewer aren't supported. For developing or evaluation you can get away with 4GB of RAM, but a production server should have 8GB minimum. You'll also need 80GB of disk storage just for the programs. Estimating the storage for data and documents is up to you.

Client PCs that will connect to SharePoint just need a web browser. Internet Explorer 7 or 8 (32-bit versions) give the best experience, followed by Mozilla Firefox on Windows. You get more basic functionality from other browsers, including Safari 4.x on a Mac.

BEFORE YOU START There are several points to consider before installation. A domain is required to deploy SharePoint Foundation 2010; you can't install to a workgroup. You can't install it as a single server with a built-in database on a Domain Controller; you must use a separate machine for this topology. You must be a member of the Administrators group on the machine. You must have internet access from the computer on which you're installing SharePoint,

because the preparation tool downloads components from the Microsoft Download Center.

1 **DOWNLOAD** Once you've followed the checks above, download SharePoint Foundation 2010. Microsoft makes this easy: head to http://sharepoint2010.microsoft.com and follow the prompts.

2 **PRE-STEPS** It takes just 16 mouse-clicks and two entries of a user ID and password to install SharePoint Foundation as a standalone server. The most exciting part is accepting the licence terms.

3 **INSTALLATION** The installer first deals with the prerequisites, rebooting the machine if necessary. Then you can start installation, choosing the Standalone type of installation rather than Server Farm. A Standalone installation will put the database in SQL Server Express on this machine. You'd want a Server Farm installation to store the database on a separate server.

4 **RUN THE WIZARD** At the end of the install process you're prompted to run the Configuration wizard, which does all the configuration for you, and then you're done. The new SharePoint site is displayed in your browser and you get to sign in and add the site to your list of trusted sites.

Microsoft

Microsoft® Office 2010
MAKE IT GREAT

I want to make it great
for my little DEVIL.

My name's Stella and my cat Charlie is wicked. I used new OneNote® 2010 to make a scrapbook all about how naughty he is. I put in a video of Charlie attacking my mum's ankles and drew little red devil horns on his picture with the pen tool. I think he liked it because he licked the screen.

> See how you can make it great with new Office 2010 at
office.com/2010

✳ ONE GOOD REASON TO EXPERIMENT WITH SHAREPOINT IS CO-AUTHORING, WHICH IS SUPPORTED BY WORD, EXCEL, POWERPOINT AND ONENOTE.

Co-authoring via SharePoint

A new feature in Office 2010 is that, in four key applications, several users can all edit the same document at the same time. This works in Word, Excel, PowerPoint (as we examine in Chapter 5) and OneNote, although it's slightly different in each application and depends on whether you're using the desktop app or the equivalent web app. The table below left shows where co-authoring is available.

Co-authoring, as it's known, won't suit everyone. To some, the idea of sharing documents is just as disturbing as sharing a dessert with one spoon. To everyone else, it's a very welcome change from seeing the all-too-prevalent message "<Document name> is locked for editing by <user name>. Do you want to: Open a read-only copy, create a local copy and merge your changes later, or receive notification when the original copy is available?" None of the above, thank you, I just want to work on the document.

Co-authoring is enabled when you store your Office 2010 documents in SharePoint 2010 – even the free SharePoint Foundation – and it adds yet another tool (along with formal document versions, the check-in and check-out procedure, and document approval) to help users collaborate on a document.

All these features help to avoid the problem of having multiple versions of a document in circulation –

perhaps some sent by email, some stored in a network folder, with version numbers noted in the filename, some just labelled DRAFT – or worse, FINAL 1, FINAL 2, FINAL 3 and onwards to infinity. It's a pain merging multiple versions of documents and deciding whether to accept or reject each change, especially when many people have all made similar but slightly different changes to the same sentence or paragraph.

What's more, that kind of change tracking has only ever been available in Word. Excel doesn't have those features, and PowerPoint has only now gained some version comparison capabilities in PowerPoint 2010. OneNote has been better, in that it's had rudimentary co-authoring for a couple of versions, but until now it couldn't tell you who wrote what in a notebook.

Let's take a closer look at how co-authoring works in each of the four Office 2010 applications that support it.

WORD To co-author a Word document, you need to store a Word 2010 file in a SharePoint 2010 document library. When two or more people open that document in Word (not the Word Web App), they all see a little balloon message over the status bar saying "<N> authors are now editing this document", and the status bar shows a couple

Co-authoring availability

	Desktop app	Web app
Word	●	
Excel		●
PowerPoint	●	
OneNote	●	●

Co-authoring now works in Word, Excel, PowerPoint and OneNote, but whether the feature is available in the full version and/or the web app varies between the applications. Only OneNote supports both.

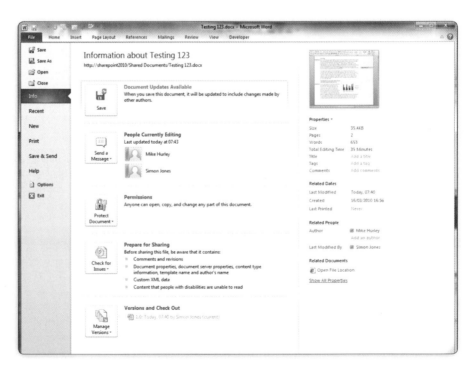

You can quickly check who's editing a Word document, and their current status, using the Backstage view.

of "pawn" icons and the number of editors. Click the pawns to see the names of the editors, with presence indicators showing if they're busy or free.

To avoid disrupting individual users with others' changes appearing as soon as they're made, Microsoft has decided that, as a user, you don't see changes from other authors until you save your own changes. An icon appears on the right of the status bar, next to the view controls, if there are updates from other editors available. When you save your changes, the new changes from other authors are merged into your document and highlighted in green.

Word marks the paragraphs being changed by each author with their name and presence indicator, so you know who's changing what. If there are updates available for that paragraph, you also see an extra icon showing refresh arrows. Paragraphs being edited are locked, so no-one else can change them until that author saves their changes and moves into another paragraph. If any conflicting changes do slip through, the last author to make changes sees a warning bar at the top of the window and a button to click to resolve the conflict, which performs a more fine-grained merge of the changes.

Since all the standard features of Word are available while co-authoring, you can use the Comment tools if you want to put a note in the document rather than changing the text, or turn on Track Changes to get a formal record of who changed what.

EXCEL Excel is the Cinderella of co-authoring in that the feature is available only in the Excel Web App, not the desktop application. This immediately limits the features and functions available, and some other features such as Undo and Redo aren't supported when there are multiple authors. Unlike with Word, there's no need to save your changes to see other users' changes; indeed, you can't save your changes, because there's no Save button: the Excel Web App saves every change as soon as you make it. Everyone's changes appear on your screen in near real-time.

POWERPOINT PowerPoint's co-authoring experience is very similar to that of Word. You open a PowerPoint 2010 presentation stored in a SharePoint 2010 document library and it just works. You see the multiple authors' pawns and the "updates available" icons in the status bar, and you save your changes to see changes from other authors.

We take a closer look at the co-authoring process in PowerPoint on p74.

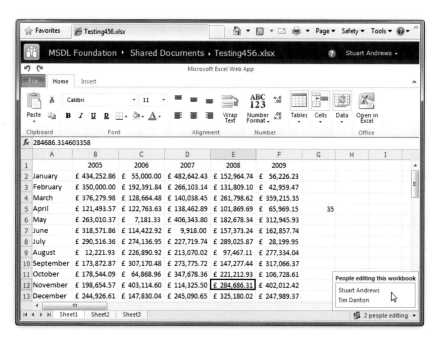

Excel's co-authoring, unlike Word's, does show changes instantly, and only works in the Excel Web App.

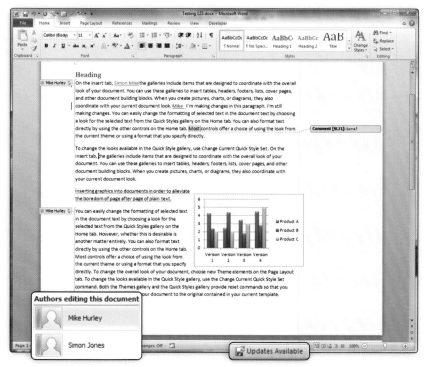

Co-authoring in Word works best with the desktop app, where it can show who's working on the document and their status. It only shows changes once the user saves the document.

ONENOTE OneNote is the best-served application for co-authoring: you can do it in either the desktop application or the cut-down web app. Again, you have to have a OneNote 2010 notebook stored in a SharePoint 2010 document library – and then it just works. There's no need to save your changes, because OneNote doesn't have a Save button. Changes from other authors appear as they finish writing a paragraph, and they're marked with a sidebar and tagged with the author's initials. You can hide the authors' initials if you prefer using View | Authors | Hide Authors.

10

Office for business

HOW LONG?

Set aside plenty of time, particularly to decide your trusted locations.

HOW HARD?

This depends on just how much control you want to take.

HOW TO...
KEEP DOCUMENTS SECURE

Office 2010 brings extra security to help prevent infection of your PC by malware contained in Office documents, and to ensure the integrity and confidentiality of data.

The first new security layer is Data Execution Prevention (DEP). This identifies areas of memory that contain data and prevents any application from attempting to run program code put there. DEP is turned on by default in the 64-bit version of Office 2010, but is an option for the 32-bit version. To switch it on, go to File | Options | Trust Center, and click Trust Center Settings | Protected View | Enable Data Execution Prevention mode.

The second layer validates Office files before they're opened to ensure they're in a valid format – not on a list of insecure, blocked file types – and don't contain any insecure ActiveX controls. If documents pass these tests, the third layer of defence is the new Protected View or "sandbox mode", where any potentially insecure files are opened in a safe, isolated, read-only environment. Here, the user is allowed to read the file and decide whether they need greater access and if they trust the file.

① PROTECT YOURSELF Protected View is used by default for documents from the internet or email, and shows itself by collapsing the ribbon to just its tabs and displaying a prominent yellow band at the top of the document. This says you're in Protected View and invites you to click a button to enable editing. Clicking this reopens the file outside the sandbox, but all the other layers of protection still remain active.

② TAKE CONTROL Network administrators will be able to control all these security settings, including setting up trusted locations on their network or SharePoint service through the Office Customisation Tool and group policies.

③ ADD TRUSTED LOCATIONS Opening documents stored in those locations won't trigger the Protected View sandbox, so it's important to get this set right and to ensure that the local SharePoint and other internal websites are in the correct Internet Explorer security zone, so documents stored there don't trigger Protected View unnecessarily.

④ DOWN TO THE USER End users can control most of the security settings, if the network administrator doesn't stop them, using the Trust Center via Options for each app. If an end user marks a document in a network folder as trusted, they're not asked again. They can't mark files received via email as trusted.

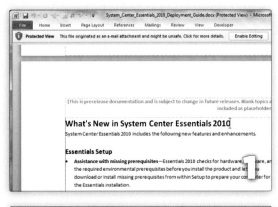

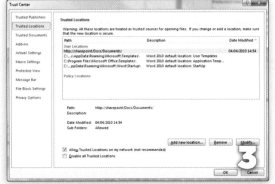

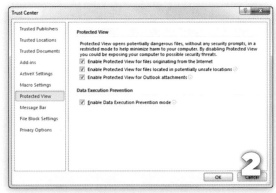

HOW TO...
KNOW WHERE PEOPLE ARE

Playing telephone tag is one of the biggest wastes of time in business. If you could see that the person you wanted was out or busy before you called, you could have sent them an email instead and awaited a reply. Or, if it was urgent, you might have found someone else to handle it.

1 **PRESENCE INDICATOR** Presence indicators across the Office apps aim to help solve these daily communication headaches. Wherever you see a person's name, on email or in a document, you could see a presence indicator. These simple coloured blocks link to Office Communicator, Windows Live Messenger or another third-party system to show you if someone is available (green), away (yellow) or busy (red).

2 **OFFICE COMMUNICATOR** You get a licence for the Office Communicator app with the Professional Plus edition of Office 2010, but it does nothing unless you buy Microsoft Office Communications Server (OCS). The current release of OCS, 2007 R2, works fine with Office 2010. Communicator and OCS give you instant messaging (IM), voice and video calls, application sharing, conferencing and more. They integrate with your office and mobile phone systems, giving great flexibility in call handling and communications. Unlike public IM systems, OCS can archive all IM conversations for compliance, so the details of IM conversations are retained in a central database, like email.

OCS will federate with any suppliers and customers who use it, making presence information available to all staff of all the organisations involved. It will also federate to other messaging systems such as Windows Live Messenger, AOL Messenger and Yahoo Messenger. This brings IM and presence information from these public systems, but gives more control than allowing free access to public IM systems from your PCs.

3 **WINDOWS LIVE MESSENGER** If you don't have OCS and Office Communicator, you can still use the public Windows Live Messenger system to give presence information and IM inside Office. Put the IM address for users in their contact information in Outlook, if different to their regular email address, and sign in to Windows Live Messenger to see presence indicators light up next to email addresses and names all over Office.

4 **CONTACT CARDS** Wherever you see a presence indicator you can click or hover for a Contact Card that lists key details about this user, such as if and when they'll be free based on their Outlook Calendar items. It also gives you quick ways to send an email, start an instant message or phone them.

HOW LONG?
Up to an hour, maybe more, if you install Office Communicator.

HOW HARD?
Taking full advantage of OCS requires plenty of expertise.

Tip

To see a Contact Card on a person's name in a Word document, right-click the name and choose Additional Actions. If you don't see "Instant Messaging Contacts" or "Person Name", click Options and enable one or both of those Actions in the AutoCorrect dialog. The IM Contacts action gives access to the Contact Card. The Person Name action has options for Send Mail, Schedule a Meeting, Open Contact and Insert Address.

IF YOU'RE A SMALL BUSINESS AND OPT FOR MICROSOFT'S VOLUME LICENCE SCHEME, THIS COULD BE THE SALES TOOL YOU'VE BEEN WAITING FOR.

Business Contact Manager

There are three things you need to know about Business Contact Manager. First, it's a module that plugs into Outlook. Second, it's only available (and free) to Volume Licence customers who buy Office Standard or Professional Plus. And third, it's a very valuable tool to help small businesses keep track of their customers.

This is true of all customer relationship management (CRM) software, but what makes Business Contact Manager interesting is the way it addresses the needs of small businesses – right down to sole traders – and the depth of its integration with Outlook. In many ways, it turns Outlook into a proper business tool, able to track your sales, marketing, contacts and projects. There's even a customisable dashboard that allows you to see at-a-glance information such as your best-selling products, your most successful salespeople and your sales pipeline.

If you've never used CRM software before, your first step should be to familiarise yourself with the tools: Microsoft creates a dummy set of contacts and businesses to play around with. After that, you can import existing contacts en masse via File | Business Contact Manager | Import and Export | Import Outlook Contacts.

To get an idea of how it works, let's say you do business with a firm of lawyers. You'd set up an account for that company, then attach any existing contacts to the account. You can then track conversations you have, record additional information (such as their birthday or preferred method of communication), and mark a date in the calendar for that post-project courtesy call. You can then share all that information with colleagues.

Or perhaps you've found a new contact. Add them to your Business Contacts, then click Opportunity on the ribbon. Fill in the form with as much detail as you need, adding the products they're interested in buying. Keep on going for all your opportunities and contacts. During this process, Business Contact Manager will automatically create a sales funnel showing your prospects.

Another nice feature is the Project Manager. It isn't too complex, so you shouldn't expect the bells and whistles of full project management software, but if you want to keep track of various projects without learning a whole new skill set, it's a good introduction.

The ability to send out and track the success of marketing campaigns is another bonus: you can design an HTML email (or base it on a Word or Publisher document), choose your target customers and track success, all within Outlook. Nor do you have to hit every person in your database: if you know people's birth dates, for example, you can email everyone who has a birthday in the next 14 days. Potentially, it's a very powerful piece of software.

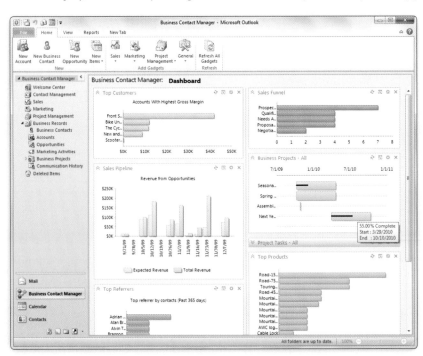

Business Contact Manager isn't designed to rival fully fledged CRM software such as FrontRange GoldMine; in fact, Microsoft recommends it for small businesses only. Considering its close integration with Outlook, however, it's an excellent introduction to CRM.

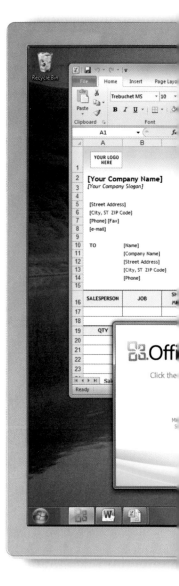

11
Office Starter

OFFICE STARTER

Completely new with the launch of Office 2010, Microsoft's Starter edition of the suite has been created specially to come bundled with new PCs and laptops. And unlike a lot of the "free" software that might arrive with a new machine, it's well worth keeping on your hard disk. We've been genuinely surprised by just how many of the full product's features have been included.

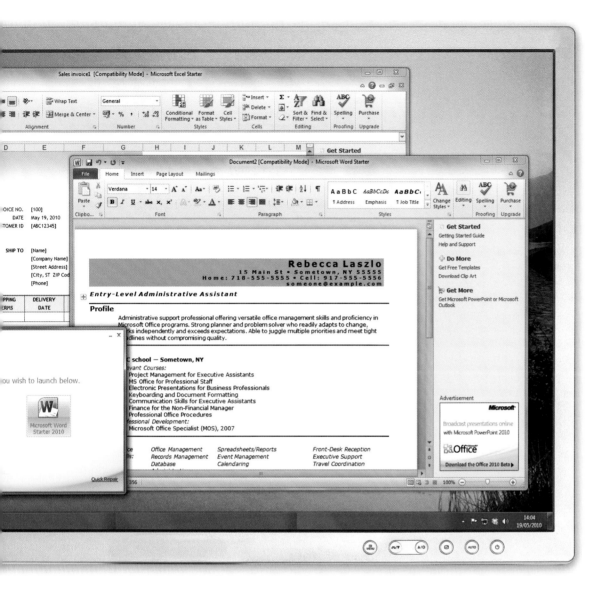

2010

Office Starter consists of just two applications, Word Starter and Excel Starter, but they're remarkably capable. In this chapter, we explain what is included and what isn't. You'll also find a comprehensive guide to the applications' ribbons, and discover the catch that makes this incredible bargain just that: a trade-off between cost and convenience.

IT SEEMS TOO GOOD TO BE TRUE: FEATURE-RICH VERSIONS OF WORD AND EXCEL FOR NOTHING! INEVITABLY, THERE ARE ONE OR TWO SMALL CAVEATS...

Introducing Office Starter 2010

We were pleasantly surprised by the features in Office Starter 2010. Compared to the annoyingly restricted Microsoft Works, whose word processor was barely worthy of the name, such a complete offering for free is amazing.

WHAT'S INCLUDED Office Starter 2010 includes cut-down versions of Word and Excel. There's no PowerPoint, Outlook or – a little disappointingly – OneNote. "Cut down" means you miss out on advanced features targeted at expert or business users. For instance, in Word that means tracked changes; in Excel, PivotTables (see p56) are absent.

All the features most people would consider essential are present, however: Word includes a spelling and grammar checker, word count, even advanced text effects. There are no niggling restrictions on printing, saving or sending: this is a fully fledged word processor.

THE CATCH Yes, there's a catch: a panel at the right-hand side, which is precisely 208 pixels wide and can't be resized or removed. Newcomers might find it handy to have the Getting Started guide and Help links in permanent view, and it also encourages you to download templates and clip-art. In reality, though, that panel is for advertising. At launch Microsoft will be pushing upgrades to the full version of Office, with an image that rotates at frequent intervals. (For instance, as we've been typing this short paragraph it's switched images three times.) This could become annoying, especially if and when Microsoft chooses to sell the advertising to third parties. It says the space will never be offered to the more dubious kind of internet advertiser, but there's still a possibility of being distracted from your work by a random, attention-grabbing ad.

The other big problem comes if space is limited. When you make Word half the width of the screen, so you can look at a web browser at the same time, those 208 pixels count. And on netbooks with screens only 1,024 pixels wide, you're losing a fifth of your screen space.

WORTH THE HASSLE? Despite the irritations, there are many good reasons to get Office Starter. For one, you'll be able to open and edit Word and Excel files created in Office 2007 or 2010 without losing any information. (You can do the same using the Web Apps, but it's a more cumbersome process.)

Plus, Starter includes the bulk of the features you'll actually need. Most of the omissions are functions you'd never use at work, let alone at home. What's more, Office Starter is an excellent introduction to Office 2010 – in a way, it gives you an elongated trial without any risk.

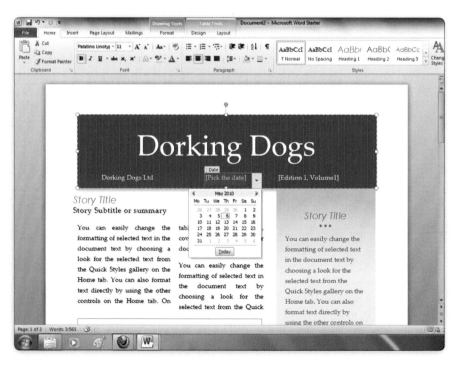

Office Starter Edition is only available preinstalled on new PCs, and gives you a remarkable number of the features of Word and Excel completely free, with no time limit. To the right of what you see here, though, is the catch: a fixed-size pane showing rotating ads.

PROS AND CONS

Starter has its frustrations – but it's still amazing that you can produce professional-looking documents for free.

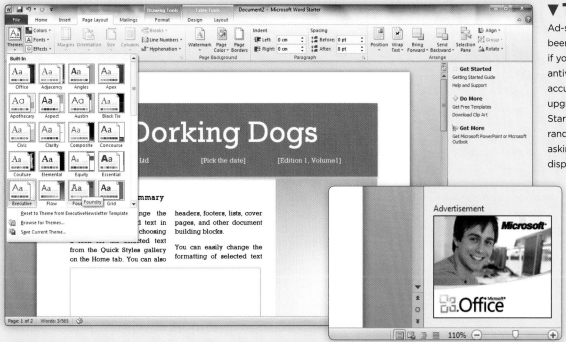

▲ The good

Some people think Microsoft has erred on the side of generosity by including so many advanced features. It could have got away with a more basic feature set, stripping away the word count or the themes. With these intact, you can still follow almost all the Word and Excel tutorials in this book. So even with Starter, you can create and edit much more professional-looking documents than would be possible in rival applications.

▶ The ugly

While that fixed-size pane on the right of Starter's program window might be bearable when you're using a large widescreen monitor, it makes it much more difficult to work productively on a small laptop – the prime example (although not the only one) being netbooks. This is particularly true when you're using two windows simultaneously; for example, if you want to copy figures into Excel from a website. Just look at the screenshot on the right to see how irritating this is in practice.

▼ The bad

Ad-supported programs have been available for years, and if you're already using a free antivirus program you'll be accustomed to the nagging upgrade screens. While Office Starter won't interrupt you by randomly popping up dialogs asking you to upgrade, it does display a small rotating ad that's always there in the corner while you're tapping away in Word or manipulating figures in Excel, and in many ways this is more annoying – you never get away from it. Those short on patience will eventually give in and upgrade, or simply stop using Office Starter altogether.

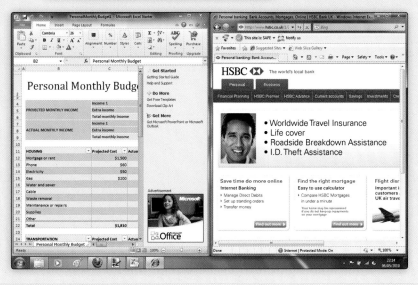

Needless to say, Microsoft would like you to move on from that trial to Office proper. A Purchase button at the right of the Home ribbon links to a web page offering the version of Office 2010 that Microsoft deems right for you. In fact, it's already on your system, just locked away until you buy a product key. Do read Chapter 1 before you buy.

Of course, Office Starter isn't the only free productivity application. OpenOffice is a strong competitor, and includes a presentation tool and database. It can't rival the Microsoft Office interface, though, and if you open

Office documents they won't always appear as intended (for example, graphs opened in the spreadsheet application might look odd). You can download OpenOffice from www.openoffice.org, or buy any edition of *PC Pro* that comes with a DVD, as we always include the latest version on the disc.

TIED UP We expect Office Starter to be bundled with most new PCs from summer 2010. Unfortunately, if you're not buying a new PC there's no way to download it (legally, at least) – this is currently the only way it's distributed.

IF YOU CAN COPE WITH A FIXED PANEL DOWN THE RIGHT AND ROTATING ADS, WORD STARTER MAY OFFER ALL YOU EVER NEED FROM A WORD PROCESSOR.

Introducing Word Starter 2010

When we heard Microsoft would be giving away a "starter" version of Word for free, we were sceptical about all the features that would be missing. Spellchecking, WordArt, built-in thesaurus – we assumed these would be thrown out in a cynical ploy by Microsoft's money-men to make people press the Upgrade button.

As it turns out, this is far from true. Microsoft has been much more generous than we dared to hope: there's very little a home user would want to do with a Word document that they can't do in Word Starter. While most people will still want the full word processor on their main system, the features that remain may well be enough for a second PC (or netbook) on which you mainly view and edit documents rather than creating them.

WHAT YOU CAN DO One of Word's great strengths compared to rival word processors is its ability to create professional documents with minimum effort. This trend continues with Word Starter, with all the key tools we covered in our guide to Word (see Chapter 3) included here. In particular, you can create themes, insert cover pages, add impact with pictures and apply styles.

Naturally, all the basics are covered too. There's a word count, spelling auto-correction, and the formatting tools everyone uses – bold, italics and underline.

We're also pleased to see Text Effects make the cut; these add advanced touches such as glows, shadows and reflections. Even if you need to whip up a professional report, the tools you need are here: headers, footers, watermarks and much more.

Perhaps most surprisingly, there's even mail merge. So if you have to send out a mailing to all the members of your club, you can follow the six-step wizard and either dispatch emails or letters; Outlook isn't included in Word Starter, but it integrates with Windows Live Mail.

WHAT YOU CAN'T DO Students and academics will be disappointed by the wholesale omission of the References tab. This takes away the nifty ability to create an automated table of contents or use citations in the meaningful way we show on p42. Likewise, the Review tab is nowhere to be seen: you can't add comments, even though you're able to view those from other people. Nor can you track changes.

A number of other small omissions may annoy, such as advanced reading views. For example, many people find it useful to opt for full-screen reading view when checking a document, to avoid distractions. All you can do in Word Starter is switch between print, web, outline and draft layouts (via the icons at the bottom right of the screen, because the View tab is also missing).

A bigger problem for power users is the lack of macro support. This doesn't just mean you can't create macros (command sequences that are used to automate tasks, which we provide a guide to on p21): even if they're already part of the Word document you're viewing, Word Starter won't run them.

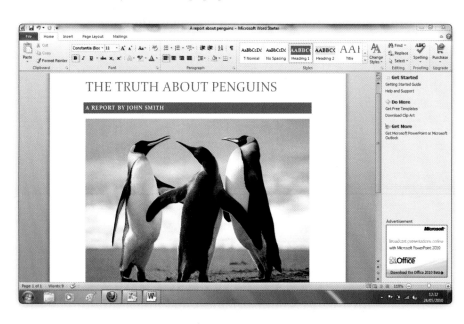

Word Starter is amazingly feature-packed for a free edition. Even advanced features you'd expect to have been culled are included. Exceptions include change tracking and macro support.

WORD STARTER 2010
HOME TAB

All the same features are included in the **Clipboard** group, including the Format Painter: select text that's formatted in the style you want it, click Format Painter, and you can then apply that formatting to any other text too.

You want to add **bullet points**? No problem. Numbered lists? Naturally. Apply a background colour behind certain paragraphs? Your wish is Microsoft's very literal command.

Spelling is the sole visual survivor of Word's Review tab, but click the down arrow and you'll see that thesaurus, word count and even translation services are still available.

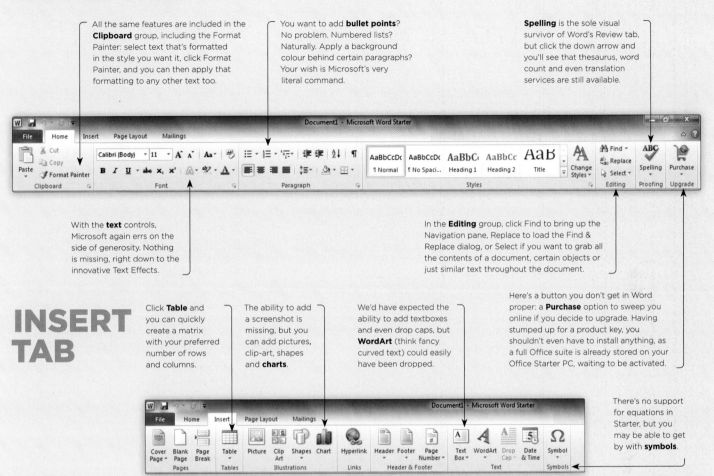

With the **text** controls, Microsoft again errs on the side of generosity. Nothing is missing, right down to the innovative Text Effects.

In the **Editing** group, click Find to bring up the Navigation pane, Replace to load the Find & Replace dialog, or Select if you want to grab all the contents of a document, certain objects or just similar text throughout the document.

INSERT TAB

Click **Table** and you can quickly create a matrix with your preferred number of rows and columns.

The ability to add a screenshot is missing, but you can add pictures, clip-art, shapes and **charts**.

We'd have expected the ability to add textboxes and even drop caps, but **WordArt** (think fancy curved text) could easily have been dropped.

Here's a button you don't get in Word proper: a **Purchase** option to sweep you online if you decide to upgrade. Having stumped up for a product key, you shouldn't even have to install anything, as a full Office suite is already stored on your Office Starter PC, waiting to be activated.

There's no support for equations in Starter, but you may be able to get by with **symbols**.

PAGE LAYOUT

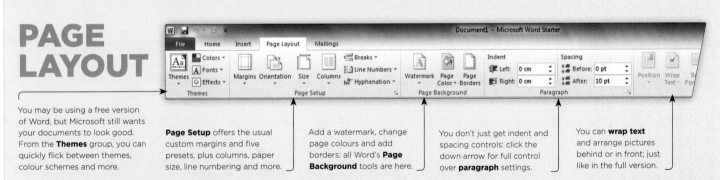

You may be using a free version of Word, but Microsoft still wants your documents to look good. From the **Themes** group, you can quickly flick between themes, colour schemes and more.

Page Setup offers the usual custom margins and five presets, plus columns, paper size, line numbering and more.

Add a watermark, change page colours and add borders: all Word's **Page Background** tools are here.

You don't just get indent and spacing controls: click the down arrow for full control over **paragraph** settings.

You can wrap **text** and arrange pictures behind or in front; just like in the full version.

MAILINGS TAB

Mail merge is one of those areas where Microsoft could have chopped out functionality to ensure advanced users pay for the full product. But no, everything on the Mailings tab is lifted wholesale from Word. There's precisely nothing you can't do in Word Starter that you can do in the full version.

Office Starter

11

Introducing Excel Starter 2010

There are many alternatives to Word that people can use happily – obvious examples being the word processor bundled with OpenOffice.org (www.openoffice.org) and Google Docs (http://docs.google.com) – but it's much tougher to find a free spreadsheet application that comes close to matching Excel.

While both OpenOffice.org and Google provide usable rivals, they lack the finesse and flexibility of Microsoft's offering. They're fine for simple tasks, such as creating structured lists, and OpenOffice even includes some quite advanced powers. However, they're little use if you want to present data in professional-looking charts, as just one example.

So can Excel Starter be a viable alternative? In short, yes. Although Microsoft omits a large number of features when you compare it to Excel proper, if you need to whip up a chart or perform simple analysis it remains a brilliant choice.

WHAT YOU CAN DO Microsoft hasn't removed any of the basics from Excel 2010 Starter. You can add the same array of colourful charts, benefit from an instant professional look courtesy of the themes, and use all the formulae found in the full-fat version. That's particularly impressive when you consider the power on offer – right down to the obscure functions that only engineers and statisticians will use.

What's really useful, though, is the inclusion of the basic formatting tools that most people need to

easily present data. Conditional formatting is one obvious example. In what would otherwise be a dry collection of numbers, for example, conditional formatting can instantly draw out "hot" data by adding a red fill to the hottest (highest) numbers and blue to the coldest (lowest) numbers.

In a similar fashion, Sparklines (see p52) can add instant trendlines to a row of data, allowing you to pick out the winners and losers at a glance.

WHAT YOU CAN'T DO You could use Excel Starter for years and never miss a single feature. PivotTables (see p56) are an omission that will be regretted by people who need to analyse data to any degree. Slicers – a debut feature in Excel 2010 – are also omitted, which means that even if you're analysing a spreadsheet that already includes PivotTables, you won't be able to add a slicer to aid analysis.

The Data and Review tabs are nowhere to be found, either. As we discuss on p58, dealing with external data is one of Excel's most advanced powers, so it's no surprise that Microsoft has removed it wholesale from Office Starter. Some of the omissions from Review are more disappointing, though: you can't add a comment to a spreadsheet in Excel Starter, nor can you protect cells – a useful tool if you want to share a spreadsheet with others, but don't want them to see the data that lies beneath, or mess up any of the formulae.

Overall, though, it's hard to argue with Microsoft's decisions. Excel Starter is a surprisingly powerful tool.

Q&A

Q: If I open a spreadsheet in Excel Starter that was created in a full version of Excel, will it lose any advanced features – like PivotTables – if I edit the file and resave it?

A: No. When you come to open that file again – for example, if you have Excel at work but only Excel Starter at home – all the advanced features will still be there. Of course, your edits might affect the results they display.

Excel Starter perhaps has more obvious omissions than Word, including some everyday functions such as the ability to protect cells from accidental editing or add comments, but remains a highly functional spreadsheet – and there aren't many of those you can get free of charge.

EXCEL STARTER 2010
HOME TAB

No surprises in the **Clipboard** group: Cut, Copy and Paste are all present and correct, along with Format Painter, which quickly copies formatting from one cell to another.

The **Alignment** group is self-explanatory: align text left or right within cells, for example, or merge cells together using the commands here. As in Excel proper, you can also set whether long text runs over into the next cell or wraps downwards, expanding its cell to fit.

The five **Editing** buttons let you sort data from lowest to highest, auto-sum a row or column of figures, or hunt for words, data or formulae.

In **Proofing**, the spellchecker, thesaurus, translator and other reference tools can all be called up by clicking the down arrow.

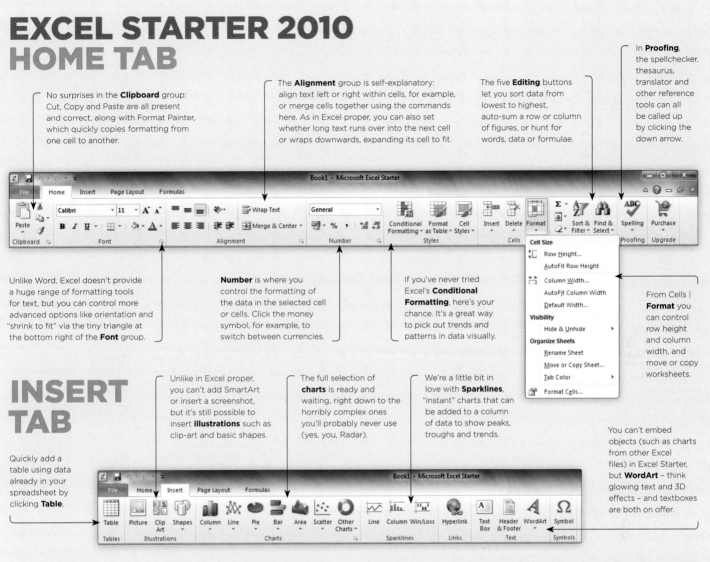

Unlike Word, Excel doesn't provide a huge range of formatting tools for text, but you can control more advanced options like orientation and "shrink to fit" via the tiny triangle at the bottom right of the **Font** group.

Number is where you control the formatting of the data in the selected cell or cells. Click the money symbol, for example, to switch between currencies.

If you've never tried Excel's **Conditional Formatting**, here's your chance. It's a great way to pick out trends and patterns in data visually.

From Cells | **Format** you can control row height and column width, and move or copy worksheets.

INSERT TAB

Quickly add a table using data already in your spreadsheet by clicking **Table**.

Unlike in Excel proper, you can't add SmartArt or insert a screenshot, but it's still possible to insert **illustrations** such as clip-art and basic shapes.

The full selection of **charts** is ready and waiting, right down to the horribly complex ones you'll probably never use (yes, you, Radar).

We're a little bit in love with **Sparklines**, "instant" charts that can be added to a column of data to show peaks, troughs and trends.

You can't embed objects (such as charts from other Excel files) in Excel Starter, but **WordArt** – think glowing text and 3D effects – and textboxes are both on offer.

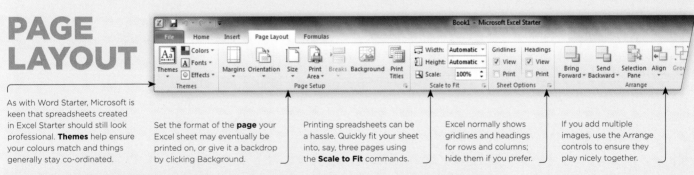

PAGE LAYOUT

As with Word Starter, Microsoft is keen that spreadsheets created in Excel Starter should still look professional. **Themes** help ensure your colours match and things generally stay co-ordinated.

Set the format of the **page** your Excel sheet may eventually be printed on, or give it a backdrop by clicking Background.

Printing spreadsheets can be a hassle. Quickly fit your sheet into, say, three pages using the **Scale to Fit** commands.

Excel normally shows gridlines and headings for rows and columns; hide them if you prefer.

If you add multiple images, use the Arrange controls to ensure they play nicely together.

FORMULAS TAB

We're very impressed that Microsoft has included all the same functions in Excel Starter as in the full version. The only omissions from the Formulas tab are auditing commands, which help you trace errors in complex formulae.

IN THIS CHAPTER

12

Office Web Apps

OFFICE WEB APP

For the first time, Word, Excel, PowerPoint and OneNote will now be available not only as desktop or mobile phone software, but also through a web browser. No longer will you need Word installed on your PC to make changes to a document, or PowerPoint on your laptop to run through your slides. All you'll need is a web browser and a broadband connection.

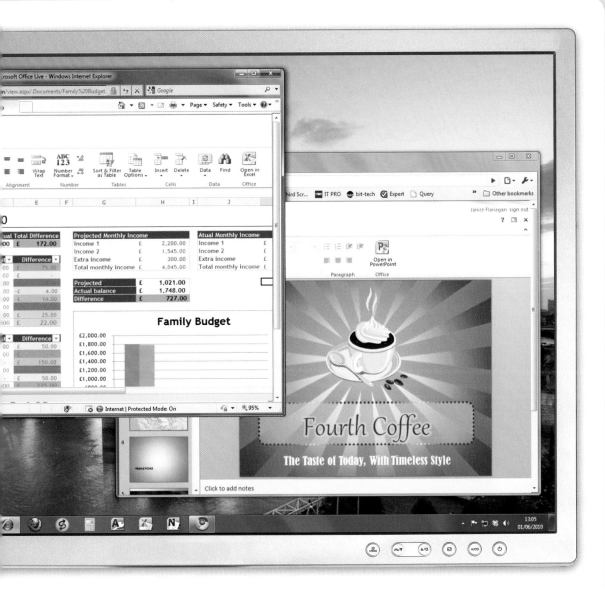

But don't be lulled into thinking the Office Web Apps could replace Office: they're more of a complement than a replacement. Most of the suite's features are unavailable if you try to create a document from scratch, although many more come into play if you're editing a file already created in Office 2010. Here, we reveal what each of the Web Apps can and can't do.

THERE'S A CHOICE OF TWO WAYS TO ACCESS THE OFFICE WEB APPS. HERE'S HOW TO GET HOLD OF THEM AND START WORKING ON DOCUMENTS ONLINE.

Where to get the Web Apps

There are two ways for people to get hold of the Office Web Apps. For consumers, they're available via Microsoft's free online storage service, SkyDrive. Businesses that operate their own Microsoft SharePoint server can also access them from their company's secure document store, mitigating the risk of leaving confidential commercial documents on the open internet or on USB sticks.

SKYDRIVE Microsoft's SkyDrive has been running for a couple of years now, providing 25GB of free online storage, with separate folders for documents, music and digital photos. While that amount of storage seems generous – it's more than enough space to hold thousands of documents in addition to most people's digital music collection – taking advantage of all that free capacity isn't as easy as it sounds.

In particular, there's a limit of 50MB on individual file uploads: while that's ample for the majority of documents, large spreadsheets and Word documents stuffed with images might fall foul of the limit. Files can only be uploaded in small batches, so there's no easy way to back up your entire documents folder. That makes it impractical as a regular online backup service, and more of a temporary holding bay for files you want to access from different PCs.

Another way to move files to SkyDrive is via Microsoft's Live Sync service (previously called Live Mesh). This allows up to 2GB of files and folders on your PC to be added to the Live Sync system, and they'll be automatically synchronised with your main PC each time you go online. If you use Microsoft's Hotmail service, any Office documents attached to emails can also be saved to your SkyDrive.

Follow the steps opposite to access the Office Web Apps from www.skydrive.com.

SHAREPOINT SERVER The 2010 version of Microsoft's SharePoint Server also includes support for the Office Web Apps. If your company runs a SharePoint server you'll know that, instead of saving files directly to your computer's hard disk, SharePoint allows you to save them to the company's servers, where you and your colleagues can access them. This allows several team members to work on the same spreadsheet, for example, without having to email each other the file or risk working on two competing versions.

With SharePoint 2010, instead of downloading the file for editing on your PC, you can work on the files directly from the web browser. Alongside each file stored on the server, you'll find a down arrow containing a dropdown menu with various options, including Edit in Browser. Only one person can edit a document at a time – apart from Excel spreadsheets and OneNote workbooks, where simultaneous editing of the same file is permitted.

Not every company will have a SharePoint server, and even those that do may still be running on older versions that don't support the Microsoft Web Apps. Check with your IT department.

Tip

Although Microsoft lets you upload only a few files at a time to SkyDrive, there are unofficial ways around the limitations. Software such as Gladinet (www.gladinet.com) treats SkyDrive like any other disk drive on your computer, allowing you to drag and drop files or entire folders into Microsoft's online storage. Be warned, though: Microsoft doesn't officially support services such as Gladinet, and the software may stop working at any moment.

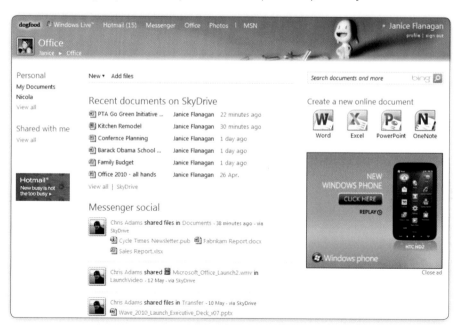

Microsoft makes it easy to create new documents once you've logged into your SkyDrive account, while listing any documents you've recently accessed.

HOW TO...
USE THE WEB APPS IN SKYDRIVE

Finding the Office Web Apps isn't as easy as you might expect. Here, we'll show you how to create a Microsoft SkyDrive account and start uploading documents.

① CREATE AN ACCOUNT To access SkyDrive, you need a Windows Live ID. If you've signed up for Hotmail or Windows Live Mail, you can use this login. If not, you'll need to register when you first visit www.skydrive.com. Registration is free, and you can sign up as many times as you like – keeping one account for work, for example, and another for personal files.

② UPLOAD A DOCUMENT Once you've created your SkyDrive account, you'll need to start uploading documents to edit. SkyDrive offers both private and public folders. Only you can access your private folders, which have a little padlock sign next to their name. The Public folder can be accessed by anyone on the internet, unless you click on the Edit Permissions link in a Public folder and restrict access to people you know.

Whether you decide to make a document private or public, the upload process is the same. If you have Microsoft's Silverlight technology installed (www.microsoft.com/getsilverlight) then you can drag and drop files into My Documents. If you don't have Silverlight, you'll have to use a more basic browse-and-pick method.

You can upload any document file type, but it's safest to save documents in the default Microsoft format if you plan to edit them using the Web Apps.

③ EDIT THE DOCUMENT You can now edit any of your uploaded documents by clicking on the file's name or icon, and selecting Edit in Browser from the next screen. The document appears in the relevant Office Web App, with the ribbon interface along the top. As we'll see on the following pages, you won't see all the buttons and features you're used to: some are withheld from the Web Apps, while others appear only when you perform certain actions, such as clicking on a picture. Any changes you make in the Web Apps are automatically saved – there's no Save button. But if you've uploaded a document, changes aren't saved back to the file on your PC. You have to download the new version.

④ CREATE A NEW DOCUMENT You can also create documents from scratch using the Web Apps. In your My Documents folder, click New and select which type of file to create from the dropdown menu. Or, click any of the four icons that sit to the right of the page, just below the search field. Note, though, that the Web Apps' biggest strengths are editing existing documents rather than creating new ones.

HOW LONG?
The most time-consuming part is uploading your files.

HOW HARD?
Step-by-step guidance makes it simple.

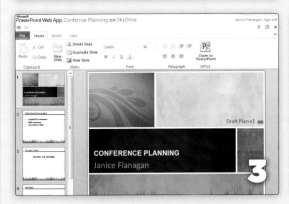

LEARN HOW TO VIEW AND EDIT DOCUMENTS – AND FIND OUT WHAT YOU CAN AND CAN'T DO ONLINE – WITH THE OFFICE 2010 WORD WEB APP.

Introducing the Word Web App

Word is probably the Microsoft Office application that most people use every day. With the introduction of the Web Apps, you no longer need to have the software installed on all your PCs to create and edit your documents. However, it isn't about to replace the desktop software, as we'll see.

WHAT YOU CAN DO The Word Web App is superb for viewing and tweaking documents you've created using the full version of Word on your PC. Documents appear in the Web App exactly as they appear in the desktop software – even long, elaborately formatted documents. That means all the fonts, tables, photos or SmartArt graphics you spent hours labouring over won't go awry, unlike with other online word processors, such as Google Docs. (Note that the editing, rather than the reading view, is far more stripped-down.)

Although there's only a limited selection of fonts available in the Word Web App when you decide to create a document from scratch, any font you've used in an existing document will be made available when you upload it to the Web App, so you'll never have to compromise on design.

The Web App is also surprisingly sprightly, even with massive documents, allowing you to scroll through dozens of pages without judder. Better still, the excellent new Find feature in Office 2010 is retained in the Web Apps, making it easy to hunt down words or phrases using the new preview bar on the left-hand side of the screen.

While it's possible to create new documents using the Word Web App, it isn't something we'd recommend for anything but the most basic of letters or reports. The limited selection of fonts, layout tools and features means it's best for hammering out chunks of plain text, not complete professional-looking documents.

WHAT YOU CAN'T DO While the desktop version of Office 2010 has seven different tabs full of features running across the ribbon at the top of the screen, the Word Web App has only three – and even they are sparsely populated. It's possible Microsoft may add to these over time, but don't be fooled into thinking this is in any way comparable to the desktop software.

Among the more notable features not to make the cut are the page-layout tools: forget about adding niceties such as page borders or margins, or changing the page orientation using the Web App. Handy reference tools such as the thesaurus are also omitted, and although the spellchecker remains, it's so rudimentary and awkwardly implemented that it's as good as useless. On the plus side, the Word Web App will still draw a little red squiggle under incorrectly spelt words, giving you a visual clue that you may have entered a typo.

Perhaps the most surprising omission from the Word Web App is the option to edit documents simultaneously with other users. This feature has been a staple of rival services (such as Google Docs) for many years, and it's difficult to see why Microsoft is unwilling to let multiple people collaborate on a Word document, when it's built the feature into the Excel and OneNote Web Apps. This facility may well be added in time.

Tip

Make sure you save documents regularly while working in the Word Web App. It doesn't have the auto-recovery features found in the desktop version of Word, and you could find you lose work if you suddenly drop your internet connection or the browser crashes.

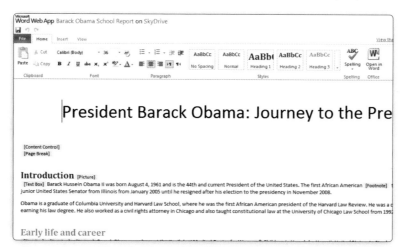

The Word Web App is a long way from being a substitute for Word running on your PC, but handy for viewing existing documents online.

THE WORD WEB APP
HOME TAB

Use these buttons to **cut, copy and paste** text. As you'd expect, you can also use the standard keyboard shortcuts: Ctrl-X, Ctrl-C and Ctrl-V respectively.

Bullet points, numbered lists and options to indent and realign text are available in the **Paragraph** section.

If you decide you need the enhanced editing power of the full-blown Office 2010 desktop software, you can always click this button to **open the document in Word**.

Microsoft
Word Web App Barack Obama School Report **on** SkyDrive

View the

| File | Home | Insert | View |

Cut — Calibri (Body) — 36

Paste — Copy — **B** *I* U abc x₂ x² ab A

No Spacing | Normal | AaBb Heading 1 | AaBbCc Heading 2 | AaBbCc Heading 3

ABC Spelling — Open in Word

The selection of **fonts** available in the Word Web App is nowhere near as extensive as the list in the desktop software, but there are still almost 50 to choose from. The ability to highlight and change the colour of fonts is also retained.

A variety of predefined **styles** can be applied to Word Web App documents, helping to maintain consistency between headings and body text in documents. Click on the down arrow on the right-hand side of the Styles box to uncover a pop-up menu containing even more options.

The **spellchecker** in the Word Web App is basic, with no option to even ignore a word and move on to the next (this may be updated over time). The Web App does at least underline misspelt words, giving you a chance to put errors right yourself.

INSERT TAB

Click here to **insert a table** into your document. A dropdown menu will appear, containing a grid of squares. Drag the mouse across the grid until you have the number of columns and rows required for your table. Don't worry if you get it wrong: rows and columns can be added or deleted later by right-clicking on the table.

This option allows you to **create clickable links** to websites without having to include the ugly web address in your documents. Insert the full web address (including the http://) into the address box and just type the site's name – or something such as "click here to see our website" – in the Display text.

VIEW TAB

| File | Home | Insert | View |

Table | Picture | Clip Art | Link

Tables | Pictures | Links

You can **insert a photo** stored on your PC into the document by clicking here. It may be wise to resize large photos first, since it can take several minutes to upload the high-quality photos produced by today's digital cameras on regular broadband connections.

A neat feature of the Word Web App is the option to **insert Microsoft-provided clip-art** into your documents. Simply choose a search term (for example, "dog" or "red") and Microsoft will hunt down photos you can use from its online vault. You'll notice that when you add a photo or clip-art, a new Picture Tools tab appears, which allows you to resize the image.

The **Editing View** allows you to make changes to your documents. Don't panic if some of the formatting, borders or background colours have disappeared in this view – they'll still be retained when you look at the document in Reading View.

The **Reading View** shows you exactly what the fully polished document looks like, with all the tables, photos and other elements intact.

| File | Home | Insert | View |

Editing View | Reading View

Document Views

THE POWER OF EXCEL IS TRANSFERRED TO THE WEB. FIND OUT HOW TO START WORKING WITH YOUR SPREADSHEETS IN OUR BUTTON-BY-BUTTON GUIDE.

Introducing the Excel Web App

Excel is a fearsomely powerful piece of software, and many doubted it could be successfully converted into a web app. Yet Microsoft has done an amazing job of preserving its features and utility. Indeed, so far, Excel is far and away the most successful of all the Office Web Apps.

WHAT YOU CAN DO The Excel Web App's great strength is the way it retains the formatting and integrity of even the most complex of spreadsheets. Uploaded workbooks look exactly the same as they do in Excel 2010, including graphs, conditional formatting and new graphical features such as Sparklines (see p52 for more on these).

What's most impressive, however, is the way the Web App almost instantly updates when data is added or altered. Changing one of the figures in the table in our example spreadsheet (below) sees the bar chart amended, the conditional colours adjusted, and the little Sparklines at the end of each row updated – each within a second or two. It isn't as snappy as the desktop software, but still impressive given the complexity of what's going on in a humble web browser. We've thrown huge, multisheet workbooks at the Excel Web App and it's coped admirably with them all.

Another standout feature of the Excel Web App is co-authoring. Two or more people can edit a spreadsheet at the same time, which is great if you and a colleague want to work on business data simultaneously, or even if one person merely wants to view a spreadsheet while the other is busy plugging in new figures. Edits are updated on both people's screens within a second or two, so there's little danger of conflicts due to two people trying to change the same piece of data.

As can be seen from the illustrations opposite, Microsoft has also covered the basics of formatting and data manipulation. You can add rows and columns, and refresh any existing data sources. But, as we'll see below, there are some obvious restrictions as well.

WHAT YOU CAN'T DO While the Excel Web App is brilliant at coping with graphs and other graphical elements already embedded into an uploaded spreadsheet, it doesn't currently allow you to create new graphs, Sparklines or Pivot Tables with raw figures. Indeed, there are only two things you can insert into your spreadsheet: tables and web links. Likewise, the handy Formulas tab is missing from the Web App, meaning you'll have to tap out complex formulae by hand if you want to start manipulating freshly entered data.

In summary, the Excel Web App is near-perfect for tweaking data in established spreadsheets that have their charts, formulae and other elements already inserted, but the cracks start showing when you try to do anything more ambitious.

Q&A

Q: I've just tried the Excel Web App and it looks different to your screenshots – why?
A: Unlike the main Office programs, the Office Web Apps are continually being updated by Microsoft, so it may well be that the interface changes over time as new features are added.

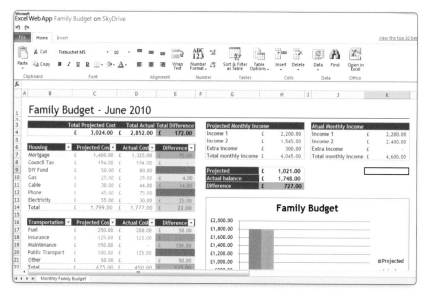

The Excel Web App is much more capable than the Word equivalent, allowing multiple users to work on the same document simultaneously.

THE EXCEL WEB APP
HOME TAB

Use these controls to **cut, copy and paste** data in your spreadsheets. Note the dropdown menu under Paste: this allows you to access advanced options, such as only pasting values or formulae.

The various **alignment** options let you alter the position of numbers and text in their cells – shifting them to the top or bottom or aligning them left or right, for instance. The Wrap Text option automatically increases the height of a cell when text runs out of space within it.

Forgotten to include some data? Use the Insert button to **add extra rows or columns** to your spreadsheet or tables. Delete eradicates unwanted rows or columns and closes up the table, so that there are no ugly blank rows in the middle of your spreadsheet.

Use these controls to change the **font, size and colour** of your text, as well as the shading behind cells. There are also options to bold, italicise and underline (or even double-underline) text and numbers.

The **Number Format** option lets you tell Excel exactly what kind of data it's dealing with – for example, currency, time or percentage – so that it handles the figures appropriately. The other two options in this box allow you to quickly increase or decrease the number of decimal points displayed in the selected cells.

To present information in a table (like the sales figures in our example), highlight the relevant data and then press the **Sort & Filter as Table** button. You can now manipulate the data in a variety of more advanced ways (see below). The **Table Options** button can be used to add or remove headings and totals rows.

Use the **Data** dropdown menu to refresh data in any PivotTables you have (see p56) or to manually refresh all the data input by different users of the Web App, so you can be absolutely sure there's no outdated information in the sheet you're working on. The Calculate Workbook button refreshes all the data in your spreadsheet, ensuring all formulae has been properly applied.

INSERT TAB

To **insert a web address** into your sheet, click this button. It will ensure users can click straight through to the site from the spreadsheet, once you've filled out the simple form.

Click here to **insert a table** into your sheet. A dropdown menu appears containing a grid of squares. Drag the mouse across the grid until you have the number of columns and rows required for your table. Don't worry if you get it wrong: rows and columns can be added or deleted later by right-clicking on the table.

FILTERS

Number Filters could be used, say, to rank stores by sales in July. Click the down arrow by the "Jul" label and pick Sort Descending. The other figures shuffle accordingly. You could also choose to show only stores that performed below average, for example.

Text Filters could be used to sort the towns into alphabetical order, in a similar way to Number Filters. The figures shift accordingly. To see the data just for, say, Manchester and Newcastle, click "Filter..." at the foot of the box and untick the others. Further options, such as only selecting stores that begin with a certain letter, are of more use when dealing with larger tables.

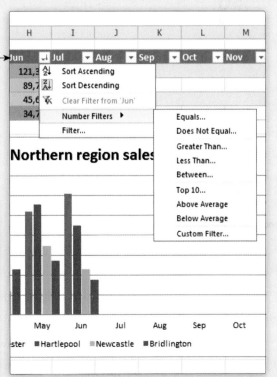

FIND OUT HOW YOU CAN SMARTEN UP AND SHOW YOUR BUSINESS PRESENTATIONS FROM A WEB BROWSER WITH THE POWERPOINT WEB APP.

Introducing the PowerPoint Web App

It may have its critics, but PowerPoint remains the de facto software for delivering slick-looking business presentations. PowerPoint is one of the most improved applications in the Office 2010 line-up (see Chapter 5 for more on its new features), and the arrival of the PowerPoint Web App adds another string to its bow.

The ability to make even quite sophisticated edits to a presentation, or rehearse slideshows, from a web browser will make the PowerPoint Web App a valuable tool for many executives and lecturers – and one they don't have to pay a penny extra for. We'll show you what the PowerPoint Web App has to offer, and highlight the things it can't do.

WHAT YOU CAN DO The arrival of the PowerPoint Web App may mean the end of having to borrow a work laptop for the weekend to finalise Monday morning's presentation. Upload your presentation to Microsoft's SkyDrive or your company's SharePoint server, and you can run through a full fidelity version of the slideshow – complete with any slide notes you may have made – directly from the web browser.

Fancy features such as photo frames, whooshing 3D transitions and animations are preserved in the browser version. The only thing that doesn't transfer well is embedded video, which is replaced with ugly black boxes instead of your chosen clips.

Making edits to slides is straightforward too – and not only minor tweaks such as changing a caption here or

there. Click on a picture, for example, and a special ribbon tab appears that allows you to add refined touches such as rounded 3D photo frames from right there in the browser. Or select a SmartArt diagram and you can change its style, colouring and content.

Admittedly, we've come across more than a couple of glitches when we've attempted to make edits, but it's early days for these online applications, and we're confident the reliability and features will improve over time.

WHAT YOU CAN'T DO The major shortfall of the PowerPoint Web App is its lack of ability when it comes to creating a presentation from scratch. While it's technically possible to do so, you'll be limited to a handful of preset slideshow themes, and this is the only way to change the background colour of slides. You're also very limited when it comes to making big changes to an existing presentation's appearance; while we do appreciate the ability to insert pictures, complete with the fancy effects described above, sometimes you need to take more drastic measures.

With web-based rivals such as Adobe and Zoho (see p156) providing the option to create better-looking slideshows without desktop software, the PowerPoint Web App is left looking underwhelming. Clearly, its main strength is as an accompaniment to the desktop version rather than as any sort of creation tool in its own right. As with the OneNote Web App, we hope Microsoft continues to develop PowerPoint over the coming months.

Q&A

Q: If I'm presenting at a venue, what equipment will I need to access my PowerPoint online?
A: As with the other Web Apps, you should be able to use any PC with an internet connection and Internet Explorer 6 or higher; other recent browsers should also work, including Safari on Macs. However, we'd always take at least a copy of our slideshow on a USB drive, in case of glitches like the connection going down.

The PowerPoint Web App will only let you create basic presentations from scratch, but it's great for viewing, testing and tweaking what you've prepared in the desktop app.

THE POWERPOINT WEB APP
HOME TAB

Use the buttons to **cut, copy and paste** items, or use the keyboard shortcuts: Ctrl-X, Ctrl-C and Ctrl-V.

These buttons allow you to **add or remove slides** in your presentation. When you click on New Slide, you'll be given a selection of different slide templates to choose from. The Duplicate Slide button allows you to create an exact copy of a slide, which is handy if you want to copy the format of a previous slide. The Hide Slide feature removes the slide from the Slideshow but, unlike deleting, keeps the content in case you later wish to reinstate it.

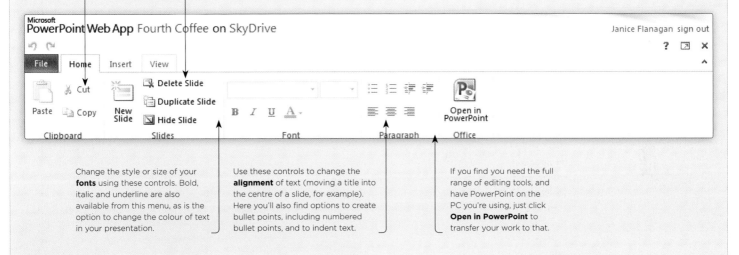

Change the style or size of your **fonts** using these controls. Bold, italic and underline are also available from this menu, as is the option to change the colour of text in your presentation.

Use these controls to change the **alignment** of text (moving a title into the centre of a slide, for example). Here you'll also find options to create bullet points, including numbered bullet points, and to indent text.

If you find you need the full range of editing tools, and have PowerPoint on the PC you're using, just click **Open in PowerPoint** to transfer your work to that.

To **move a slide** to a new position in your slideshow, simply drag and drop its thumbnail into the desired slot in the list.

Use this button to **insert a photo** stored on your computer into a slideshow. PowerPoint accepts photos in most of the common formats, including JPEG, TIFF and GIF.

INSERT TAB

This allows you to insert a selection of business-orientated graphics, dubbed **SmartArt**, into your slideshow. When you click the button, a dropdown menu appears with a wide variety of elements to choose from. Once you've made your choice, the SmartArt Tools tab will appear, providing even greater control over the layout of the graphics.

VIEW TAB

The **Editing View** allows you to make changes to the text, photos, SmartArt or other elements within your presentation.

The **Reading View** is the best way to skim through your presentation while viewing any accompanying notes. Click the Notes button at the foot of the screen to make the relevant notes appear in a pane beneath your slides.

Click here to start a **full-screen slideshow** of your presentation. This feature lets you present without bringing anything along with you, as long as internet access is available on the venue's PC, and could be a lifesaver if your laptop fails on the way to a meeting or the boardroom projector won't work with your machine.

Click this button to **add presenter notes** to a particular slide. These notes aren't visible to your audience during the slideshow; they're intended to be used as an aide memoire, to help prevent you running dry during a talk.

ONENOTE IS SOMETIMES OVERLOOKED WITHIN OFFICE, BUT THE WEB APP IS A GREAT WAY TO SHARE MEMOS AND NOTEBOOKS WITH COLLEAGUES ONLINE.

Introducing the OneNote Web App

OneNote is the rising star of the Office suite, elbowing its way in alongside Word, Excel and PowerPoint as a key member of the line-up. Its growing status is reinforced by becoming only the fourth app to be converted into an Office Web App, leapfrogging long-established stalwarts such as Access and Publisher. So what does the OneNote Web App have to offer?

WHAT YOU CAN DO Although the other Office Web Apps do a pretty good job of retaining all the information stored in documents created on the desktop, OneNote falls remarkably short in this respect (as we'll see later). That said, it faithfully preserves any typed text, photos or web clippings, which is all that the majority of OneNote pages will contain.

Along with Excel, OneNote is only the second Web App that allows co-authoring, meaning more than one person can edit the same notebook at the same time. That could come into its own in brainstorming meetings, where several people are trying to jot down ideas for a project simultaneously.

It also keeps track of which person edited which boxes on a page, so you'll never be left in the dark about who suggested a certain idea. The OneNote Web App also allows you to tag text or pictures stored in notebooks, which means you can mark an item as "important" or a good "idea". This is especially handy when multiple people are working on the same notebook, since it allows you to get instant feedback on your ideas from co-workers.

WHAT YOU CAN'T DO This is Microsoft's first stab at the OneNote Web App, so it's likely to improve in the future, but so far the number of items that the online software can't display is a disappointment. Any drawings, shapes or handwritten annotations added to OneNote pages aren't displayed in the web browser, which could result in critical parts of pages going missing when they're stored online.

Multimedia content is also conspicuous by its absence. Although it's possible to add audio and video clips to notebooks using the desktop software, they're stripped out online. In its defence, the Web App does show a warning message if there are parts of the page it can't display, so at least you're not left completely in the dark – and you have the option to download the full page into the desktop version of OneNote if there's a video you really must see.

In conclusion, the OneNote Web App shows early promise, but we hope Microsoft will continue to bulk out the features and display options as the software evolves.

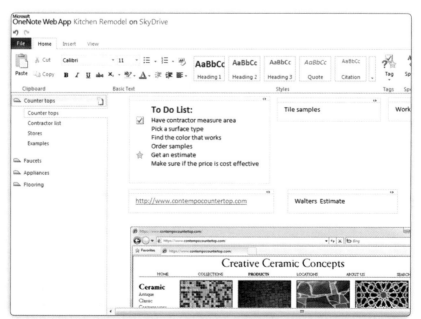

OneNote is potentially very handy to have as an online app, especially with the facility to edit notebooks at the same time as other users. However, a lot of the features we'd like and expect to see are still missing.

THE ONENOTE WEB APP
HOME TAB

Use these buttons to **cut, copy and paste** items to and from OneNote notebooks. Alternatively, you can use the familiar keyboard shortcuts: Ctrl-X, Ctrl-C and Ctrl-V.

Tags allow you to mark up certain text or images within a notebook. So, for example, you could place the little lightbulb icon next to a piece of text to show it's a good idea, or put a star next to a box heading to emphasise its importance. Tags are exceptionally handy when working in groups, as other people can see what you think of their suggestions.

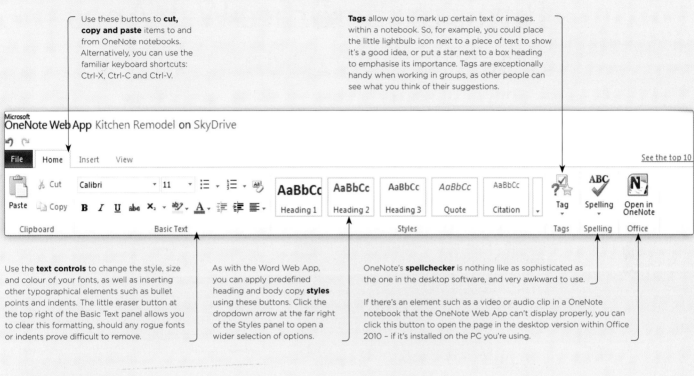

Use the **text controls** to change the style, size and colour of your fonts, as well as inserting other typographical elements such as bullet points and indents. The little eraser button at the top right of the Basic Text panel allows you to clear this formatting, should any rogue fonts or indents prove difficult to remove.

As with the Word Web App, you can apply predefined heading and body copy **styles** using these buttons. Click the dropdown arrow at the far right of the Styles panel to open a wider selection of options.

OneNote's **spellchecker** is nothing like as sophisticated as the one in the desktop software, and very awkward to use.

If there's an element such as a video or audio clip in a OneNote notebook that the OneNote Web App can't display properly, you can click this button to open the page in the desktop version within Office 2010 – if it's installed on the PC you're using.

INSERT TAB

Microsoft provides a free library of **clip-art** images that can be used to brighten up your notebooks. You'll get the option to resize the graphic when it's inserted into your page.

Click here to **add a new page** to the notebook. You'll be prompted to insert a title for the page, which will be saved automatically.

Use this button before inserting **web links** into your pages to ensure other users can click straight through to the website from OneNote. This option also allows you to shorten ugly URLs – for example, replacing http://www.bbc.co.uk/sport with "BBC Sport website".

VIEW TAB

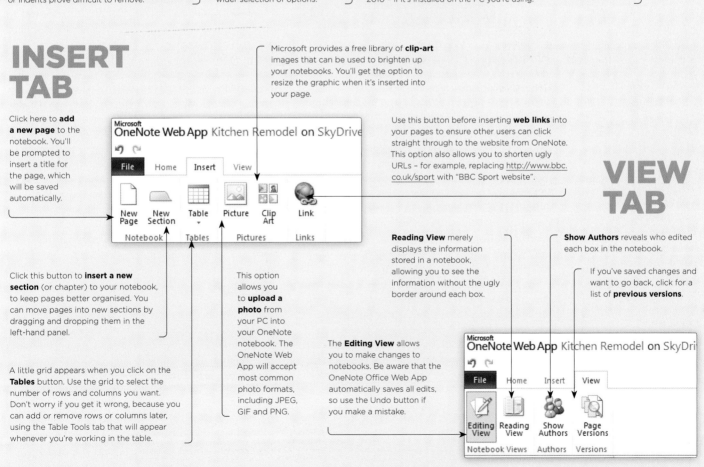

Click this button to **insert a new section** (or chapter) to your notebook, to keep pages better organised. You can move pages into new sections by dragging and dropping them in the left-hand panel.

This option allows you to **upload a photo** from your PC into your OneNote notebook. The OneNote Web App will accept most common photo formats, including JPEG, GIF and PNG.

Reading View merely displays the information stored in a notebook, allowing you to see the information without the ugly border around each box.

Show Authors reveals who edited each box in the notebook.

If you've saved changes and want to go back, click for a list of **previous versions**.

A little grid appears when you click on the **Tables** button. Use the grid to select the number of rows and columns you want. Don't worry if you get it wrong, because you can add or remove rows or columns later, using the Table Tools tab that will appear whenever you're working in the table.

The **Editing View** allows you to make changes to notebooks. Be aware that the OneNote Office Web App automatically saves all edits, so use the Undo button if you make a mistake.

MICROSOFT ISN'T THE ONLY COMPANY PRODUCING FREE OFFICE APPLICATIONS ON THE INTERNET. SEE WHAT'S ON OFFER FROM THREE OF ITS COMPETITORS.

Rivals to the Office Web Apps

The Office Web Apps are among the new features of the 2010 suite, but Microsoft's rivals have been providing online office suites for years. Many of them offer features that simply aren't available in Microsoft's products – and best of all, they normally do it for free.

So before you commit to using Office Web Apps, it might be worth considering one of the alternatives, whether it's from a well-known company such as Google or Adobe or a little-known newcomer such as Zoho. Here's what you'll find in these three vendors' suites.

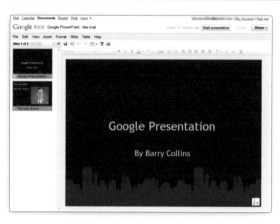

Google Docs

Google's online software is probably the best-known alternative to Microsoft's Web Apps. It includes a word processor, spreadsheet, PowerPoint-like presentation software and more.

The key advantage Google's online word processor holds over that of Microsoft, at least for the moment, is simultaneous editing: documents can be shared with as many colleagues as you wish, and they can all make changes to the document at the same time. That may sound chaotic, and it certainly isn't ideal if two people attempt to tweak the same piece of text at the same time, but it's a wonderful tool for brainstorming, when you want multiple people to contribute ideas to a project.

However, the Google word processor also shares many of the Word Web App's faults. Creating professional documents from scratch is almost impossible, due to the limited selection of fonts and formatting options. While you can upload neat-looking documents created in the desktop version of Word, much of the advanced formatting is discarded by Google Docs. A ridiculously tight upload limit of 500KB per document also means Google Docs may not accept documents with a smattering of photos or other graphics, such as brochures.

Google Spreadsheet is improving all the time, and is increasingly used by publications such as

The Guardian to share large amounts of data with its readers, such as tables of MPs' expenses and school league tables (www.guardian.co.uk/data-store). The spreadsheet formatting options are more advanced than those in the word processor, but it often struggles to cope with complex formulae in documents from Excel.

Once again, it's a brave executive who tries to create a presentation using the rudimentary themes and formatting options in the Google Presentation tool, but the online app does a good job of preserving most of the transitions and effects in presentations created with PowerPoint. At the very least, that makes Google's service a decent free backup in case your laptop fails on the way. http://docs.google.com

Zoho

Zoho is without question the most powerful online office suite we've come across. All of its myriad applications have full, desktop software-like toolbars, putting the likes of Google Docs to shame with a vast range of features and formatting options.

Zoho Word is reminiscent of Word 2003 in its design and features. Although that may sound old hat, the features on offer are more than capable of producing documents that look like they've been created by using desktop software, unlike both the Word Web App and

Tip

Make sure you don't leave your only copy of vital documents stored in online services. Always save a copy to your computer or an external hard disk if possible. Although most online services have excellent reliability records, there's no guarantee the service won't suddenly close or that files won't be deleted from your account. As ever with data, it's always wise to have a backup.

Google Docs. And while no-one could argue that Zoho is as responsive as desktop software, it's certainly no slouch on a decent broadband connection.

Documents can be shared online with other Zoho users, emailed or published on a website. Innovatively, it also allows you to embed your documents into your own website, so you can publish the company's annual report on the About Us page, for example.

Aside from the usual word processing, spreadsheet and presentation apps, Zoho has a battery of other online applications, including calendars, project management tools and email. Not all of them are magnificent, but Zoho should be the first port of call for anyone considering a shift to online applications.
www.zoho.com

Adobe Acrobat.com

Adobe's stock in trade is making pages look good – this MagBook was designed using its InDesign software. So it should come as little surprise that Adobe's online word processor places aesthetics above all else. There might be a limited selection of fonts in Buzzword, but they all boast a notable typographical elegance on the printed page.

Adobe's other area of expertise is photography, so inserting images and making text flow neatly around them is also a cinch with Acrobat.com's word processor. If your chief priority is to make a document that's easy on the eye, Buzzword should be top of your list of online

applications. Better still, Adobe allows you to export those documents in its PDF format when complete, making them easy to email to other people.

In addition to Buzzword, Acrobat.com also offers presentation and spreadsheet apps. The presentation software is nowhere near as powerful as PowerPoint's desktop software, but the limited selection of themes once again makes slides look attractive and businesslike. While no self-respecting professional would create a presentation from scratch using Office Web Apps or Google Presentation, Acrobat.com's presentations wouldn't leave anyone sniggering in the boardroom. One particularly nice feature is the option to easily drop in images from photo-sharing site Flickr (www.flickr.com).

Acrobat's spreadsheet table feature is, on the other hand, elementary and only really of use to people looking to store basic data – such as wedding invitation lists – on the web. There's no way to create a graph from your data, for instance, although the tables are clearly presented and easy to manipulate.
www.acrobat.com

Acrobat.com (above and top left) takes a more visually led approach to online office apps. Unlike the PowerPoint Web App, this is a tool you could use to build a simple but impressive presentation from scratch.

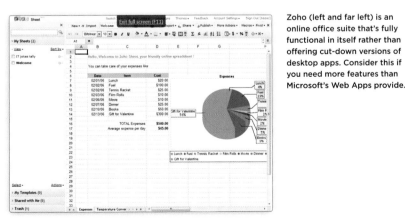

Zoho (left and far left) is an online office suite that's fully functional in itself rather than offering cut-down versions of desktop apps. Consider this if you need more features than Microsoft's Web Apps provide.

YOU'RE PROBABLY FAMILIAR WITH "WORD" AND "EXCEL", BUT WHEN IT COMES TO THE NITTY-GRITTY, HERE ARE SOME OF MICROSOFT'S LESS FAMILIAR TERMS.

Office jargon explained

Add-in
A downloadable program that can add extra features to individual Office applications. For example, Excel has an add-in called PowerPivot that allows extremely complex data analysis to be performed. Add-Ins can be developed by Microsoft and other companies.

Animation
In PowerPoint, this describes a movement applied to text or other elements. For example, a bullet point may "fly in" from the bottom of the page.

Clip-art
Simple, often cartoon-style pictures that may be used free of charge, or – if supplied by a company other than Microsoft – bought for a low fee.

Conditional formatting
A feature in Excel that looks for trends or patterns in figures and applies formatting accordingly. For example, you might use green for high figures and red for low to give an at-a-glance view of "hotspots" and "coldspots".

Group
Microsoft groups commands together in the ribbon to make it easier to find the one you're looking for. For example, in Word, all the illustration commands – such as Insert Picture, Clip Art and Charts – can be found in the Illustrations group on the Insert tab.

Linked notes
A feature that ties Internet Explorer, Word or Publisher to OneNote. When a OneNote page has been linked to any of these programs, it automatically provides links to where you were on the source document at the time you took the note.

Mail merge
A mail merge allows you to send a large volume of emails (or letters) to a list of contacts in both Word and Publisher. You can personalise using people's names, companies and any other information you hold about them.

Picture Tools
A new set of image-editing controls available in most Office apps, allowing you to tweak images without using a separate program.

PivotTable
A powerful tool in Excel that analyses data in spreadsheets and can then drill down into details. You can also create PivotCharts. See p56.

Quick Access Toolbar
A small group of shortcut icons that sits above the ribbon at the left of the screen (it can move below the ribbon if you prefer). It usually includes Save, Undo and Redo by default, but you can also customise it by adding your favourite shortcuts.

Ribbon
Replaces the old menus of Office 2003 and earlier. See p18.

SharePoint
Installed on a server or group of servers in a business, Microsoft SharePoint gives all employees a space to share documents – and collaborate on them. SharePoint Foundation is the free version; SharePoint Server adds extra features such as wikis.

SkyDrive
A file-sharing service that's part of Microsoft Windows Live. Each user can store up to 25GB of files on their SkyDrive.

SmartArt
Think flowcharts with added intelligence. For example, you can design a graphic depicting interlocking cogs that move by themselves to demonstrate dependencies.

12	October	55	39	76	85
13	November	63	41	87	43
14	December	171	33	115	42
15	*Total*	1017	336	760	563
16					
17					

Sparklines
A new feature in Excel 2010 (pictured above) that creates instant trend graphs to be placed at the end of a row or column of data, for example.

Styles
A way to apply formatting repeatedly to text and paragraphs. For example, in Word the Normal style will usually be in the Calibri font at 11 point, with an extra line space at the end of each paragraph. By setting up your own styles you can make your documents distinctive yet consistent. Styles can also be linked to themes.

Q: Microsoft's website is huge – how can I find answers to my questions about Office?
A: There's a large amount of content to trawl through, but a handy summary of the Office-related sections can be found at http://support.microsoft.com/ph/8753 – this includes links specific to each Office application.

Style Set A collection of predefined styles.

Tab Microsoft's name for the headings that form the ribbon. Typical tabs are Home, Insert and View, all of which are then split into groups (see left).

Template Each new file is based on a template that establishes common elements such as page size: in Word, for instance, it's a predefined document complete with page settings, styles and colour schemes.

Text Effects New refinements that can be applied to text in most Office apps, including soft shadows, outlines and bevels.

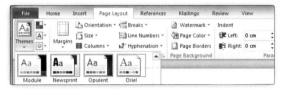

Themes A way to change the colour palette and fonts throughout a document. In conjunction with Styles and Style Sets, these can drastically change the appearance of a document with only a couple of clicks.

Transition In PowerPoint, the move from one slide to the next is called a transition. A wide variety of effects can be applied to make the transition more interesting.

Undo/redo Most Office applications offer the ability to either undo a command (such as deleting some text). If you change your mind again, press Redo to re-apply it.

Windows Live Microsoft's name for its collection of software and online services, such as SkyDrive, which allow users to communicate, exchange files and even co-operate on documents while online.

Web Apps New versions of some of the Office applications that you can run in a web browser via Windows Live. See Chapter 12.

WordArt A way to create highly stylised text warped into preset shapes, with colours and effects.

The Ultimate Guide to Office 2010

EDITORIAL

Editor
Tim Danton editor@pcpro.co.uk

Managing Editor
Adam Banks

Production Editor
Priti Patel

Sub Editor
Simon Petersen

Design and layout
Adam Banks adam@adambanks.com

Group Art Editor
Bill Bagnall

Contributors
Stuart Andrews, Barry Collins,
Simon Jones, Mark Whitehorn

LICENSING & SYNDICATION

International Licensing
Winnie Liesenfeld +44 20 7907 6134

Syndication
Anj Dosaj +44 20 7907 6763

ADVERTISING & MARKETING

Advertising Manager
Ben Topp +44 20 7907 6625

Digital Production Manager
Nicky Baker +44 20 7907 6056

MagBook Manager
Dharmesh Mistry +44 20 7907 6100

Marketing Manager
Claire Scrase +44 20 7907 6113

MANAGEMENT +44 20 7907 6000

Publishing Director
Ian Westwood

MD of Advertising
Julian Lloyd-Evans

Production Director
Robin Ryan

Newstrade Director
Martin Belson

Chief Operating Officer
Brett Reynolds

Group Finance Director
Ian Leggett

Chief Executive
James Tye

Chairman
Felix Dennis

To order multiple copies of this MagBook, please contact Michelle Marsh 020 7907 6140.

MAGBOOK™

The "MagBook" brand is a trademark of Dennis Publishing Ltd, 30 Cleveland St, London W1T 4JD. Company registered in England. All material © Dennis Publishing Ltd, licensed by Felden 2010, and may not be reproduced in whole or part without the consent of the publishers. The Ultimate Guide to Office 2010 ISBN 1-907232-54-0

Printed by
BGP, Bicester, Oxfordshire

Index

Q&A

Q: How can I help make the next version of this guide even better?
A: If you have ideas on how we can improve the guide, we'd love to hear them. Email editor@pcpro.co.uk with your suggestions.